Negotiating with Imperialism

Negotiating
with
Imperialism

∾ THE UNEQUAL TREATIES
AND THE CULTURE OF
JAPANESE DIPLOMACY

MICHAEL R. AUSLIN

HARVARD UNIVERSITY PRESS
Cambridge, Massachusetts, and London, England

First Harvard University Press paperback edition, 2006

Library of Congress Cataloging-in-Publication Data
  Auslin, Michael R., 1967–
     Negotiating with imperialism : the unequal treaties and the culture of Japanese
    diplomacy / Michael R. Auslin.
      p.   cm.
    Includes bibliographical references and index.
    ISBN13 978-0-674-01521-0 (cloth)
    ISBN10 0-674-01521-5 (cloth)
    ISBN13 978-0-674-02227-0 (pbk.)
    ISBN10 0-674-02227-0 (pbk.)
    1. Japan—Foreign relations—19th century—Treaties.   2. Japan—Foreign relations—
  United States—Treaties.   3. United States—Foreign relations—Japan—Treaties.   I. Title.
    DS881.45.A97 2004
    327.52073'09'034—dc22
    2004054126

For Ginko and Benjamin

.

Contents

Author's Note

Japanese names are given in traditional order: surname first, given name second. Following Japanese convention, however, certain individuals are referred to in the text by their given name; in particular, Hitotsubashi Keiki as Keiki (similarly after his shogunal name change to Tokugawa Yoshinobu as Yoshinobu), his father Tokugawa Nariaki as Nariaki, the lords of Satsuma Shimazu Nariakira and Shimazu Hisamitsu as Nariakira and Hisamitsu, Matsudaira Katamori as Katamori, Matsudaira Keiei as Keiei, and the artist Hashimoto Sadahide as Sadahide.

For convenience's sake, all dates have been changed to the Western calendar.

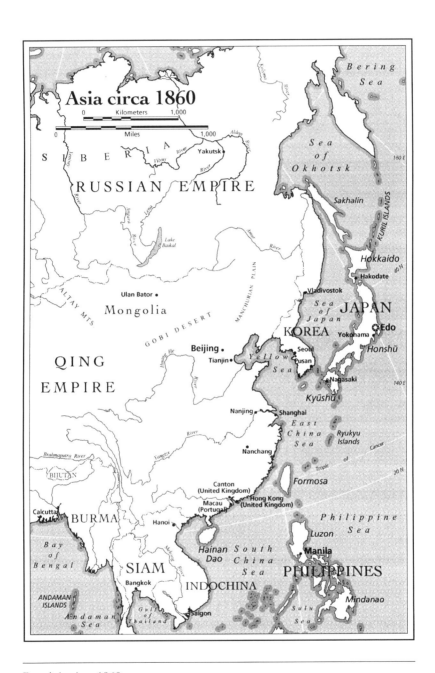

East Asia circa 1860

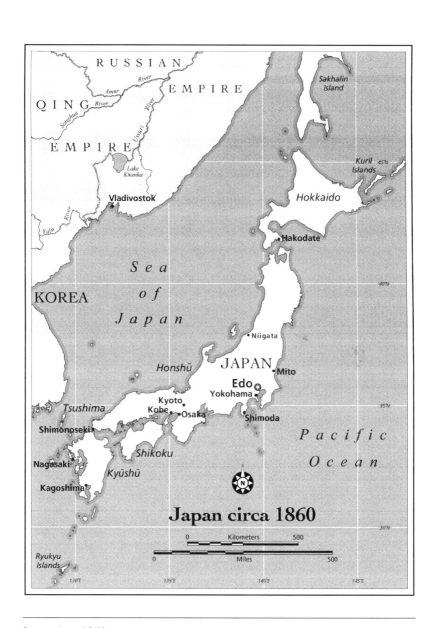

Japan circa 1860

Melians: Well, then, if you risk so much to retain your empire . . . it were surely great baseness and cowardice in us who are still free not to try everything that can be tried, before submitting to your yoke.

Athenians: Not if you are well advised, the contest not being an equal one, with honor as the prize and shame as the penalty, but a question of self-preservation and of not resisting those who are far stronger than you are.

Melians: But we know that the fortune of war is sometimes more impartial than the disproportion of numbers might lead one to suppose; to submit is to give ourselves over to despair, while action still preserves for us a hope that we may stand erect.

THUCYDIDES, "THE MELIAN CONFERENCE," *THE PELOPONNESIAN WAR*

Introduction

Japan's modern international history began on July 29, 1858. That morning, accompanied by Western-style cannon salutes and marine honor guard, Inoue Kiyonao and Iwase Tadanari, commissioners of maritime defense for the Tokugawa bakufu, boarded the U.S. warship *Powhatan*. In a short yet formal ceremony, they signed the Japan–United States Treaty of Amity and Commerce, which they had negotiated during the past months with Townsend Harris, the U.S. consul to Japan.[1]

The ceremony, which took place in Edo Bay within sight of the Tokugawa shogun's castle, marked the beginning of a new era in Japanese history. The treaty served as a template for Edo's subsequent pacts with Great Britain, Holland, Russia, and France, all of which were initialed in the summer and autumn of the same year. Officially, these agreements were known collectively as the "Ansei treaties," so named for their signing in the fifth year of the Ansei era; unofficially, later generations would denigrate them as the "unequal treaties." At first blush, the Ansei agreements indeed appeared to be "unequal." They seemed to mirror other imperial pacts, particularly those that Great Britain had extracted from China by force. They contained provisions for extraterritoriality, they denied the Japanese the freedom to set their own tariff rates, and they included most-favored nation (MFN) status for the Western signatories but not the Japanese.

Yet the unequal treaties were far more than simple diplomatic instruments. They served as the bridge between early-modern and modern Japan, and the challenge of responding to them shaped Japanese history. In the fifteen years after that first signing in Edo Bay, the worldview of Japanese underwent a transformation that ultimately led to fundamental changes in the country's politics, economics, and society. Indeed, due to the evolution of treaty policy, the general direction of Japan's history was largely set by 1872.

That change in worldview during the decade and a half after 1858 came about largely through the emergence of a new diplomatic culture shared by officials and understood by many ordinary Japanese. Culture, in general, I take to be the ideas, beliefs, values, and customs particular to a given group at a specific historical moment. The concept of a distinct diplomatic culture extends these broader "structures of meaning" to the set of accepted interpretations and beliefs about the relationship between the foreign and the domestic, and the traditional patterns of interacting with the outside world.[2] The thesis of this book is that the transformation of diplomatic culture led to sweeping changes in Japanese society as a whole. Moreover, at the level of national politics, the birth of a new diplomatic culture directly helped bring about the end of the 250-year-old Tokugawa era and the start of modern imperial Japan under the Meiji leadership. The diplomatic culture thus transcended, yet both influenced and derived from, two different political regimes.

At its most immediate, however, the influence of the treaties could be measured in its effect on the mindset of the leaders who now were forced to choose either to defend their traditional beliefs or to embrace a new world. Both the bakufu and the Meiji government adopted the same strategy in treaty relations, namely a defense of specific ideological, intellectual, and physical boundaries. These boundaries had protected Japan's central rulers from domestic challenge while simultaneously insulating the country from the outside world.[3] The key tactic the Japanese employed in this strategy was negotiation, which allowed them a voice in treaty relations. However, once negotiation reached its limit, at different times for different issues, the strategy began to falter and ultimately to collapse.

Nor were treaty relations merely a battleground pitting Japanese against Westerner. Their domestic impact was just as great, exposing strains in the Tokugawa polity and bringing Japanese into conflict with Japanese. Indeed, challenges to the bakufu's strategy came from within as well as without. In the government's attempts to maintain its sole control over foreign affairs, it not only fuelled the alienation of some of Japan's most powerful regional lords, it made success or failure in foreign relations a key prop of its continued legitimacy. Thus, when the strategy began to fail, the boundaries protecting Japan's diplomatic culture were transgressed and the course of Japanese history, both domestic and foreign, changed.

However, the end of the old world and the beginning of the new did not result solely from the events comprising diplomacy, foreign affairs, or domestic dissent. Rather, the profound change in the Japanese, and especially the leadership's, shared understanding of the nature of the world and Japan's place in it was the catalyst for the upheavals of the nineteenth century.

This book is more than a study, then, of a change in policy or tactics. It illuminates the process by which the key factors shaping the Japanese interpretation of the world changed. At one level, it is an analysis of the leaders and thinkers whose experience of treaty relations led them to a new conception of the international environment. At another level, it is a story of how Japan attempted to play a role in the Western-dominated nineteenth-century international system. At a third level, it traces the emergence in Japan of an international culture centered on Yokohama, the largest treaty port, and on the way nonelite Japanese and Westerners interpreted that culture in various media. In short, this is a study of the beginnings of Japan's modern international history and the lasting changes it brought to all Japanese.

Culture and Strategy in Japanese Diplomacy

Japanese diplomacy was not an uncoordinated hodgepodge of reaction to threats from the West. Both the Tokugawa bakufu and the Meiji government pursued a rational course of action informed by a distinct, if changing, diplomatic culture. Equally important, bakufu and Meiji diplomacy was not monolithic, and was itself negotiated among a variety of interests inside the government and out. By identifying this culture we can turn the "noise" of a welter of apparently disparate bakufu and Meiji actions into a "coherent voice" responding to the challenge of the West.[4]

This reconstruction of a coherent voice, which Mary Wright long ago suggested in the case of China, points us toward its expression in an equally complex diplomatic strategy. This strategy operated according to tradition and yet was also fully articulated as a counterpart to the new challenge posed by Western powers.[5] This policy, one of maintaining Japan's physical and intellectual boundaries, showed itself to be both flexible and overzealous at various times. Prioritization, what some might call triage, was central to this strategy, and allowed policymakers to respond flexibly to a range of pressures. This response shifted between foreign and domestic threats, depending on the interpretation by the policymakers of the time.

The key to the strategy was negotiation, which the Japanese saw as the best weapon to defend themselves from the West. Negotiation was more than mere dialogue with the treaty powers, however; it encompassed the response to the West. In the Japanese case, negotiation is better understood as a form of resistance. Resistance, clothed as diplomatic policy, especially by the bakufu, has either been downplayed or portrayed as ineffective by most historians.[6] Yet a shift in our frame of reference illuminates a more complex story and reveals the importance of the Japanese case in understanding global history during the period of imperialism. Since Tokugawa Japan was not a centralized, modern nation-state, its policy does not fit neatly with more traditional ways of interpreting state-to-state encounter. Nor did Meiji Japan emerge sui generis, with a modern stance toward the world untainted by the previous years of bakufu contact with the West. In fact, much like subelite classes in colonized lands at the same time, Japanese officials selectively employed tactics designed to frustrate Western plans while maintaining the fiction of adhering to the treaties. Investigating such resistance provides a crucial insight into the limits of both Japanese autonomy and Western power, and allows us more properly to judge the efficacy of Japanese policy.[7]

This indigenous strategy reflects what James C. Scott calls "practical resistance," which is a "constant testing of the equilibrium" that is established between two actors with asymmetrical power capabilities.[8] Such resistance encompasses everyday practices of "noncompliance, foot dragging, and deception" in order to make one's political presence felt.[9] As Scott notes, such an approach treats seriously the "immense political terrain that lies between quiescence and revolt," a perfect description of Japanese policy circa 1860.[10] As one investigates Japanese resistance, as expressed through the indigenous strategy, the dynamic nature of the treaty regime is laid bare. The treaty system was neither stable nor monolithic. Treaties and the relationships they created changed over time. Japanese resistance was sometimes unilateral, in direct contravention of the treaties, but more often negotiated, an attempt to use the treaty structure itself to frustrate further Western moves. The result was a relationship in which "history from below" played a prominent role.[11]

This particular type of negotiation, then, was the core of the Japanese–Western relationship. Through the Western acceptance of negotiation, norms of conduct were established and protected by both sides. Employed in the early years by the Japanese against certain provisions of the treaties, however, negotiation could also backfire, as it did in 1872. Regardless of its viability at any given time, negotiation was in fact the only tool available to the Japanese to protect themselves.

This, too, is a point that should be more appreciated. Lacking military power equal to the West, an economy that could ignore or influence the Western trading system, and the protections of an international system in Asia, the bakufu and imperial governments had no weapon but diplomacy. They embraced it because there were no other options, and they treated it seriously as the only realistic means to preserve their national (and sometimes more parochial) interests.

Yet one aspect of negotiation clearly exposed the various levels of interaction that were at play. As seen from the viewpoint of the international system, the Tokugawa bakufu was, in effect, a "subelite" actor, positioned between the global elite of the imperialist powers and the "nonelite" Japanese actors, from daimyō (feudal lords) to peasants. The bakufu thus was forced into a balancing role, interacting in one way with global powers and in another way with its domestic opponents. This dynamic was present from the beginning of the treaty regime but played an increasingly important role in the mid and late 1860s, as those nonelite actors challenged bakufu authority with ever more vigor. The Meiji government did not initially face such a challenge, having itself been the domestic opposition to the treaty structure in the years before 1868, but it did face a groundswell of opposition to its policies in the late 1870s and throughout the 1880s, a period not covered by this book. It is clear, though, that the intermediary position of the bakufu was a wildcard that interfered with its diplomatic strategy.

Ultimately, a diplomatic culture changes due to the failure of the strategy that it animated. Once the barriers protecting that culture are breached, new interpretations and new meanings are constructed to respond to the loss of a coherent understanding of the world. In Japan's case, this process straddled two political regimes, thus giving rise to earlier interpretations that only after 1868 did any significant change in worldview occur. But change began long before the fall of the Tokugawa, and the Meiji leaders initially shared with their predecessors much of their understanding of the world, an understanding itself influenced by the peculiar experience of treaty relations.

The Problem of Treaties

Treaty relations pose an interesting problem for those trying to place them in their historical context. Treaties are not simple instruments unrelated to the world they try to order. They are inherently political in nature and are based in speech, as negotiations. The relations ordered and guided by treaties are also assumed to be political in nature, that is, based on rational, verbal exchanges between the signatories. Yet the treaties between Japan and the West masked three different and distinct problems.

The first problem was the collision between the rhetoric of treaty making and the reality of the unequal power relationship that existed between the signatories. Japan, like all non-Western nations to varying degrees, was forced into opening trade relations with the West. Yet when the actual relationship was inaugurated, a ceremony of equality, respect, and even partnership was constructed, utterly at odds with the very conditions that brought about the association. Indeed, the Westerners entered into relations with Japan through a ritual all but indistinguishable from that employed amongst themselves, thereby further implying equality. In the particular case of Japan, moreover, the Ansei agreements were not peace treaties imposed after war, but ostensibly compacts freely entered into by both sides.

But relations between the two, of course, were not based on parity, no matter what type of common memory diplomatic ritual sought to create. A struggle by Japan to assert its autonomy was almost pre-ordained, yet there was no legal standing in the treaties, beyond the renegotiation clause, to support any moves to make the treaties truly equitable. If the treaties, then, rhetorically celebrated the creation of an equal partnership between the contracting parties, how did that affect attempts by Japan to equalize the relationship or by the Western powers to maintain their superior advantages? Were the treaties open to further negotiations, could they logically be backed up with force?

The Westerners had no clear answer to this problem, and it was Japan that first forced the issue over how the treaty regime should evolve, especially in the early 1870s. The treaty powers had not come to Japan to colonize, for the country was part of that larger sphere of informal empire tied to Western, mainly British, commercial interests. Given the lack of Western interest in the final sanction of colonization, how was this treaty relationship to proceed, based as it was on imperfect precedent? Both the Tokugawa and the Meiji saw that only through action on their part could the treaties be brought more into line with Japanese interests. Yet such an occurrence had repercussions far beyond Yokohama and Edo, potentially reaching the very core of imperialist power. Ultimately, the experience of treaty relations with Japan forced the Westerners to conceive a new type of international relations, one in which the supposedly subordinated, uncivilized partners played a true role, expressed through negotiation.

The second problem with treaty relations was an intra-Western issue. Since Japan was not to be colonized, the Westerners treated Japan from the beginning more "equally" than they did colonized states, such as India, or semi-colonized nations, such as China. They took no territory in Japan, and did not carve out spheres of influence for themselves, in which only one nation was the primary power and prevented other states from engaging in trade or military actions (the classic example being Europeans in late-nineteenth-century Africa). They were thrown together into small trading outposts, only one of which, Yokohama, was of any importance. As a result, all the Western powers ultimately were bound by the same set of agreements with Japan, and found no room for typically imperialist competition with any other treaty power. The Ansei treaties thus played the key role in regulating not only Japanese-Western relations but, uniquely, also intra-Western relations in Japan.

This situation, paralleled only in Siam, arose out of the West's inexorable expansion across the globe. There was no mechanism in place for ordering or stabilizing great power relations in Asia, and if the Concert of Europe experience did not extend to the Ottoman Empire, how much less was it applicable to Japan.[12] Moreover, at this very moment the Concert itself was beginning the slow collapse which would result in the cataclysm of 1914, as the 1854-56 Crimean War pitted the system's great powers against each for the first time since the Napoleonic conflict a century previously.

Thus, the farthest reaches of the "Great Game" were hesitantly played out in Japan. Here however, each power was constrained by the treaties it had signed with the bakufu, though the treaties played no official role in ameliorating the Game's competition. What was new was that the lack of territorial issues meant that the Westerners had to learn to deal with each other on a more equitable, and intimate, basis than they did in other overseas regions. At the same time, the existence of treaties that equally bound all the foreigners both provided Japan with the opportunity to play the treaty nations off each another and offered the Westerners the raw material for creating a common ground, which in turn could be used against the Japanese.

The third problem with the Ansei pacts came from the more general nature of treaties noted above, that they were rational instruments designed to operate in a stable environment. Yet the treaties themselves undermined domestic stability in Japan. The country began to slide into violence, and more particularly, violence directed against the sectors of society (the bakufu and the Westerners) that based their relations on agreed norms of rational conduct. The more the treaty signatories attempted to preserve the agreements, and bring their notion of stability back to Japan, the more the domestic situation disintegrated. In the end, both government and foreigner were reduced to employing force to try and stamp out the threat to the dialogue of treaty relations. As Hannah Arendt pointed out, violence, by its nature is voiceless, and therefore cannot interact with the political or rational.[13] It can only undermine and destroy them. This was the fate of the Tokugawa shogunate, ultimately weakened by assassinations, uprisings, and battle, a trajectory that moved from inchoate violence by masterless samurai to large-scale conflict with the powerful domains of Chōshū and Satsuma.

In this vortex, how are we to place treaty relations? The treaties never ceased being what they were—political instruments—but they operated according to a logic increasingly different from that sweeping through Japan. It is for this reason that the story of treaty relations often gets marginalized in accounts of the fall of the bakufu and the rise of the Meiji regime.

In reality, treaty relations continued to operate regardless of domestic political upheaval, and did so by the logic inherent in them. Thus, the Tokugawa, until their collapse, continued to negotiate and communicate with Westerners, while Westerners never seriously contemplated abrogating the treaties and imposing pure force on Japan. While the bakufu still existed, Westerners never considered any other power in Japan as a legitimate authority in foreign affairs. After 1868, similarly, the Meiji government found itself tied into the existing framework of relations that it dared not renounce; indeed, it soon discovered that its cherished goal of revision itself operated according to the logic of timetables included in the treaties. The point, simply, is that to understand treaty relations, we must understand how those relations worked and what type of structure they created. We can then fit them into their historical milieu, not assuming that they were passively buffeted by domestic events.

To argue that treaty relations encapsulated some type of logic, however, is not to claim that the signatories were somehow guided along predetermined paths toward ever-freer economic or cultural exchange. Treaty relations were a feature of daily life for those who participated, not a predetermined story written according to the abstract rules of imperialism. The decisions, fears, and hopes of the Japanese were singly birthed, nursed, and buried according to an incalculable variety of factors. Just as merchants attempted to record the excitement of life in Yokohama, policymakers struggled to understand the new world in light of their shared beliefs and concerns.

It was in this space that Japanese policymakers acted. Western imperialism did not seem to them an unstoppable historical force that deprived them of their autonomy. Rather, men such as the Great Councillor Ii Naosuke saw the Western challenge as a problem to be solved. Perhaps his and others' estimation of their power was overrated. Perhaps Ii did not fully understand the limits the treaties imposed on his freedom, and in that light his actions were ineffective or quixotic. Whatever one's view of these events, to assume the failure of the Japanese from 1858 (or 1854) on, to interpret a multitude of actions solely in the light of Japan's ultimate historical development, is to deny history its due. As the historian Ronald Syme wrote about the fall of the Roman Republic, "The tale has often been told, with an inevitability of events and culmination, either melancholy or exultant. The conviction that it all had to happen is indeed difficult to discard. Yet that conviction ruins the living interest of history and precludes a fair judgement upon the agents. They did not know the future."[14]

Within these chapters a common theme emerges, perhaps more strongly in the beginning but present throughout: for the Japanese, nothing superseded defending the ideological, intellectual, and physical boundaries between themselves and Westerners. This was the overriding concern of both the bakufu and the Meiji government, and it encompassed both political and cultural features. The first line of defense, not surprisingly, was control of Japanese territory, for both concrete and symbolic reasons. This was the main motivating factor in the formation of Japanese treaty policy and in the struggles between Japan and the West. Economics, seemingly very important, was largely subordinated to these political and cultural concerns. For the West, economics, as trade, was the sine qua non of treaty relations, but for the Japanese, trade and economics were secondary to maintaining control over Japanese land and minimizing the physical intrusion of the West. With the breach of this boundary, the ideological and intellectual ramparts soon fell, and the goals of policymakers began radically to change.

The result was a period of complex interaction, formal process, and political and cultural evolution. As William Beasley noted, "1858 marked the beginning, not the end, of [Japan's] real struggle with the West."[15] In order to understand that struggle, this book simultaneously proceeds at two levels of analysis: the local, from the viewpoint of Japanese policymakers; and the systemic, which integrates the Japanese case into the larger pattern of nineteenth-century international relations. The particular path the Japanese took—the continued emphasis and reliance on negotiation—is an underappreciated and unique feature of Japan's encounter with the West, and one that, in the end, led to a reenvisioning of that encounter.

CHAPTER ONE

The Style and Substance of Treaty-Making

Elaborate ceremonies filled the Japanese summer and autumn months of 1858 as the Tokugawa bakufu concluded nearly identical trade treaties with the United States, Great Britain, France, Russia, and Holland. For the Japanese, the imposing ceremonies marked the end of over two centuries of tradition and the beginning of a new phase of foreign relations, while for the Western powers, they bespoke the high hopes held for the new trade relationship with Japan.

Laurence Oliphant, secretary to Lord Elgin when he concluded Britain's pact with Edo in August, later described the ritual of creating this new international relationship. "The signing of the Treaty," he wrote, "was a most solemn and serious operation, employing copies of the agreement in Dutch, Japanese, and English in triplicate, and requiring a total of eighty-four signatures."[1] Then, as the London *Times* dramatically reported, "Not only was the Treaty ratified, but the instrument itself was carried in solemn procession under a silken canopy through the principal streets of the capital, escorted by an imposing guard from a British man of war."[2] To commemorate the event, the Japanese signatories gathered in the courtyard of the Kanagawa magistrate's office for a group photograph. The print was carried back to London, where it lay forgotten in the Victoria and Albert Museum for more than 140 years.[3]

Culture, Ritual, and Diplomacy in Europe and East Asia

Diplomacy has a complex nature, being at the same time hard-hearted and visionary, realistic and utopian. It is the tool by which a government seeks to achieve strategic goals, yet it also raises hopes for a more peaceful and prosperous future. Diplomacy not only reflects the cultures of its practitioners, it becomes a culture of its own with shared meanings and symbolism. For European diplomats, as the above descriptions attest, treaty signing was the apex of international relations and had been so for centuries. Treaties, as the stepchild of diplomacy, represented the honor of a nation hazarded on fragile vellum.

European-instigated treaty signings were thus carried on quite solemnly, for the inculcation of such feelings of reverence served as a symbolic, and often emotional, underpinning of the treaties themselves. The finery of the ambassadors, the opulence of the gifts, the minute ballet of diplomatic audience, all symbolized the gravity of such moments and indeed served as a prophylactic to protect the infant treaties. These agreements not only ordered the relationship between the parties, they also embodied through words and signatures the honor of each sovereign. They were, in short, personal bonds between the bodies of the sovereigns extended to their larger societies.

As European nations expanded their influence across the globe, their particular style of formalizing relations was transferred to societies with no such tradition. The Europeans knew well that such transfer was not a simple process, but they rarely questioned the appropriateness of treaties as the key instrument of diplomacy. Oliphant, for example, reflected in his memoirs on the "sacredness of treaty-obligations" and questioned whether the Japanese and Chinese could understand their importance.[4] Rutherford Alcock, the first British minister to Japan, perhaps best encapsulated the relationship between treaties and the Western notion of national honor when he wrote in 1862 that "the reputation of the British name . . . cannot be upheld or preserved untarnished if Treaty rights in any direction are modified or foregone."[5]

In East Asia, the Western practice of signing treaties was relatively new, a result of sustained contact, and often conflict, with the West. Nonetheless, diplomatic ceremony was, if anything, the essence of the region's international relations. The most important feature of traditional East Asian diplomacy was the formalities enacted before sovereigns or among representatives of nations linked in a hierarchical relationship. For all intents and purposes, ritual *was* the relationship.

Townsend Harris discovered this in Bangkok in 1855. On his way to Japan, he had stopped in Siam (Thailand) hoping to sign a commercial treaty in the footsteps of the British. Harris recorded that when he went to present the United States' formal request to the king, his retinue was brought to the Siamese palace in ten boats, with the letter itself coming first in a vessel of its own. A complex twelve-stage process was followed simply to get Harris into the royal precincts. One month later, at the signing of the treaty, the ceremony itself lasted more than three hours and employed more than 108 seals and signatures.[6]

Perhaps unique among Asian nations, the Siamese believed that treaties were repositories of history, not merely diplomatic instruments. Harris was surprised, and offended, by a request to include in his treaty a history of the previous thirty years of Siamese diplomacy, including the names of those nations with which the Siamese had relations and of the envoys previously sent to Bangkok.[7] To the Siamese, a treaty was a document that reflected their nation's past as well as its future. It glorified the sovereign and served as a testament of his stewardship over the nation's collective memories and goals.

The cultural role and ideological content of East Asian diplomacy was perhaps most developed in China. From the time of the Han emperors, Chinese leaders conceived of the world ideally as a hierarchy reflecting Confucian and Neo-Confucian cosmology. The main mechanism of the Chinese "world order," which reached its apotheosis during the Qing dynasty (the seventeenth to the twentieth centuries), was the tribute trade system. This system comprised ideological, political, economic, and diplomatic elements, all of which holistically interacted. The proper observance of diplomatic protocol, what James Hevia terms "centering," identified the emperor as the locus of all diplomatic authority and the protector of a cosmologically derived order of hierarchy.[8] This ideological construct allowed for the smooth functioning of Chinese foreign relations, and provided cover for the Qing practice of bribing warlike peoples on its borders to leave it in peace.

This ideology was paralleled in early modern Japan. Japan's traditional diplomatic culture comprised ideological, intellectual, and physical boundaries. The innermost ring, the ideological boundary was the elaborate system of diplomatic ritual established by the Tokugawa bakufu after 1600. This system culminated in the person of the shogun, who replaced the emperor as the fundament of Japanese ideology.[9] The bakufu served as the instrument of shogunal power in foreign relations, and around it was erected a barrier keeping all non-bakufu influences outside the walls of decision-making. As a result, domestic actors isolated from policy councils sought various means of influencing those holding power, sometimes by appealing to them, sometimes by going around them.

The intellectual boundary around Tokugawa diplomacy was an inversion of the geographical hierarchy employed by the Qing dynasty. This intellectual ordering of the world placed Japan at the center of the physical realm, and relegated the Chinese to a position on the barbaric fringes. Information from abroad was strictly controlled, and officially, knowledge of the world was neither sought nor valued. All that had to be known could be found inside Japan's borders, and without explicit government approval no one could attempt an intellectual journey outside the nation's boundaries.

This intellectual boundary led to an inward-looking culture, for the most part, yet one that eagerly accepted new forms of knowledge when they proved beneficial, as in the rise of Western medical studies in the late eighteenth century. The Tokugawa controlled information, considering it a source of power. From the earliest days of the bakufu, as Ronald Toby has shown, foreign information reached Japan from several sources: Chinese merchants in Nagasaki, reports on China from the Ryūkyū (Okinawan) islands, information from Korean embassies and Korean traders with the island of Tsushima, and intelligence on the West from Dutch traders on Dejima in Nagasaki.[10] The information then flowed to Edo and the senior council, the highest bakufu policy-making body, which upheld the ideology of shogunal supremacy.

Finally, the physical boundary of Japan's diplomatic culture served, Janus-like, as the first line of defense. One face was domestic, supporting the ideological basis of Tokugawa power. Its physical symbol was Edo Castle, the center of the realm. The locus of temporal authority rested inside the citadel, and the flow of information and trade tribute into, and orders out of, the fortress gave the impression of the shogun's complete control over foreign affairs, and hence the world. The moats, gates, walls, and towers of Edo Castle served as a visible reminder to daimyō and commoners alike of the physical barriers that protected the Tokugawa ordering of the realm and world.

The other face of the physical boundary looked out onto that ordered world. Erected through the maritime exclusion edicts, this boundary protected Japan's national security and supported the intellectual boundary established by the Tokugawa. The edicts, completed during the 1630s, forbade Japanese egress from the realm and tightly controlled foreign ingress. In a further inversion of the Chinese ideal, the bakufu accorded Korea and the Ryūkyū islands diplomatic status while granting the Dutch and the Chinese only limited trading rights.

This boundary's physical manifestation was the trading complex at Nagasaki, on the southern island of Kyūshū. Here was Japan's traditional window on the world, and here two boundaries served to seal off the realm, at least officially. Nagasaki first and foremost was closed to those whom the bakufu wished to keep out of Japan. Yet it also contained a second boundary between Japan and those foreigners who were allowed to enter for trade. The Chinese were segregated in their own quarter of town, while the Portuguese, and later Dutch, traders were isolated on the fan-shaped island of Dejima, which had been specifically constructed to hold them. Once a year, later changed to once every four years, the shogun commanded the Dutch to come to Edo to pay personal tribute. The Dutch journeyed to the capital as though a bacillus in a container—guarded, herded along predetermined routes, and shuttled into and out of Edo Castle with military precision.

Here trade entered into the picture, as it did in China, as a supporting element of each boundary. Trade did not exist by itself, as a purely economic exchange of goods. Rather, it was camouflaged as diplomatic ritual. When Korean embassies came to send greetings to a new shogun, tribute was offered by the visitors and goods were granted by the hosts, all to underline in Japanese eyes the shogun's supremacy, while the physical barriers raised between Japan and the outer world served to reinforce the shogun's right to control contact with the foreign. There was no concept of free trade, for merchants, occupying the lowest status level in official ideology, could play no possible foreign role, while other domains were to be denied the fruits of international commerce. Edo, of course, turned a mostly blind eye to the activities of outer domains that carried on trade surreptitiously with Korea, the Ryūkyūs, and China. Overt Western demands for free trade would thus threaten the entire edifice of foreign policy in the nineteenth century.

These were the boundaries of Japan's diplomatic culture. It had been designed to bolster the Tokugawa claim to domestic authority in the aftermath of a century of civil war. Its complex nature and inter-related features made this ideological conceit and its attendant appa-ratus a system through which bakufu leaders spoke a shared language for interpreting and acting on the world, and for isolating their ac-tions from domestic interference. Accordingly, Tokugawa Japan had but one diplomatic strategy: to protect and preserve its diplomatic culture.

Both Qing China and Tokugawa Japan thus conducted foreign af-fairs according to a long-held "strategic culture."[11] Both were heavily influenced by Neo-Confucian thought and sought to replicate a cos-mological order in the temporal realm. China's hegemonic position in East Asia and Japan's isolation preserved these cultures until both were confronted with the technological insistence of the Western mar-itime powers. While they functioned, however, the two countries' strategic cultures were a closed system, subsuming all knowledge of and action in the world within their boundaries. A challenge to these cultures, then, struck at the very heart of political authority.

Both Japan and China sought to limit the impact of European diplo-macy on their traditional cultures. At gravest risk was the central prop of their systems, the ideological hierarchy of realms. The Europeans claimed equality as the guiding principle among nations, except in the cases of course where one party was uncivilized. This was the language suffusing their treaties. Treaties themselves were radical innovations for East Asians. Such legal compacts between states were all but unknown in the region (the one major exception being the Treaty of Nerchinsk, signed between China and Russia in 1689). Perhaps most radical of all was the European practice of mixing traditional ceremony, well understood by all East Asian states, with the signing of formal treaties, complex agreements that sought to define precisely the universe of re-lations between peoples. It is no surprise that things did not always go as smoothly as the façade of ritual suggested.

As the Europeans attempted, in their view, to rationalize Asian diplomacy, the reality of international relations often sharply deviated from the sanctity of ceremony. Treaties were as often honored in the breach as in the observance. Long service in China and Japan had taught Alcock this lesson. As he noted in his memoirs, "To make a treaty is indeed only the first and the least of the difficulties, as all his-tory and experience prove. The real touchstone of success lies in the practical working."[12] This practical working lay in communication and verbal intercourse—in other words, dialogue—even if in actuality the parties misunderstood each other with alarming regularity.

Such was the case of mid-nineteenth-century Japan. Although idealized by Japan and Western nations alike as inviolate, the 1858 Ansei treaties were far from being sacrosanct legal documents; rather, they proved to be a field of battle between the signatories. Over the years, a distinct Japanese diplomatic approach emerged: the desire to preserve the bakufu's traditional diplomatic culture meant that the treaties were considered fluid documents subordinate to the actual relationship; for Western powers, however, the treaties were prior to relations, creating and guiding them. Treaty relations as a whole, therefore, encompassed both contestation and accommodation. Though the Japanese held goals often antithetical to the Westerners, they dared not violate the treaties directly. Both the Tokugawa government and its successor Meiji regime thus worked to maintain the dialogue of treaty relations. The Japanese reacted in this way because they realized that they had entered a relationship unlike any they had encountered before.

The Nonrevolutionary Nature of the Perry Treaty

The romantic appeal of Commodore Matthew C. Perry's arrival in Japanese waters in July 1853 maintains its hold after a century and a half. To Japanese and Americans alike, the appearance of the "Black Ships" appears to be a watershed in Japan's foreign relations. In reality, however, Perry's Treaty of Peace and Amity (also known as the Treaty of Kanagawa), signed in March 1854, far from "opening" Japan, was quite limited in nature, and did not herald a revolution in Tokugawa diplomacy.

Perry, of course, was hardly the first contact Japan had with Western civilization. For centuries, the country had been drawn increasingly closer to the West, a process under way at least since the first arrival of Portuguese off the southern island of Tanegashima in 1543.[13] The six decades before Perry's appearance, in particular, witnessed a vast increase in Japanese contact with the West. The bakufu was primarily concerned with repeated Russian probing from the north. Since Adam Laxman's arrival in Hokkaido in 1792, Edo had worried about the Russian threat, fears brought to life in the early 1800s by Russian depredations in northern Japan.[14] As for the "southern" maritime powers, Britain had sent a powerful ship of the line into Nagasaki in

1808, during the Napoleonic Wars, in search of Dutch shipping, while American whalers appeared as early as 1791 and sporadically thereafter. Clearly, the world was shrinking, and the bakufu was acutely aware of that fact long before Perry arrived.

Perry undoubtedly pitched his performance expertly, given previous American failures to open relations with Japan, and there is no question that his appearance marked a turning point for Japan. In terms of actual effect, though, the Perry episode represented a transition moment in Tokugawa diplomacy. It should not be forgotten that Perry was denied an agreement during his first visit, and that he was forced to return the following spring; since nothing concrete had changed, there was no assurance that the commodore would actually return or that Edo would not be able to maintain its current foreign policy. Once Perry did return, his hurried negotiations over two weeks ended with the American squadron promptly sailing away after the signing ceremony.

Perry's 1854 treaty resulted in what was primarily a tentative pact between the two countries. Although it was the first formal treaty signed between Japan and a Western power, it was predicated on chance and impermanence: the chance that U.S. ships would have a need for Japanese ports and supplies, and the transitory nature of such contact. In addition, it merely provided for the possibility of appointing "consuls or agents" to reside on Japanese soil (Article 9); nothing in the treaty mandated long-term contact.[15] It did not in itself create permanent trade or diplomatic relations.

What was significant about Perry's intrusion was that it caused the bakufu to inch toward expanded maritime relations with Western nations, specifically with the Dutch and Russians, until the formal trade treaty with Townsend Harris a half-decade later. This was the transition that Perry sparked, resulting in Japan's slow enrollment into the larger international treaty structure of the mid-nineteenth century. Though, as we will see, the Harris treaty heralded a new age, it was in many ways a composite of these intermediate conventions of 1854–1857. As such, the bakufu leadership saw negotiations with Harris largely as a continuation of its traditional, gradualist strategy. This belief was fueled by an understanding that, despite the challenges posed by the Perry precedent, the particular pattern of Japan's treaty relations allowed it significant latitude, especially in contrast to China.

The Chinese Comparison

Despite the threat inherent in Perry's arrival, the Japanese faced a challenge far different from that confronting the Qing Empire. China's refusal to allow unfettered British trade and the importation of narcotics had resulted in the Opium War from 1839 to 1841. The Chinese were defeated, and the Qing Empire now labored under a treaty dictated by Britain. Through the 1842 Treaty of Nanjing (Nanking), London imposed Western law to establish its right to conduct trade in China. The British also believed that both their trade and their rule of law would help spread "civilization" in that country. This first treaty, according to John King Fairbank, was essentially a charter of rights for British merchants that established a trading system on the Chinese coast.[16]

The Nanjing treaty system, however, was both radical and yet limited. Chinese dynasties throughout history had often implicitly, and sometimes explicitly, granted rights of residence and trade to foreigners, particularly in the vast expanse of lightly controlled Inner and Central Asia. The Chinese pursued order by bribing, threatening, or coercing foreigners to participate in the tribute system, through which non-Chinese affirmed the ideologically superior position of the Chinese emperor, whether he was Tang, Ming, or Qing. The "barbarians" were kept under a "loose rein" (*qi mi*) policy, by which China never assumed full responsibility for policing or controlling them.[17] In fact, the Chinese acceptance of the Treaty of Nanjing came from the Qing's experience in the 1830s of maintaining control over the western desert region of Xinjiang (Sinkiang).

Joseph Fletcher identified China's "first unequal treaty" as the 1835 agreement between the Qing and the khanate of Kokand.[18] Kokand had moved aggressively in the early nineteenth century to expand its control over trade at some of the main Xinjiang outposts, particularly Yarkand and Kashgar. The Chinese were unable to suppress Kokand, and agreed to a settlement, essentially a treaty, in 1835. Qing concessions included allowing Kokand to place a diplomatic agent at Kashgar; granting extraterritoriality for Kokand merchants in Xinjiang; recognizing consular powers for Kokand officials in Xinjiang; establishing a "fair and regular" tariff; permitting free trade without interference from Qing monopolies (the cohong), implicitly granting most-favored-nation (MFN) status; and tacitly declaring national equality between Kokand and China.

The Qing, Fletcher explained, ultimately sought to simplify their administrative and political problems on the far reaches of the empire. Thus, they did not consider the treaty "unequal." China had already recognized the equal status of other nations, for example that of Romanov Russia in the 1689 Treaty of Nerchinsk. Moreover, extraterritoriality did not appear to be an imposition on Chinese autonomy; rather, it freed the Qing from dealing with foreign criminals, yet did not diminish the emperor's claim to universal political primacy. Finally, the MFN clause was a perfect example of the practice of "imperial benevolence," granting Kokand whatever rights other barbarian nations had in their dealings with China.[19]

The Qing court relied on its Central Asian experience when confronted with the European demand in the 1840s for access to China's trade markets. Consciously transferring its policy from one end of the empire to the other, Beijing appointed numerous officials from Central Asia to deal with the Europeans. By 1843, the temporary governor-general of Shanghai, who was responsible for opening the city to trade, was an official who had cut his teeth in Kokand in the early 1830s.[20] According to John King Fairbank, the major initial change brought about by the Europeans was that, until the Treaty of Nanjing, the rights of foreign residence and trade were never formally or fully codified.[21] As in Central Asia, though, the Qing believed concessions such as MFN were in China's best interest, since they helped to ensure that no one foreign power gained a preponderant position.[22] In this way, the Qing would be able to keep the barbarians in a state of equality vis-à-vis each other and employ the traditional method of "using barbarians to control barbarians."

Because of Japan's geographical propinquity to China, and because the Japanese treaties were chronologically contemporaneous to the various Chinese treaties, it has often been argued that China and Japan thus occupied the same position in the international system. Most Japanese scholars have followed Inoue Kiyoshi, who labeled Japan a "semicolonized" nation (*hanshokuminchi*).[23] Ishii Takashi, the leading historian of bakumatsu foreign relations, also believed that Japan, like China, was brought into the nineteenth-century international capitalist system as an "economically subordinated state" (*keizaiteki jūzokukoku*). Japan, in this scheme, occupied the lowest rung of that system, being primarily a supplier of raw materials and a market for European goods.[24]

The cases of China and Japan, however, were fundamentally different. As Katō Yūzō argues, one cannot underestimate the crucial fact that the Treaty of Nanjing (and later the 1858 Tianjin [Tientsin] Treaty) was a "treaty of defeat" imposed on a beaten nation, while the Harris agreement was a "negotiated treaty" in which the threat of force, but not force itself, was used.[25] Though the Qing retained their overall sovereignty, treaty relations in China proceeded from a situation of military defeat, while Japan from the beginning conducted its treaty relations through bilateral and multilateral negotiation.

The crucial change in Sino–Western relations came with the 1858 Tianjin Treaty imposed by Britain after the Arrow War. This new treaty was vastly more punitive and intrusive than the Treaty of Nanjing and materially reduced Chinese sovereignty. Katō thus agrees with Fairbank's assertion that the years 1842 to 1860 represented the first phase of China's treaty relations with the West, in which the institutional structure of relations was gradually worked out. Fairbank sees the 1858 Tianjin Treaty as codifying the new state of relations between China and Europe, but it was not until the Franco–British invasion of Beijing and the burning of the Summer Palace in 1860 that the Qing finally accepted the new system.[26]

The treaty Japan ultimately signed with Harris in 1858 resembled the 1842 Treaty of Nanjing in several key respects: trade was limited to a small number of ports (five) and cities (two); foreigners were allowed to live there, but not to travel freely in the interior; and freedom of religion was allowed only at the port settlements. The differences between the contemporaneous Ansei and Tianjin treaties, however, were substantial. Under the Tianjin Treaty, ten new ports were opened, three of which were in the Chinese interior; the British received the right to send warships anywhere in China's coastal waters and interior waterways, in order to suppress unrest; Christianity was allowed to be preached openly and was to be protected by the Chinese; European holders of valid passports could travel anywhere within China, and free travel thirty miles from any treaty port was allowed; official communications were to be in English; and the right to sell opium was reinforced.[27]

In clear contrast, under both the Perry and Harris treaties the bakufu did not allow the importation of opium, did not cede any land outright, did not allow Christianity outside the ports, prohibited travel in the interior, and paid no indemnity to the West. In short,

Japan escaped the harsh conditions of an imposed treaty.[28] Moreover, by refusing Western ships access to the interior, including the Inland Sea, the bakufu denied the imperial powers the key means by which they had expanded their control over colonized areas.[29]

In fact, China was less a model for Japan's treaties with the West than another Asian nation. By viewing the treaty from the vantage point of the international system, one notes a global influence on the Japanese treaties, including strong similarities between Japan's case and that of Siam.

The Siamese Comparison

In many ways, the kingdom of Siam played a role analogous to that of Japan, albeit starting thirty years previously. Though neither country was the direct target of colonial aspirations, each was positioned contiguous to or close by crucial territorial holdings or interests of European powers, especially Great Britain. Siam, in fact, was strategically located on two fronts. To its northwest lay Burma, an object of intense British concern due its location next to British India. To the east lay Indochina, which was to become the site of the greatest concentration of French forces in Asia, and thus in British eyes a potential threat to the same Indian holdings. Initially, though, Siam's proximity to Burma meant that Britain wanted to keep the kingdom quiescent and integrated into its growing Southeast Asian commercial network.

In 1824, stung by Burma's refusal to open up to trade and its threatening moves against Indian border territory, London launched the first Burmese war, which lasted for two years. This was a major effort and costly: 15,000 of the 40,000 British imperial troops sent to fight perished of injury or malaria and other tropical diseases.[30] Despite this, the British were victorious, and when the outcome was assured, London approached the Siamese court with a request for commercial relations, stressing that it entertained no territorial designs. The first Anglo–Siamese pact, known as the Burney Treaty, was signed in 1826. It placed high tariffs on many British goods and restricted British merchants primarily to the port of Bangkok.[31] Britain's presence in Siam, then, was relatively limited, given its immense interests just across the Bay of Bengal.

During the next several decades, however, Siam became more incorporated into the Southeast Asian trading network. This network—centered on China, Singapore, and the Malay states—served a crucial function in facilitating British commercial expansion in the region. Participation in the network allowed Britain to further knit together its China coast trade with the Indian subcontinent. It was, in fact, Singapore commercial interests that pushed for an expanded British trade presence in Siam, although London remained committed to its policy of territorial nonintervention.[32]

By 1851, Britain was once more at war with Burma. This time, their outstanding differences were resolved by Britain enrolling most of Burma formally into the empire. As a result, British territory now abutted Siam, and the old Anglo-Siamese commercial treaty was deemed insufficient to protect British interests. Sir John Bowring, governor-general of Hong Kong, crafted a revised pact with Siam's new ruler, the energetic reformer King Rama IV (Mongkut). Mongkut was a realist who had witnessed the British use of force in Burma. In order to preserve his formal political authority, and the territorial sovereignty of his core lands, he negotiated his way to a balance of interests with Bowring.

The second Anglo–Siamese treaty was signed early in 1855. It substantially expanded British rights in Siam, but maintained Siamese control over its own land. The new treaty opened all domestic ports to trade, though it retained the residency limit of Bangkok, thus holding in check the physical expansion of British traders in Siam. The treaty further allowed free trade throughout the whole country and free travel if one was in possession of a joint Anglo–Siamese passport. British subjects, however, were prohibited from buying land within four miles of Bangkok's walls until they had resided in the country for ten years.[33] The treaty effectively ended the Siamese state's monopoly over trade, thus allowing regional elites as well as wealthy native merchants to participate. Britain was given de facto control over Siamese shipping and the import-export trade.[34]

Siam, then, by 1855 was firmly ensconced in both the indigenous and the British commercial networks of Southeast Asia. In negotiating two commercial treaties with the British, it had surrendered much of its economic autonomy, but had induced Britain to recognize the importance of preserving Siamese native political authority. The Siamese court now found itself supported by a British policy that increasingly depended on a stable Siam to protect the eastern borders of British

Burma. As a result, the structure of the Siamese state itself evolved. A more modern, centralized bureaucracy was established, and the court extended its control over loosely affiliated frontier regions.[35] In essence, the institutions of the Siamese state and their attendant policies were, as Ian Brown points out, shaped by the need to accommodate the demands and interests of the British military and commercial classes.[36]

Negotiation, informal empire, limited expansion, state evolution, and a balance of interests all marked Siamese international relations in the nineteenth century. The Japanese experience was very similar, from negotiations with Western powers engaged in military action in Asia to the complex interplay of domestic and foreign interests. By the time Harris presented to the bakufu his draft treaty in December 1857, Edo had a wealth of intelligence and experience to inform its diplomatic strategy.

The lessons of China and Siam were clear: negotiation with Westerners could preserve a state's territorial autonomy, while refusal could lead to war. By choosing negotiation, the bakufu could help determine the treaty structure itself. An imposed treaty, however, would remove from Japan the ability to influence its formation. Like Mongkut in Siam, bakufu policymakers chose to opt in to the global system before they were forced in, and they adopted diplomatic convention to Japan's advantage wherever possible.

The Language of "Inequality"

In Japan, foreign affairs were inseparable from domestic political legitimacy. As the shogun claimed universal primacy, that extended to control over the outside world and determination of the means to exercise that control. This central feature of Edo's rule could not but be challenged by the intrusive American demands to formalize relations. Perry's 1854 treaty, then, no matter how limited, thus directly raised the question of shogunal legitimacy to the level of a national issue.

As a result, Perry's demands polarized the political elite. Abe Masahiro, head of the senior councillors, himself weakened the ideological boundary protecting the shogun by requesting the opinions of the daimyō in the interval between Perry's visits in 1853 and 1854. This was contrary to all precedent and exposed both the weakness and the lack of self-confidence in Edo. In response to Abe, the daimyō arrayed themselves across the political spectrum, some desiring more contact with the West, many urging the bakufu to fight.[37] This lack of consensus only highlighted how contentious foreign policy was becoming, but it did not halt the bakufu's expansion of its foreign relationships, for Japan now was affected by the pressure of an international system that prized interconnectedness, not isolation, among its parts. Despite this reality, Edo did not see the decision to sign a treaty as an irrevocable move toward permanent relations. Indeed, the rhetoric of many top Japanese leaders inside the bakufu and out did not change in the years after Perry's intrusion, as they constantly vowed to build up Japan's shore batteries and drive the foreigner back across the seas, or at the least, keep the foreigners out of Japan by sending trustworthy Japanese to Western lands.[38]

That rhetoric could not efface reality soon became clear to all knowledgeable Japanese, for Perry's treaty opened the floodgates to a wave of new pacts. Within three years, Edo agreed to the 1854 Stirling Convention with Great Britain, the 1855 Russo–Japanese Treaty of Amity, the 1855 Dutch Preliminary Convention, the 1857 Shimoda Convention with the United States, and the 1857 Dutch Supplementary Treaty. Yet even in the wake of this apparent shattering of precedent, the bakufu could claim that nothing fundamental had changed, for none of the post-Perry agreements allowed free trade or even addressed the issue. Although Japan was being drawn ever further into the Western trading network in Asia, the maritime relationships to which the shogunate had so far acquiesced maintained the traditional restrictions on trade and forbade foreign residence outside of Nagasaki.[39]

Nonetheless, both the language and the substance of Japan's new foreign relations interacted in complex ways with the bakufu's diplomatic culture. The language of diplomacy, for example, required adapting existing words or inventing neologisms. Specialized terms, such as "consul," "tariff," and "extraterritoriality," had no specific counterpart, and often no analogous meaning, in Japanese. As late as 1867, for example, the Japanese had no word for consul. The early treaties referred to the diplomatic agents of the West as *kanri* or *rijin*, which simply meant an "official." During negotiations with Harris, the bakufu transliterated terms such as consul ("conshuraru" or "conshuraru jeneraru"), minister ("minisuteru"), and agent ("ajento").[40] Bakufu documents used these terms interchangeably throughout the rest of the Tokugawa period.

Another ill-defined term in the early treaties was "consulate." The word was sometimes translated as *shōkan*, or trading house, which reflected conditions in Nagasaki, where there was no Dutch consular or diplomatic corps separate from the traders. In the Perry treaty, it was referred to as *kansha*, which simply means "building." It is not clear if the bakufu clearly understood, as it negotiated the early pacts, that a diplomatic presence separate from temporary Western visitors to Japan, and invested with specific rights and privileges, would occupy a permanent place on the Japanese landscape.

Sometimes, however, unfamiliar Western terms reflected, if imperfectly, more traditional Japanese approaches to foreign relations. Indeed, some of those issues that became the most contentious after the 1870s caused no alarm two decades earlier. Extraterritoriality is a case in point. During the Meiji period, extraterritoriality, more than almost any other facet of the treaties, was seen as an infringement on Japan's autonomy and an insult to national honor. Yet, as Richard Chang has demonstrated, not until 1875 did the first serious problem with extraterritoriality emerge.[41]

In fact, the bakufu attitude toward extraterritoriality was rather similar to that of the Chinese: merchants were to be left to their own devices, since they were physically controlled at fixed residence areas. The Japanese were under such a system in Korea, at the *wakan* (Japan House) trading post in Pusan. Within Japan, as early as 1613, the bakufu mandated that any employee of the English East India Company in Japan who committed a crime was to be held accountable only to the head of his factory.[42] This was less clear-cut than it may have seemed, for the head of the British factory could try lawbreakers only in conformity with bakufu regulations.[43]

The Dutch were given similar responsibilities, but by keeping them virtual prisoners on the man-made island of Dejima in Nagasaki, and by allowing only a handful to reside there at any time, the bakufu ensured that there would be little opportunity for any interaction between Dutch and Japanese that could lead to the commission of a crime. In contrast, the limited nature of the Perry treaty meant that there was no reason to address extraterritoriality. As noted earlier, this agreement made no provisions for regularized trade, and the bakufu did not foresee that in the future, Americans would permanently live in Japan.

By early 1855, however, the Russians and Japanese explicitly accorded each other extraterritorial status in Article 8 of their Treaty of

Amity, agreeing that malefactors would be punished "according to the laws of their own country."[44] It would seem that, as it slowly expanded the trading rights of foreigners, the bakufu codified its traditional reliance on extraterritoriality. Such a change could be justified since Edo still had not granted foreigners the right of permanent residence. Yet the increase in ships visiting Nagasaki because of the new pact likely made it desirable to spell out clearly how to deal with foreign criminals.

The practice was reaffirmed in the Dutch–Japanese Preliminary Convention of Commerce of November 1855 and again in the Dutch Supplementary Treaty of October 1857. By this time, moreover, the bakufu had received a copy of the 1855 Anglo–Siam treaty, which granted extraterritoriality to British subjects while still restricting their place of residence in Siam.[45]

Thus, when Harris secured extraterritoriality for Americans in his June 1857 Shimoda Convention (Article 4), the bakufu had already incorporated its use into Japanese diplomatic strategy. Harris noted that when he requested that Americans who had committed crimes be placed under the consul's jurisdiction, "to my great and agreeable surprise this was agreed to without demur."[46] Later, during negotiations in early 1858, Harris raised the issue of establishing formal consular courts as the mechanism underlying extraterritoriality. No bakufu opposition was aroused, and the only discussion on the subject occurred when the Japanese inquired whether the courts would be physically located in the consul's residence, and asked about the restriction on movements of repeat offenders.[47]

Yet unlike the pacts enumerated above, Harris in 1858 demanded permanent residence for American merchants, a condition which ostensibly would bring about a completely new pattern of relations between Japanese and foreigners. Yet still, the bakufu unhesitatingly accepted the establishment of legal alienation of foreigners and the imposition of foreign courts on Japanese soil. Two reasons can be adduced for Edo's acceptance of both: first, it genuinely believed in the benefits of extraterritoriality; and second, the bakufu already was beginning to focus on how to isolate the Americans, as at Nagasaki. In effect, the Japanese leadership did not believe that more foreigners necessarily meant freer or uncontrolled encounter with Japanese, and thus consular courts would have few, if any cases, actually to hear.

On the whole, Western nations did not consider the attainment of extraterritoriality a great victory; rather, it was the accepted order of international relations, and a necessary evil. Merchants had been practicing some type of consular jurisdiction in Europe since the twelfth century.[48] By the mid-nineteenth century, there existed enough distrust of the behavior of merchants and sailors abroad to lead the *Times* of London to remark that the Japanese "throw upon us the odium of punishing our own rogues, and take the same office upon themselves."[49]

MFN status similarly raised no Japanese objections. Later excoriated by domestic critics as an oppressive means of keeping Japan in thrall to an ever-expanding number of treaty partners, the MFN clause had been granted to Perry in the ninth article of his 1854 treaty. Though a mention of bilateral MFN status was included in Harris's draft, it would be left out of the final 1858 pact. Rather, being enumerated in Perry's convention, it was simply assumed by both sides to be still in force.[50] Only with the Elgin treaty was an explicit, one-sided MFN clause finally inserted; this, it should be of no surprise, was identical to the MFN clause Britain secured in the just-completed Tianjin Treaty as well as in its 1855 Anglo–Siamese agreement.

Why was there no Japanese resistance to MFN? One answer may be that Japan had inherited the traditional Chinese attitude of ensuring that no barbarian was superior to another. The Tokugawa system of diplomacy, it will be recalled, had formalized diplomatic relations only with Korea and the Ryūkyūan kingdom; both China and the Dutch were accorded only trading status. Yet the shock of both the Opium War and the incursion of several Western nations at roughly the same time prodded Edo to conceptualize new security strategies, particularly those that would least tax the strength of the bakufu.

In that vein, Bob Wakabayashi has written of the late Tokugawa thinker Aizawa Seishisai's calls for Japan to "use barbarians to control barbarians." Unlike the strident nationalistic tone of his 1825 *Shinron (The New Theses)*, Aizawa's later writings urged the bakufu to adopt a Japanese version of "China among equals," used when the ruling dynasty was too weak to defend its interests. In such times, the Qing recognized rival states as equals and attempted to ensure that no one power gained superiority over the others. For Aizawa, such a reliance on balance-of-power alliances would help ensure that barbarians were kept concerned with one another's position, and thus not focused on swallowing Japan whole. This was China's traditional policy of "loose rein" and it seemed a logical way to face the crush of numerous powers at once.[51] It was also, as has been shown, the policy of Siamese leaders, including Mongkut, who realized that the British desired a stable Siam precisely as a counterpart to any other European, particularly French, aspiration in the region.

Some officials close to the bakufu center of power read the international situation in the same way. In 1844 and 1851, books by the Chinese intellectual Wei Yuan were passed through Nagasaki to the bakufu. His *Sheng Wu Chi (Imperial Military Exploits)* was read by then-head of the senior councillors Abe Masahiro, and it kindled in him an increased fear of Western expansion. Also translated was the famous *Haiguo Tuzhi (Illustrated Treatise on the Maritime Kingdoms)*, which extolled the policy of using barbarian versus barbarian, and also employing Western technology to build up China's maritime power.[52]

Matsudaira Keiei, lord of Fukui and an influential leader in bakumatsu Japan, wrote to the senior councillors just before the commencement of formal negotiations with Harris that "it is quite clear that present conditions make national seclusion impossible. . . . The thing most to be feared is not the influx of other countries, but the rivalry *between* England and Russia. . . . That one of these two might sometime seek privileges that would inevitably endanger the State is the thought that fills me with the greatest concern."[53] For the bakufu, being able to keep the powers at a level of equality vis-à-vis one another was a logical policy, and thus made the MFN clause seem a benefit to Japan, not a detriment.

Japanese Territory and Geopolitics

The issue of central concern to Edo was territorial sovereignty—the defense of its physical boundary. Certainly bakufu leaders understood Japan was being absorbed into a regional trading system that was supplanting traditional exchange networks. Yet the workings of that structure were still a mystery, and hence a threat. It would take several years after Perry for the bakufu to appreciate that Great Britain was the dominant Western power in the East Asian regional system. Nor could Edo's policymakers initially have understood that London was committed in general to keeping itself at arm's length from entrapment in foreign problems. Indeed, commercial expansion by British merchants could turn into imperial control if local conditions interfered with what London considered to be normal market practices— other words, if a territory's government could not or would not ensure smooth trade.[54] This was the lesson of the Opium War, information about which had flooded Japan back in the 1840s.

It was Britain's nonintervention policy, however, that marked relations with Japan from the start. The first British pact with Japan was a naval one, negotiated by Admiral James F. Stirling, and from it the bakufu immediately discerned just how limited the British presence would normally be. Stirling's 1854 convention and its later emendations contained a strict proviso that British warships were not allowed to use Japanese ports except in case of emergency, and even then they could not proceed into the interior. Stirling made clear Britain's negligible interest in territorial expansion in the islands, and he reported back to London that British neutrality toward, and friendship with, Japan were "matters of vital importance to Britain's interests in adjacent seas."[55] The bakufu was able to interpret the British strategy through its familiarity with the 1855 Anglo–Siamese treaty. There, too, Britain eschewed territorial expansion; Siamese lands were inviolable, and British warships were restricted from trespassing into the interior.[56]

In London's eyes, Japan played a geopolitical role similar to Siam's. The British initially were interested in keeping the country a stable and independent polity in the emerging East Asian trading sphere. In a variant of informal empire, they knew they could not have a trading monopoly in Japan, so they sought instead to deny any other Western state the ability to use the islands as a base from which to attack British interests in China or Southeast Asia.[57] Thus Japan was initially viewed by the British primarily as a strategic point in East Asia, and not as a trade center itself. Due to the relative proximity of the China Station, Britain's Asian naval squadron, London could more easily ensure that Japan remained a "healthy" part of the system.

It was the Americans, however, who first forced Japan to sign a trade treaty, and their global outlook was very different from the British. In approaching Japan, Washington on the one hand had neither the desire nor the ability to colonize the country; in this, it accorded with British designs that have come to be called informal empire. Yet on the other hand, the Americans did not view Japan as part of a larger network of interlinked territories, some colonized, some not.

Having expanded across the American continent and now the Pacific, Washington's interest in Japan was purely economic, as a source of supplies for whalers and a potential coaling station for U.S. naval ships. That a demand for free trade could undermine domestic Japanese stability, and thereby cause the country to become a problem in regional politics, was not a concern of either Commodore Perry or consul Harris.

In fairness, even had Harris been sensitive to the issue, there was no way he could have understood how foreign issues were tied so deeply into Tokugawa domestic politics, and therefore how unsettling his proposal would be.

Once Harris made clear that he would demand nothing less than free trade, though, Edo was faced with a completely new threat to its diplomatic culture. Harris in this sense represented the end of the post-Perry transition period, and indeed was the herald of the end of the traditional Tokugawa state. The call for free trade throughout the country forced the issue of clearly defining just what comprised Japanese territory and, even more, the limits of Tokugawa authority. This was so because the borders of the realm were not yet fixed in nineteenth-century Japan.[58] In the north, for example, the bakufu had an administrative apparatus for the island of Hokkaido (called Ezo), which was at that time still populated largely by indigenous Ainu tribes. Edo, however, did not physically control the whole island, despite its desire to deny the Russians a foothold there.[59] Similarly, the Ryūkyū islands, though of long-standing concern to the bakufu, were not yet claimed by Japan, and were not absorbed until 1879.

More important, perhaps, the system regulating relations between Edo and the 250-odd domains was in many respects a type of international order.[60] Edo was the paramount power, and seemingly impervious, but fundamentally the bakufu was merely the house organization of the most powerful territorial lord, the Tokugawa, and thus not a "national" administration in the way that the Meiji government was to become. The most powerful outer domains, such as Satsuma in Kyūshū and Chōshū in western Honshū, were all but autonomous, even though they followed the centuries-old alternate attendance system and largely deferred to Edo's authority in foreign affairs. Harris's call for free trade throughout Japan would force Edo not only to allow these domains to participate in international commerce, but also hinted at irresolvable questions over how the bakufu would administer trade and assert control over the outer domains with respect to this new type of foreign affairs. Letting the genii of authority out of the bottle of tradition could result in conflict that might well cause the kind of regime destabilization that Edo had always feared and that Great Britain was eager to guard against.

Worries over how to square the circle of the shogunate's domestic limits and foreign responsibilities, however, began long before the specifics of Harris's plan were known. The bakufu had been weakened throughout the nineteenth century by the costs of dealing with famines, reconstruction efforts, and popular insurrections. Tensions with domains small and large were increasing in conjunction with efforts to extract more resources and maintain traditional elements of central control. Then, as the Western threat in Asia became clearer, some voices began to call for fundamental changes in Japanese domestic and foreign policy leading to the bakufu having total authority over the entire realm. Hayashi Shihei, for example, had argued in the early 1790s that the bakufu must protect Japanese territorial integrity; the way to do this was to control Ezo and the Ryūkyūs, as well as Korea, not to mention all the main Japanese islands.[61] From this enlarged power base, he wrote, Japan would be able to confront any threat.

Never before, however, had the question of Japan's international boundary directly been pressed from the outside. Bakufu officials had mapped the main islands and, as noted earlier, ended their jurisdiction in the southern part of Hokkaido. Evfimii Putiatin's 1855 mission to conclude a maritime convention, one of the wave of post-Perry pacts, included a demand to settle the boundary between Japan and Russia. The second article of the treaty took up the border question, and the bakufu found itself for the first time agreeing, at least on paper, to the definition of its lands. The agreement gave Japan the entire Kurile Island chain stretching northward from Hokkaido to the Kamchatka peninsula, while the two governments split the island of Sakhalin, although they deferred setting a precise latitudinal break.[62]

Thus, by the time the bakufu sat down to craft a trade treaty with Townsend Harris in 1858, top officials understood both that they had to protect Japan's physical boundaries and that they had to adapt their strategy in order to do so. If the bakufu refused to agree to trade, the Western powers could use it as a casus belli. Moreover, the European states could demand the inclusion of the outer domains in any trading system. This in turn raised two crucial problems: first, if Satsuma or Chōshū refused to trade, the foreigners could hold Edo culpable; and second, the bakufu obstinately did not want to share the potential riches of trade with the outer domains. Edo's economic policy was essentially mercantilistic, and enriching the Tokugawa's most powerful hereditary enemies was to be avoided at all costs. What trade ultimately threatened was the loss of bakufu territorial control, either to the foreigners or to hostile outer domains.

At the head of the bakufu stood Hotta Masayoshi, successor to Abe

Masahiro and leader of the senior councillors since November 1855. Hotta had refused to meet with Harris after his arrival in the summer of 1856, and indeed kept him waiting for sixteen months. By the end of 1857, though, he bowed to Harris's repeated entreaties, and opened up direct contact with the American. On December 7, 1857, Harris was granted an audience in Edo with the shogun himself. In a world in which ritual was all, this meeting represented perhaps the gravest breach hitherto in Tokugawa diplomacy. Even Perry, at the head of the Black Ships, had not been allowed inside Edo's precincts and had not met with anyone higher than the Kanagawa magistrate. But Harris, alone in Japan except for his secretary, Henry Heusken, nonetheless crossed the moat of Edo Castle on that December morning. The bakufu had tried to ignore him, and perhaps ironically it was Harris's very isolation that made Hotta believe he could contain Harris's demands. This American seemed so much less a threat than Perry had, and the prints that recorded his embassy to Edo portrayed a rather ordinary man respectfully doffing his cap as he entered the castle, in contrast to the fire-breathing demon that was the commodore.[63]

Hotta was persuaded to interview Harris both by the American's doggedness and by news of the latest British military engagement in China. Yet implicit in his reception of Harris was the negotiation of some kind of more comprehensive trade treaty with the United States and by extension, with the major European powers. Informed partly by the Siamese model and partly by the Japanese view of extraterritoriality and MFN discussed earlier, Hotta did not see his actions as a surrender that would bring Japan either completely uncontrolled trade or a permanent Western presence.[64] Negotiations, while unavoidable, would be like walking a tightrope, but it could be done.

To the bakufu, the challenge to its traditional policy was clear: its diplomatic culture would stand or fall on its response to Harris's key demand, free trade. Bakufu negotiators quickly understood the most important issue to be where they would allow such trade to occur, for those spots would be the actual intersection of the two civilizations, the place where the raw material of relations would meet and mix. To control this new type of interaction, and thereby protect Japan, meant maintaining a voice in treaty relations, and that in turn meant controlling the location of the treaty ports and cities. The negotiation of space now became the focus of the Japanese.

CHAPTER TWO

Negotiating Space:
The Meaning of Yokohama

The physical boundary between Japan and the outer world had been the bakufu's first line of defense since the early seventeenth century. As such, it remained perhaps the crucial component of Japan's diplomatic culture in the early modern period. Townsend Harris's presence itself was a breach in this boundary, but his free-trade proposal threatened to destroy it completely. The defense of Japanese space became Edo's overriding concern.

What resulted was a series of shifting and parallel negotiations within the bakufu, between the bakufu and domestic interests such as the court, and between the bakufu and Westerners. Negotiation now became a regular part of the diplomatic experience of the shogunate. These parleys sometimes were contemporaneous, sometimes flowering in response to other negotiations.

Diplomatic Culture and the Crystallization of Policy

Although Harris had arrived at Shimoda with Henry Heusken in August 1856, he languished there, battling disease and his own nerves, until late 1857. Finally on December 7, he presented U.S. President Franklin Pierce's letter to the shogun, Tokugawa Iesada, in an unprecedented and impressive ceremony in Edo Castle. Attired in a florid pseudo-naval uniform, with Heusken carrying the letter covered in silk in an ornate box, Harris advanced between rows of top bakufu retainers to the base of the shogun's raised platform. Both exchanged pleasantries, the first time any Westerner had done so as a diplomatic equal.[1]

Once past the ritual, Harris was eager to achieve his long-held goal, and he tried to convince the head of the senior councillors, Hotta Masayoshi, quickly to sign a treaty with the United States. Harris knew that in his isolation he posed little threat to the bakufu. So, despite his sense of competitiveness with the British, he did not hesitate to stoop to the level of invoking the European specter to advance his cause. In his first substantive meeting with Hotta, a week after the ceremony in Edo Castle, Harris intimated that the British, fresh from defeating China in the Arrow War, might well sail gunboats into Edo Bay and force the Japanese to accept inequitable trading terms.[2] Harris hoped the thinly veiled threat would force the bakufu to recognize that Japan's best interest lay in accommodating the United States first. Hotta quickly relayed the message to various bakufu officials, setting in motion a massive internal debate.

Once news of Harris's threat circulated, the bakufu was flooded with advice. Such unsolicited opinion was itself a threat to Edo, whose external boundaries to isolate foreigners was mirrored by internal boundaries to eliminate domestic interference in its traditional prerogative to conduct foreign affairs. Key diplomatic questions, as for all policy issues, were decided by a tiny group of officials. Public input was neither sought nor allowed, for the bakufu did not consider foreign affairs a realm appropriate for any sectors of Japanese society other than itself. No scholars of Western studies, no domainal officials, and certainly no commoners were given any type of access to the bakufu officials charged with diplomatic policy. In response, public opinion made itself known in various ways, primarily through a vibrant publishing culture that circulated mass-produced woodblock prints commenting on the key issues of the day. The greater the amount of public discourse, the stronger the bakufu attempted to control policy-making. A static diplomatic culture was almost guaranteed to emerge, and such a culture was now deeply strained by the twin poles of Western encroachment and domestic discontent.

Only once before had this arrangement been disrupted, when Abe Masahiro, Hotta's predecessor, had polled the whole of the daimyō estate on the appropriate response to Perry.[3] In addition to calling into question Edo's ability to conduct foreign affairs, Abe had given de facto legitimization to the idea of a civic realm, no matter how circumscribed, in which great issues could be publicly debated. Not only had no firm policy been decided, daimyō, long marginalized from foreign affairs, were in essence invited by the bakufu itself to comment on, and undoubtedly criticize, Edo's strategy.

Hotta's actions in 1857 can be interpreted as an attempt to restore Edo's traditional diplomatic culture. Thus, he sought to limit effective input on Harris's information to the bakufu's top bureaucrats. Most of these sat on a body called the *hyōjōsho*, which normally functioned as the bakufu's highest tribunal. The tribunal consisted variously of the three top bureaucratic ranks of magistrate: magistrate of temples and shrines, city magistrate, and finance magistrate, whom the senior councillors often consulted on major policy issues. In addition, officials holding the important lower ranks of chief inspector, inspector, and maritime defense official also sat on the tribunal.[4]

Of the groups composing the tribunal, the finance magistrates were, on the whole, the least willing to relax restrictions on trade, and sought only the most limited relations possible. Responsible for bakufu finances, they were primarily concerned with the effect of trade on Japan's domestic economy and the bakufu's economic position. The maritime defense officials, however, concerned by the weakness of Japan's coastal defenses, were more sensitive to the need to maintain peaceful relations with the West. Yet the dynamics of bakufu politics often put them on the defensive, so a key part of their negotiating strategy within Edo Castle was to stress the benefits that more trade could bring to the shogunate. Among the finance magistrates and maritime defense officials, however, a few individuals stood head and shoulders above the rest. The most important response to Harris's threats, and the one that was to frame subsequent debate, came from the most prominent maritime defense official, Iwase Tadanari.

Iwase was born in 1818 to mid-level samurai but soon was adopted into a family of slightly lower rank. He attended the Shōheikō, the official bakufu school run by the Hayashi family, along with two other boys who would become key diplomats, Hori Toshihiro and Nagai Naomune.[5] After various assignments, he was raised to the rank of inspector and became an Abe protégé. During the crucial years of 1853–1854, Iwase was given a senior appointment along with Egawa Tarōzaemon to build an offshore battery in Edo Bay, in essence the last line of military defense before Perry's expected return. As the project neared completion, in February 1854, Abe appointed Iwase a maritime defense official. The following year he was one of the first appointees to the new Institute for Western Studies (*Yōgakusho*), being named along with the finance magistrates Kawaji Toshiaki and Mizuno Tadanori and the chief inspector Tsutsui Masanori. He stayed in the same position when the Yōgakusho became the Institute for the Study of Barbarian Books (*Bansho shirabesho*) in March 1856. By the late 1850s, Iwase had become a coordinator of the bakufu's new military-diplomatic apparatus, and one of perhaps five key men working on foreign affairs.

Iwase favored expanding trade with the West, though keeping it under bakufu control. Hotta, who succeeded Abe as head of the senior councillors in November 1855, picked Iwase to go to Nagasaki in May 1857, along with fellow institute member Mizuno Tadanori, to discuss trade issues with Dutch representative Donker Curtius. Iwase and Curtius eventually convinced the cautious Mizuno to sign a more liberal, yet still restrictive, trade treaty in October 1857. An almost identical supplementary treaty with the Russians was completed the same month. The two agreements raised the cap on the number of trading vessels allowed each year but continued to restrict all other forms of contact, limiting trade to the cities of Nagasaki and Hakodate (see chapter 1).

It was while returning from Nagasaki that Iwase received by courier a copy of Harris's crucial December interview with Hotta. In a hastily drafted letter to the senior councillors (and a parallel one to his fellow inspectors in Edo) of December 21, Iwase forcefully presented the case for opening up Japan to freer trade.[6] Understanding both Japan's weaknesses and the depth of domestic opposition to such a plan, he linked his argument to an overall strategy for strengthening bakufu control over both domestic and foreign issues.

Iwase saw trade as a way to reassert the control over diplomatic relations that Edo had lost in the years since Perry. Regaining control would in turn maximize the shogunate's domestic authority. Implicitly referring to the bakufu's symbolic powers, Iwase overtly pitched his argument to the senior councillors in political and economic terms. He acknowledged that there was no choice but to open Japan to a trading system even more expansive than the one he had just negotiated with the Dutch. That being the case, the crux of the matter was to maintain the idea of boundaries and to center trade at a spot near Edo. This would prevent foreign trade from falling into the hands of Osaka merchants and outer lords, who would be able to circumvent bakufu regulations in the more open atmosphere of that mercantile city. "Should eighty or ninety percent of the country's trade fall into the hands of the Osaka merchants, first Edo and then the rest of the country will wither, and only Osaka will prosper,"[7] warned Iwase, arguing instead that controlling trade near Edo would benefit all Japan.

The link between foreign affairs and economics took center stage because Iwase knew that he would have to negotiate his plan with the finance magistrates. Like all other bakufu diplomats, Iwase's understanding of the effects of trade was informed by the experience of the past two centuries, whereby trade was subsumed within a diplomatic framework. Free trade was inconceivable to the bakufu, for such activity had no referent beyond itself; it did not serve any political purpose, and thus did not make sense to bureaucrats. In addition, Tokugawa ideology taught that the rise of merchant princes was to be feared, while domestic political stability mandated preventing the enrichment of domains antagonistic to the bakufu. Free trade could engender both these undesirable outcomes. This was already a problem with the powerful Shimazu family in Satsuma, which had for centuries been conducting a semilegal trade with the Ryūkyūs and China.[8]

Iwase's solution was to give the foreigners what they wanted, but to construct a new boundary around them, much like in Nagasaki. "For this reason," he proposed, "we should open the village of Yokohama, in Musashi province."[9] Yokohama was still a fishing village, positioned on a spit of land across the bay from the nearest town, the post station of Kanagawa. Kanagawa sat on the Tōkaidō, which traversed the country from Edo to Kyoto, and was thus the main transport artery in Japan.

Iwase argued that merchants and all foreign diplomatic representatives should be restricted to Yokohama, where they would be isolated from Edo by nearly a day's ride. At the same time, though, since Yokohama village was close to the capital, the bakufu could easily resolve any problems that cropped up and limit potential fallout. Iwase thus called for centering Japan's new foreign relations at Yokohama, thereby keeping bakufu control over both domestic and foreign trade, ensuring that the bakufu and not major daimyō or uncontrolled Osaka merchants profited, and creating the basis for a "national renewal" (*chūkō ishin*).[10]

Key to winning the bakufu internal negotiation was an important, if subtle, argument over the symbolic importance of his proposal. Yokohama, Iwase did not have to point out, was the very spot where Perry had signed the 1854 Treaty of Peace and Amity. Since then, the growing nationwide schism between *kaikoku* ("open the country") and *jōi* ("expel the barbarians") adherents turned on whether to allow foreigners to pollute Japanese soil. Within the bakufu, the split between different camps was engendered by the debate over how far and where to allow the foreigner to intrude in Japan. "Trade" often became the code word for the ultimate question of foreign relations, namely how to preserve Japan's independence and purity in the face of foreign threat.

In choosing Yokohama, Iwase was urging the bakufu to restrict the foreigners to where they had already set foot. In such a scheme, there was no problem with keeping Nagasaki and Hakodate open to trade, as those sites had already been granted, and they thus formed part of Japan's traditional boundaries containing foreigners. No new land, however, would be given, and certainly none in the district of Kyoto, abode of the imperial family. Iwase was drawing a line beyond which the foreigners could not go. If the bakufu implemented his plan, then Hotta could claim that Edo was, in reality, making no new concession of territory. Such an assertion could be used against both domestic critics of the bakufu and the foreigners, thus addressing the larger issues of national sovereignty and bakufu authority. There is little other explanation for why Iwase, one of the emerging experts on foreign relations, should have chosen the small, isolated fishing village of Yokohama, out of the entire Kantō (or even Japanese) coastline.

The counter to Iwase's proposal came from his Nagasaki negotiating partner, Mizuno Tadanori. Mizuno was born in 1815, the son of an indebted *hatamoto*, or direct retainer of the shogun. Starting out in the Tokugawa historical records office, he rapidly rose through the bureaucracy.[11] In 1852 he was made Uraga magistrate, which at the time was a key post because of the expected arrival in Edo Bay of a squadron from the United States. A month before Perry arrived, however, Mizuno was promoted to Nagasaki magistrate, traditionally a senior appointment. In that capacity he was the bakufu's point man for dealing with the Russians and Dutch in the days after Perry's departure. In 1854 he reached the top bureaucratic position of finance magistrate and also was appointed to the Institute for the Study of

Barbarian Books. Like Iwase, Mizuno was one of the bakufu's top diplomatic hands, but by temperament he was far more conservative. He grudgingly accepted the need for limited trade, but sought even more than Iwase to isolate the foreigners.

Mizuno's letter of January 2, 1858, to the senior councillors presented an uneasy alternative to Iwase's brief of the month before. He stressed not only keeping foreigners out of Kyoto and Osaka but also keeping them as far from Edo as possible: "The best course would be for the foreigners to reside in outlying ports like Nagasaki and Hakodate, but even if they go elsewhere, it is my hope that the bakufu will designate places some distance removed from Edo."[12] Mizuno had trouble, however, firmly dealing with one of Harris's new demands, namely, that a U.S. diplomatic minister or agent should reside in the capital. He opposed such an arrangement, believing that such proximity would enable the agent to harass the bakufu. Such officials should be forced to live in the open ports, he argued, but he also realized they would most likely refuse to live in a city as isolated as Nagasaki. Therefore, to ensure that agents were kept out of Edo itself, the open ports could be located close to the capital, but only if unavoidable. Mizuno, though, made it clear that he favored a harder line than Iwase.

After weighing the proposals of his two top policy advisers, Hotta settled the internal bakufu debate by selecting Iwase to serve as one of the two negotiators for the upcoming meetings with Harris. Accompanying Iwase would be the Shimoda city magistrate Inoue Kiyonao, brother of Kawaji Toshiaki, a high-ranking finance magistrate also connected with foreign issues. Inoue was ostensibly the lead representative, but Iwase quickly emerged as the main negotiator and strategist.[13] Hotta charged the two on January 17, 1858, with negotiating a treaty, and the next day they met Harris for the first time. Hotta's instructions and Iwase's beliefs would shape the bakufu response to the Western challenge.

First Negotiations: Containing Harris

The negotiations over where to locate the open ports occurred over a period of eighteen months, from January 1858 to July 1859. The issue had both material and symbolic significance, and led both sides to negotiate not just port location, but the very nature of treaty relations itself.

Harris passed over his draft treaty at the first meeting. It called for opening the cities of Osaka, Nagasaki, Hirado, Kyoto, Edo, Shinagawa, and Hakodate, and two sites on the Japan Sea to be named later, to residence and trade, and requested in addition one coaling station on Kyushu for American steamers.[14] At these sites, Americans would be allowed to rent land and buy buildings. Shimoda, open to U.S. ships under the Perry treaty, would be closed six months after either Edo or Shinagawa opened.

Harris knew that distinct foreign settlements located in large towns were the norm for trading posts in Asia. Such settlements offered protection for Americans, as at Shanghai and Penang, but also allowed merchants to interact with native populations. Along with extraterritorial rights secured through tradition or force, this arrangement prevented U.S. citizens from being placed under foreign laws and was thus entirely a voluntary "isolation" on their part.[15] This, of course, perfectly suited Japan's traditional strategy, as well. It was not the existence of foreign settlements that troubled Harris and the bakufu, then, but rather their location and the extent of their isolation.

The Japanese negotiating strategy relied on obfuscating details and using delaying tactics if necessary to institutionalize as much as possible the isolation of the Americans. Despite Harris's threat of British gunboats sailing over from China, Iwase and Inoue refused simply to accept the U.S. treaty proposals. As negotiations commenced, Harris found that the issue of the open ports became the "Sebastopol of the Treaty."[16] The most sensitive point quickly became the location of the Kantō region port, the one that would be located closest to the shogun in Edo.

Harris initially proposed constructing a foreign settlement and port at Shinagawa, which served as the "doorstep" to the capital. That town was the first post station on the Tōkaidō and abutted Edo itself. For the Japanese, this was too close to the capital. Their minimum concession in response was to keep Westerners at least half a day's ride from Edo, which meant farther down the Tōkaidō. Inoue and Iwase claimed that Shinagawa was a poor anchorage, and Harris soon agreed to drop the site, accepting in its stead Kanagawa post town, located two stops farther west on the Tōkaidō, about twelve and a half miles from Shinagawa.

From this point on, ambiguity haunted the negotiations. Harris referred to the location of the proposed site as "Kanagawa," apparently meaning the post town itself. Iwase and Inoue, however, initially referred to it in Japanese as "an area in Kanagawa Bay," but later simply "Kanagawa." On top of this confusion, Harris himself now broached the idea of opening the village of Yokohama, though he was ignorant of Iwase's decisive memorandum on this issue of only a month before.[17] Neither Iwase nor Inoue mentioned the site until Harris brought it up. Harris and the Japanese were now talking about at least three distinct physical locations, and neither Iwase nor Inoue attempted to make Harris clarify his position.

The bakufu negotiators also employed a further tactic to ensure the physical isolation of Americans, namely forbidding any type of mixed residence in the port. This would, in essence, seal the foreign settlement within a bubble, which was the centuries-old policy applied to the Dutch in Nagasaki. Once apprised of this plan, Harris bitterly wrote in his journal that "under such regulations as they proposed, trade was impossible."[18]

This tactic of outlawing mixed residence further confused the issue of port location. Harris sought to evade the residency restriction by securing the right for Americans to live in Edo while trading. The Japanese balked at such an idea, however, demanding that Harris follow the precedent set in his Siam treaty, whereby American merchants were permitted to live only in the official trading port. During the following week of discussion on this issue, Harris and the Japanese interchangeably used "Kanagawa" and "Yokohama" in discussing the exact location where American merchants and their consul would live.[19] In the beginning of February, Inoue and Iwase finally "acquiesced" to Harris's proposal that the consul should live in Edo and Americans trading in Japan should reside at Kanagawa.[20] Little mention is made of the site after this, and the final draft treaty of February 23, stipulated that "Kanagawa" would open for trade on July 4, 1859.[21]

Harris clearly thought that "Kanagawa" referred to the post town of the same name on the Tōkaidō. After all, his primary concern was to locate American merchants where trade would be most profitable. Why, then, did he himself bring up Yokohama as a site for merchant residence? Harris gave a hint in his journal entry of November 28, 1857, which he wrote while on the road to Edo for his first meeting with the shogun: "At noon stop at Kanagawa. . . . This is an interesting spot to me as it was the scene of Commodore Perry's negotiations.

From my house I look across the bay to Yokohama, the place where his fleet was anchored."[22]

Harris, however, was mistaken, for Perry actually conducted his negotiations at Yokohama after being refused permission to land at Kanagawa.[23] Perry's 1854 convention was known, though, as the Treaty of Kanagawa. It originally was written in four languages, vernacular Japanese, Chinese-style formal Japanese, English, and Dutch, none of them being considered the original. The vernacular copy made no mention of where the treaty was signed, though in an attached report to the senior councillors the maritime defense officials noted *Yokohama-mura* (Yokohama village) as the location of the signing. The English and Dutch versions both named Kanagawa as the site of the signing ceremony. Only the formal Japanese version accurately recorded that the treaty was signed at Yokohama village.[24]

Perry himself knew well that he concluded his treaty at "Yokuhama." F. L. Hawks's report of his mission noted that Perry wanted the signing to occur at the post town, but after repeated pleadings from Japanese officials he settled for Yokohama, which he estimated to be about three miles from Kanagawa proper and nine miles from Edo.[25] There is no explanation why Perry inserted "Kanagawa" instead of "Yokohama" in the treaty. It is possible that the Japanese, during arguments over where to sign the pact, informed him that Yokohama village was part of a larger administrative sphere called "Kanagawa." This was a strategy the bakufu later adopted against Harris.

Harris therefore must have thought that the Perry treaty was signed at the post town. His sense of history likely led him to desire including Yokohama as a place where Americans could live, but he clearly considered it a minor add-on. Trade was to be conducted and merchant residences were to be built at the post town, which he described in his November journal entry thus: "Kanagawa has the air of a flourishing town and has much increased since Kaempfer described it. It is the nearest harbor to Yedo [Edo], and must become a place of great importance whenever Yedo shall be opened to foreign commerce."[26] There was no ambiguity in Harris's mind.

Once agreement on Kanagawa seemed to be reached, the rest of the treaty was quickly drafted. Iwase, Inoue, and Harris used an amalgam of existing pacts and Harris's Siamese treaty to cover the many provisions. Objectively, the treaty seemed to signal a radical rupture in Japan's relations with the outside world.[27] Of particular import were the following eight features:

1. Article 1 provided for a *permanent* diplomatic agent to reside in Japan (as well as a Japanese agent to live in the United States).

2. Article 3 established the rights of Americans to live in designated port cities, lease land, and buy buildings therein.

3. Article 3 also granted Americans the right to trade freely with Japanese in the open port areas.

4. Fixed tariff rates were provided for and calculated in Article IV and subsequent appendices; Japan was thus denied tariff autonomy.

5. The sixth article established the principle of extraterritoriality in the foreign settlements, thereby freeing Americans accused of crimes in Japan from judgment by Japanese authorities.

6. Article 8 allowed Americans the free exercise of religion, overturning a two-century ban on any practice of Christianity within Japan's borders.

7. Article 13 established renegotiation procedures for the treaty, but provided for no date of expiration.

8. Most-favored-nation (MFN) status was carried over from the 1854 Perry convention.

Negotiation complete, Hotta asked Harris for a two-month delay before signing the pact, during which he would obtain imperial sanction for the treaty. This was a calculated gamble on Hotta's part. On the one hand, he had conducted negotiations with no domestic input, following the dictates of the bakufu's diplomatic culture. Yet Hotta knew that the shogunate no longer had the prestige to sign the treaty on its own authority, regardless of its official prerogative. The treaty was too new, too radical a statement for the bakufu to risk domestic backlash, even though Edo's long-term plan was to keep conditions as similar as possible to the past.

In a tacit admission that Japan's diplomatic culture had irrevocably changed, Hotta felt that he had no option but to gain imperial approval for the bakufu's seemingly new policy. Whereas Hotta had attempted to reduce any domainal influence on foreign policy-making, he now breached from the other side the ideological boundary protecting the shogun's diplomatic primacy. A journey by the head of the senior councillors to seek imperial approval of a crucial foreign policy change could be read by society at large only as Edo's acknowledgement of its subordinate status to the court.

Riding the tiger of domestic politics, Hotta clearly hoped to maintain the bakufu's superiority over all sectors of society precisely by using the prestige of Kyoto. Were the emperor to approve the treaty, the bakufu would have a powerful tool with which to tame the feared domestic opposition. At a deeper level, though, Hotta had to understand that his journey to Kyoto would open a Pandora's box. Diplomacy was forcing a reevaluation of the fundamental basis of bakufu rule, and at the same time was being transformed by that change.

Hotta traveled confidently to Kyoto in mid-May, expecting quick approval. Yet challenges to the shogunate's domestic authority now erupted, and the treaty became entangled with a looming shogunal succession issue in which the bakufu found itself forced to vie with a group of powerful reformist daimyō over replacing the ailing Tokugawa Iesada.[28] Hotta ultimately failed to win imperial approval, and returned to Edo on June 1, his power gone. Daimyō allied to the Tokugawa called for a strong leader, one able to preserve the prerogatives of the bakufu against the reformist machinations of anti-Tokugawa great lords. Three days later, the senior councillors, acting in the name of the shogun, appointed Ii Naosuke as *tairō* (great councillor).

Ii Naosuke and the Return to a Traditional Strategy

Ii was the lord of Hikone, largest of the *fudai* ("hereditary") domains allied to the Tokugawa, but one much smaller than the domains of the major outer or blood-related lords.[29] His family traditionally had been one of two to occupy the highest nonshogunal position in the bakufu, great councillor, which was filled only during times of crisis. Ii was born in 1815, and was forty-three when he took over the bakufu. His major goal was to resolve the shogunal succession crisis in favor of his own candidate and thereby secure his position against those powerful lords, Shimazu Nariakira of Satsuma and Tokugawa Nariaki of Mito among them, who hoped to put in a reformist candidate more sympathetic to an enlarged bakufu-domain power-sharing arrangement.

As such, Ii soon came into conflict with his newly inherited diplomatic negotiators, the maritime defense officials. Led by Iwase Tadanari, the officials largely supported the reform party candidate Hitotsubashi Keiki, son of the Mito lord, Tokugawa Nariaki. Ii, however, pushed the young Tokugawa Yoshitomi, who would be a pliable, even negligible, presence. Yet Ii's opposition to the maritime defense officials was not based solely on considerations of domestic policy. He held strong opinions regarding foreign relations, being disdainful of foreigners and reluctant to open Japan to broader trade. There was bound to be a clash with the pro-trade group of maritime defense officials led by Iwase.

The months after Ii's accession saw an internal bakufu struggle over diplomatic strategy. The struggle was precipitated by news from Harris in the spring of 1858 that the British had just defeated China in the Arrow War and could be on their way to Japan. Ii was forced to prioritize the threats he faced and he chose to risk domestic opposition over possible foreign war. Turning his back on Hotta's strategy of accommodating the court, Ii decided to sign the U.S. commercial treaty without imperial approval. Once the treaty was signed, he could leisurely work to thwart it and simultaneously control the domestic response. War with the West, however, would remove his options. Moreover, by signing the U.S. treaty first, the bakufu would create a template for future pacts, the same way that the British and U.S. agreements with Siam formed the basis for Harris's proposals. Thus, despite lacking imperial approval, Ii authorized Iwase and Inoue to sign the treaty on board the *Powhatan* on July 29.

Ii's decision set the basic mold of the bakufu's response: boundaries might be expanded, for example in considering the bakufu's relation to the court or in allowing foreigners greater trading privileges, but they would nonetheless be maintained. Appeasement, thwarting, and control on both the foreign and domestic levels were the new tactics. With the newly signed treaty mollifying Harris, Ii turned to enhancing his domestic power base in preparation for controlling the expected internal response. He first secured control over the highest organ of bakufu policy-making, the senior council. He forced Hotta's resignation on August 2 and filled the council with his handpicked supporters.

Once in control of the inner circle at Edo Castle, Ii moved to reduce the influence of Iwase and his colleagues, the maritime defense officials. In mid-August, the position of maritime defense official was abolished and a new post of foreign magistrate (*gaikoku bugyō*) was created. The first foreign magistrates were Hori Toshihiro, Inoue Kiyonao, Iwase Tadanari, Mizuno Tadanori, and Nagai Naomune.[30]

The introduction of the foreign magistrate position was more than a mere administrative shuffle. By creating a new post, Ii sought to break the influence of the maritime defense officials over the formulation of foreign policy. The office had been introduced in 1845 at the beginning of Abe Masahiro's term of leadership. Two years later, thirty-one officials held the post.[31] The maritime defense officials of the late 1850s were, in effect, the foreign policy brains of the bakufu, but their potential influence over strategy was much broader. Because they dealt with issues of military reform and trade liberalization, they operated at the intersection of domestic and foreign affairs. By 1858, the maritime defense officials appointed by Abe and Hotta, along with other mid-level bureaucrats, pushed trade liberalization policies and the domestic reform program favored by the lords of Satsuma and Mito.

When Ii came to power, the leading maritime defense officials were Hori, Iwase, and Nagai, who had known each other in their youth and had all come from families with direct lineage to the Tokugawa.[32] Ii, therefore, was faced not merely with a bureaucratic front, but also a social cohort made up of members with long-standing connections to one another. Conservative finance magistrates, such as Mizuno Tadanori, could help dampen support for more concessions to the foreigners. Yet until now, finance magistrates were not members of this group and were often isolated from policy-making, despite their senior position.

Ii reduced the power of the maritime defense officials not only by including finance magistrates in the new foreign magistrate position, but by making them simply bureaucrats charged with implementing bakufu policy toward the West. By these means, Ii hoped to kill two birds with one stone and secure both his domestic and foreign policy agendas. To ensure his influence over the new foreign magistrates, Ii appointed the conservative Mizuno as a balance to Iwase. It was in his new position that Iwase signed commercial treaties with the Dutch on August 18, the Russians on the following day, and the British on August 26, all three based on the Harris treaty.

Ii, however, was not content only with controlling the bakufu's top bureaucratic positions. His view of trade relations considered treaties as pliable instruments to be manipulated on behalf of bakufu foreign-policy goals. Ii early on had decided not to let any provisions of the treaties hinder the policy of isolating foreigners in the new ports. Indeed, he would translate the vague desire for isolation into concrete plans.

On August 29, three days after the British treaty was signed, Ii dispatched Inoue, Iwase, Nagai, and Hori to Yokohama village to survey the ground for a foreign settlement. Before the four departed, the senior councillors gave them a map of the proposed foreign settlement, on which Yokohama was demarcated a part of Kanagawa.[33] Yokohama and the villages surrounding it were not actually bakufu land, but were part of the domain of Musashi held by a *fudai* daimyō. The foreign magistrates' orders were to survey this area, known as Kanazawa, and begin preparations to buy the land from its holders.[34]

Iwase and Inoue quickly saw that the senior councillors planned to

Japanese foreign magistrates after the signing of the Anglo–Japanese treaty, August 26, 1858. Standing, left to right: Iwase Tadanari, Mizuno Tadanori, Tsuda Mamichi. Sitting, left to right: Mori Takichirō (interpreter), Inoue Kiyonao, Hori Toshihiro, Nagai Naomune. Courtesy of the Victoria and Albert Museum, London.

restrict foreigners to Yokohama and to bar them from Kanagawa post town. The two felt that such a proposal was a contravention of the treaties. Even though Iwase initially had advocated Yokohama, his treaty was broader, and Ii's plan was not what he had negotiated with Harris or the other powers.

Ii now found himself forced to negotiate with his top diplomats, precisely the result he had hoped to avoid by attempting a further centralization of policy-making. After returning from Yokohama in mid-August, the foreign magistrates met with Ii and the senior councillors.[35] At this meeting, both Iwase and Inoue strenuously claimed that, because the treaty they had negotiated with Harris explicitly listed Kanagawa as a place of settlement, the bakufu could not simply exclude foreigners from the town. Ii argued in response that Harris would have to be convinced to give up Kanagawa, just as he gave up Shinagawa, reiterating how the senior councillors intended to isolate the foreigners "across the bay," a physical and metaphorical substitute for "across the ocean."[36] Ii made clear that Yokohama was to be a second Dejima, a place to absorb foreigners and quarantine them from the Japanese. The image Ii proffered was drawn from a shared cultural template, in which the foreign was kept either outside Japan's borders or controlled within them. It harked back to the early days of the shogunate, and yet all involved knew it was less and less applicable to the encroaching world.

Ii was not convinced that he had won this debate and he felt forced to ensure that his vision of treaty relations prevailed. Negotiation with his diplomats would go only so far, and then Ii would use the power of his position. Two days after signing the Franco–Japanese Treaty of Commerce and Friendship on October 9, Iwase suddenly was relieved of his diplomatic duties and transferred to overseeing the construction of temples and shrines. Six weeks later, with Iwase out of the way, Ii placed the foreign magistrates in charge of preparing Yokohama as the settlement site. On November 28, the senior councillors assigned several inspectors, city magistrates, and finance magistrates to assist the foreign magistrates with the more specialized tasks inherent in ensuring that Yokohama would be a functioning port by July 1859.[37] Debate within the bakufu was now essentially silenced, though a few of the foreign magistrates, particularly Inoue and Nagai, continued to believe that Kanagawa would be opened in some way to foreign residence.

Iwase's demotion ended the career of one of the bakufu's most able and experienced foreign affairs specialists. He was the essential mover of the Abe–Hotta vision of Japan's foreign policy and perhaps the most experienced negotiator in the bakufu. Though he initially advocated limiting foreigners to Yokohama, he later came to embrace a broader vision of trade relations in which the bakufu would not only enrich itself but also strengthen its authority over all Japan. He knew his country had entered a new age, and its diplomacy could no longer operate as the closed system inherited from the 1630s. He further understood that Western nations considered treaties to be inviolate, and he argued strenuously for adhering to the letter of the treaty. His exclusion from the councils of power marked the end of influence for the Abe–Hotta clique.

Resistance as Negotiation

Not until March 1859 did Harris learn that the bakufu was disregarding key treaty provisions. More than a year had passed since he and the negotiators had finalized the site of the foreign settlement, and he was unaware that Ii unilaterally had altered the decision. Other than an aborted visit in late January 1859, Harris did not return to Kanagawa until March 2, when the visiting U.S. warship *Mississippi* brought him there.

Harris met with Inoue, Nagai, and Hori at the Kanagawa governor's residence on March 5. The next weeks of intense negotiation revealed the importance of the territorial issue for both sides. When the foreign magistrates presented Harris with a map showing the proposed area, he immediately understood that the bakufu planned to locate the main foreign settlement on a spit of land by the small fishing village of Yokohama. Harris conceded that the village might offer a better anchorage than Kanagawa, but he objected that it was more than five miles from the post town and the Tōkaidō.[38] The whole point of relations, he reminded the foreign magistrates, was trade, and if the Americans were shunted off from the main road leading to Edo, trade could not flourish. Moreover, he complained, the proposed site was hardly even a village, so that "for every one person that passes by Yokohama, one hundred will pass by Kanagawa."[39] The Japanese ignored his complaint, as well as his suggestion of two alternate sites, assuring him that "once Yokohama is opened . . . [it] will surely see much growth."[40]

Being boxed in, Harris chose to negotiate through threat, warning the magistrates that, even if he acceded to the new site, he was sure that Britain, France, and Russia would refuse to accept Yokohama. In response, the magistrates employed the traditional tactic of using foreigner against foreigner, invoking the spirit of Article II of the treaty, which stated that "the President of the United States, at the request of the Japanese Government, will act as a friendly mediator in such matters of difference as may arise between the Government of Japan and any European Power." They assured Harris that once he had accepted Yokohama as the site of the port, he would be able to intervene with the Europeans and persuade them to acquiesce.[41] To the magistrates, this was a key line that had to be held. Even though all the Ansei treaties listed Kanagawa as being the only Kantō port site, the bakufu had to make sure that all foreigners indeed were limited to one location. Were the Westerners somehow able to establish independent settlements for each trading country, the bakufu's foreign boundaries would be fatally compromised.

Thus only reluctantly during these negotiations did the magistrates express one of their main concerns, which revealed the critical link between domestic and foreign affairs in Japan. Kanagawa was unacceptable, they told Harris, precisely because it was on the Tōkaidō.[42] As such, it was constantly filled with Kyoto nobles traveling between the imperial capital and Edo. An even greater, though not mentioned, threat was the antiforeign daimyō who plied the Tōkaidō on their semiannual pilgrimages between Edo and their home territories. As Ii had noted in his August 1858 meeting with the foreign magistrates, the bakufu feared that violence would erupt if Westerners met antiforeign elements among the nobles and daimyō on the road. The shogunate could not afford such a threat to domestic stability. This admission of weakness, of course, still obscured Ii's overall policy of isolating foreigners at all costs.

The magistrates' negotiating tactics were not limited to arguing the merits of Yokohama versus Kanagawa. They also consciously employed the ambiguous use of place-names. This was a holdover from the original negotiations a year previously, when Harris and the Japanese referred to the proposed settlement sites by various names. By 1859, the magistrates steadfastly maintained that Yokohama could not be conceived of as an independent locality, but that the town name was at best a term of convenience. During mid-March meetings, for example, they raised the Perry precedent, claiming that while Perry had signed his pact at Yokohama, it was known as the Treaty of Kanagawa.[43] Inoue in fact told Harris that "Kanagawa and Yokohama are the same, as Yokohama is within Kanagawa; therefore, I can erase 'Yokohama'" from the map of the settlement.[44] The magistrates asserted not only that Yokohama was administratively part of Kanagawa but also that its very designation was merely a "subname."[45]

From the amount of time spent debating the issue, and its importance to the central participants, one can only conclude that, whether Yokohama was in fact a subname for Kanagawa, all those involved understood there was a very real difference in the physical location of the two sites and this difference would have a profound effect on trade relations. Ii maneuvered to keep foreigners at the fishing village and Harris steadfastly refused to accept such a restriction.

In fact, not all the foreign magistrates were convinced that Yokohama equaled Kanagawa. Inoue and Nagai, who continued meeting with Harris, began to question the policy and Ii again was faced with dissension in his ranks. Accordingly, while the two were meeting Harris on March 15, Ii gathered the remaining foreign magistrates, Mizuno, Hori, and Muragaki, to argue that foreigners must be held to Yokohama; he then sent them to relieve Inoue and Nagai. Two days later, Harris confronted this new set of officials, and the debate wound down to a close.

These last days of negotiation turned seriocomic and, to Harris, exasperating. When, for example, Harris argued that the fishing village was neither a town nor a port, as required by the Franco–Japanese treaty, Mizuno refused to equate "towns" simply with the presence of houses. By the end of this lexical exercise, the magistrates had negotiated Harris to a standstill and secured his agreement to postpone a final decision until just before the port was to open.[46]

Harris undoubtedly was exhausted from the grueling schedule and from meeting for hours each day. In contrast to Siam, where he followed in the wake of the British, in Japan he was attempting to break new ground, and the Japanese could focus all their energy on him alone. Moreover, he and Henry Heusken were isolated, being the only foreigners in Japan outside of Nagasaki, and to Harris fell the burden of mastering myriad details in the negotiations. No doubt his disdain for Japanese officials echoed Henry Adams's view of British diplomats during the U.S. Civil War: "Words were with them forms of expressions which varied with individuals, but falsehood was more or less necessary to all."[47]

Despite knowing that the port issue was at best undecided, Harris reported to U.S. Secretary of State Lewis Cass that he had defeated a Japanese attempt to alter a key provision of the treaty, writing that "I placed Yokuhama [*sic*] out of consideration."[48] In reality, the site was nearing completion, and foreign merchants were preparing to sail from Hong Kong and Shanghai to take up residence in Japan. Ii, having presumably triumphed over both domestic and foreign opposition to Yokohama, now conceived a fallback plan. He decided that, should his negotiators fail and Kanagawa indeed become the site of the foreign settlement, the bakufu would change the course of the Tōkaidō itself. This would effectively make Kanagawa as isolated as Yokohama.[49] To Ii, this was as acceptable a style of "negotiation" as were formal talks.

Politically, Ii refused to negotiate with his own diplomats any longer. He had exiled Iwase to bureaucratic obscurity, and just ten days after the last encounter between the foreign magistrates and Harris, he reassigned Inoue and Nagai, the two negotiators with the greatest reservations about the Yokohama plan. Four months later, after Yokohama had successfully opened, Hori was demoted to Hakodate magistrate, ostensibly charged with solving problems at the port there, but since almost no trade existed, he had very little to do. Ii's new appointments were all undistinguished men, and this left Mizuno as the only foreign magistrate with direct diplomatic experience, until he was transferred in September 1859. Foreign magistrates from this time on played no significant role in foreign policy formulation and the senior councillors controlled Japan's diplomatic strategy uncontested.

Constructing Yokohama

As Yokohama's opening date approached, Ii faced one more Western challenge. Rutherford Alcock arrived from China as Great Britain's minister plenipotentiary in late June 1859. Not until July 1 did he go to inspect the site of the settlement. Alcock was shocked to find that the port at Kanagawa was nowhere to be seen. He was then gently turned around and his gaze directed across the bay, toward Yokohama. In consternation, he immediately returned to the new British legation in Edo.[50]

Despite Alcock's refusal to acknowledge Yokohama, British traders arrived to begin their activities as soon as permissible. At British urging, trade started on July 1, rather than July 4, 1859, as Harris's patriotic treaty had stipulated. In Kanagawa, the day passed with little notice, the town's narrow streets looking much like they had for more than two centuries. Over in Yokohama, however, the representatives of European firms in China, such as Jardine Matheson, anchored their ships and disembarked to a warren of newly constructed, if spartan, buildings, warehouses, and wharves. In addition, a Japanese side of Yokohama had sprung up, filled with representatives of the bakufu's licensed merchants (*ton'ya*) and various small traders who had moved in during the preceding weeks. Finally, a Japanese administration was in place, complete with city and finance magistrates and superintendents of construction to oversee the daily affairs of the town.

Yokohama was meant to be the physical manifestation of the bakufu's diplomatic strategy. Its guiding principles reflected the culture of boundaries championed by Ii. It was a constructed urban site, not one that evolved naturally. It was in many ways an analogue to Edo, the capital of the Tokugawa, itself a small village before becoming the headquarters of a minor warrior in the late fifteenth century. A century and a half later, Tokugawa Ieyasu rescued it from oblivion and in short order constructed what was then the largest city in the world.

Yokohama, of course, did not rival Edo in size or importance, nor was it meant to. Rather, it shared with Edo the same origin of being carefully planned and laid out. The town was divided in two, with the foreigners' settlement distinctly separated from what came to be known as the "Japan town." The Western merchants originally were given about one-third of the total area of Yokohama. The existing housing in the settlement meant, of course, that Westerners would not have to bear the expense of erecting dwellings and warehouses. They were able to select lots, lease the housing, and move in immediately, all of which compared favorably with their experiences in China, where the British, for example had had to build up Hong Kong from scratch.

Bakufu planning extended far beyond the foreigners' settlement. A wide avenue running south from the wharf divided the two sides of Yokohama, making a clear boundary between Japan and what might have seemed a holding pen for resident foreigners. Fronting the pier and physically separating the two sides of the town was the bakufu government office and customs house. At each of the major intersections, wooden gates were erected; by these means individual wards on both sides of the town were sealed at night, as in Japanese castle towns. Nor was the bakufu thinking only of the business to be transacted in daylight hours. A narrow avenue led from the southern edge of town into a bordering swamp where the bakufu had erected a substantial pleasure quarter. Here, as in Edo, prostitution would be regulated and the excess physical energies of the merchants channeled into safer currents.

In addition to these man-made controls, the bakufu counted on nature to do its bidding. Kanagawa Bay fronted the north side of the town, while to the west a large river inlet separated the site from the mainland. A branch of this river curved east to form a southern border across which lay a swamp leading to rice paddies. Finally, to the east a cliff soon known as the Bluff (*Yamate* in Japanese) led to uncleared highland. Other than the Japanese side of town, the settlement strongly resembled Dejima, as noted by the more perspicacious Westerners.

Yokohama was thus an enclosed system, making equally clear political and ideological statements. Otherness, newness, and threat could be concentrated there, giving foreigners no room to expand. Physically they might be allowed into Japan, but their impact would be lessened. The final piece in this system of control was provided by the Ansei treaties, which set twenty-five-mile travel boundaries radiating from Yokohama. Only accredited diplomats received the privilege of unfettered travel throughout Japan. The overwhelming majority of Westerners could neither go as far as Edo nor travel anywhere of consequence along the Tōkaidō. The merchants unwittingly obliged in this scheme, for they apparently were unaware that they were supposed to be in Kanagawa and they seemed unconcerned over their lack of freedom of movement. Focusing solely on their trading opportunities, they were impressed with the adequate anchorage at Yokohama and left no record of demands to be allowed to live in the post town as per the treaties or to travel beyond the narrow treaty limits.

The bakufu had correctly calculated that it could drive a wedge between the merchants and their official representatives. The Western diplomats soon saw that without support from their nationals, they would stand alone in insisting on their legal treaty rights. Harris, of course, had already been through all this, and he now merely demanded that the U.S. consulate be located in Kanagawa, while he and Heusken were to live in the legation in Edo. To back up his claim, Harris named E. M. Dorr as temporary U.S. consul and the office duly opened. Bitterly taking back his confident report to Washington of late March, Harris had to confirm that the bakufu had outmaneuvered him, informing Cass that Yokohama "can only be considered a new Desima" [*sic*].[51] The old merchant, defeated over years of negotiations with the bakufu, stood on principle: he refused to set foot in Yokohama, did not recognize it as the legitimate site of the settlement, and passed through only once, on his way home to the United States in May 1862.

For Alcock, the battle was new. For more than twenty-five years, he had successfully expanded British influence in China, often through the threat, and sometimes the employment, of force. In his eyes, the Japanese were no different from the Chinese, and would have to be handled the same way. A product of the China coast, he placed little stock in "Oriental" honesty and saw gunboats as a preferred means of negotiation.

Even while traveling to his new post, Alcock's experience convinced him that the Japanese were as unfaithful to treaties as had been the Chinese. Arriving in Nagasaki in mid-June, he found that no foreign settlement had yet been erected, though trade was slated to start the following month. Moreover, the Nagasaki magistrate provided him with a map indicating that the bakufu intended literally to build another Dejima, this time for the British, Americans, and French. Yet with the issue of Chinese acceptance of the Tianjin Treaty in doubt, Great Britain was keeping its naval strength concentrated in Hong Kong. Alcock was discovering not only that treaty relations were far from a settled issue but also that he did not have at his disposal the material force that he had in China. In the end, Alcock, too, was forced to negotiate with the Japanese, a novel situation for him.

The greatest threat to the Japanese treaty, in the minister's eyes, seemed to be the existence of Yokohama itself. Alcock quickly reported the problem to London, writing the Earl of Malmesbury, British foreign secretary, on July 9, 1859:

> on the lower edge of the bay, at a distance of some three miles from Kanagawa, a new settlement, consisting of wood huts and streets of shops extending three-quarters of a mile, with a Custom-house . . . appears to have been just created. . . . I mention these facts, as calculated

to convey . . . a correct impression of the determined and vigorous efforts made by the Japanese Government, and the large expense they have incurred before my arrival, with a view of locating foreigners on this spot, without choice or discussion on the part of the Consuls or Diplomatic Representatives, who by Treaty are, nevertheless, entitled to a deciding voice in the matter.[52]

A week later Alcock sent his first extensive complaint to the bakufu, stating that Yokohama's isolation appeared to limit "the dealing of foreigners to such Japanese merchants and traders alone as the Japanese Government may choose to license or permit to take up their residence there."[53] One week after this, he insisted on his right to select a site in Kanagawa for a permanent settlement.[54]

By this time, however, it was clear that the bakufu strategy would prevail. For all of Alcock's sound and fury, neither Western merchants nor Japanese officials seemed very concerned with the specifics of treaty port location. Ii now wisely chose to be magnanimous in victory. Negotiating with Alcock in the spirit of the treaty, he formally acceded to the British demand. Kanagawa was "opened" for settlement and Alcock wrote jubilantly to the new foreign secretary, Lord John Russell, on September 7, 1859, reporting "the final and satisfactory termination of the long-protracted discussions with the Japanese authorities, as to the selection of a site for the location of foreigners at Kanagawa."[55] His celebratory letter neatly skirted the bitter truth: the right was obtained, but the settlement stayed at Yokohama. London, still beset with problems in China, took a low-key approach and merely urged Alcock to remain at Kanagawa and to warn British merchants against allowing themselves to be confined in Yokohama.[56]

Despite the de facto admission of being bested, Western representatives sought to avoid the appearance of defeat. They attempted to create the illusion that this most important of provisions in the treaty was indeed followed to the letter. Thus, the Americans built their consulate at Kanagawa, as did the British, although Alcock soon moved it to Yokohama, where the merchants, and the markets, were. Determined to save some face, in London if not in Japan, the British catalogued all official consular correspondence until 1888 as coming from Kanagawa, even though they often dated the actual letters to and from Yokohama.[57] The Americans attempted to efface the difference until the mid-1860s by dating many of their dispatches from a hybrid "Kanagawa, Yokohama."[58]

The substitution of Yokohama for Kanagawa was not a minor event in the early days of Japanese–Western treaty relations. Rather, it revealed the bakufu strategy of negotiating at various levels, domestic as well as foreign. To the bakufu, the "negotiation" it had entered into was a struggle to impose its own stamp on treaty relations. These first years thus saw the formation of a clear bakufu strategy and its encounter with an equally clear Western policy. The clash of the two afforded Edo the chance to see how successful it could be in negotiating the pace and structure of relations. The bakufu chose to challenge a key part of the 1858 pacts while upholding the framework of the treaties itself. While it may seem a minor affair more than a century later, those at the time considered it a momentous issue.

The Japanese view can be summed up in a letter to the court penned by Ii Naosuke's fellow senior councillor, Manabe Akikatsu. Writing in early January 1859, seven months before Yokohama opened but long after the site had been selected, Manabe noted that in the new port the Westerners would be just as isolated and tightly controlled as at Nagasaki. This would give Japan time to build up its military defenses and eventually return to *sakoku no ryōhō* (the good policy of isolation).[59] The court would understand that Japan's boundaries had not in reality been breached. There was every hope that, in the short term, the West's influence would be limited and that, in the long term, Japan would be able to purge itself of the unwanted intruders.

Most crucially, Ii refused to accept a preordained outcome to Japan's encounter with imperialism. Partly out of conviction, partly out of political expedience, he presented himself as the one man who could turn back the tide of the foreigners. In the end, of course, he could not, but he nonetheless built barricades that affected the new relationship.

Alcock's 1863 memoirs of his first years in Japan reflected a similar train of thought. He noted that at the end of 1861 the foreign community numbered only 126 people at Yokohama (55 of them British), while a mere 39 lived at Nagasaki, and that trade had developed far more slowly than anticipated.[60] Yokohama, which he referred to back and forth as Kanagawa, bore primary blame for the small amount of trade and traders. He rued, "How admirably the situation had been chosen for isolation and espionage, for a system of control and surveillance. . . . If Yokohama is not another Decima [*sic*], it is at least a very excellent imitation."[61]

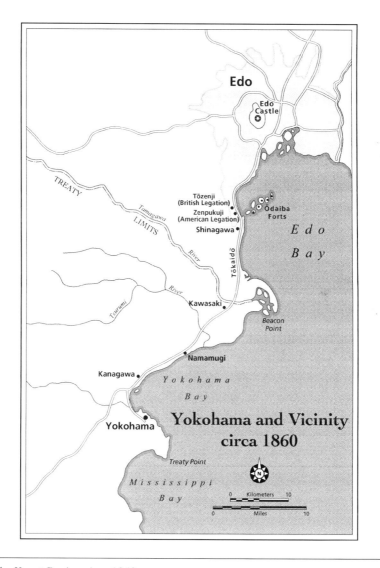

The Kantō Region circa 1860

In diplomacy, as Alcock would have been the first to acknowledge, perception often counts as much as reality, and as Ishii Takashi notes, Ii successfully returned Japan's atmosphere, if not reality, to the days before Harris's treaty, at least for the time being.[62] A crucial part of this strategy involved reshaping the memory of recent events within Japan. The bakufu, so sensitive to domestic opinion, sought to bolster its traditional authority over foreign affairs by canonizing a favorable view of its negotiation with the West. Thus, in September 1860, the senior councillors wrote to the court that

> the bakufu did not grant the five foreign powers permission to trade merely out of a passing whim. As we have reported time and again, officials who had long been responsible for such matters gave the question careful thought; and the present agreements were reached in the end by steadily whittling down the foreigners' demands.[63]

For now, the bakufu seemed to be in control of both domestic and foreign response to the new international situation. Japan's diplomatic culture had met its first test and had bent, but had not broken. The next years would see the bakufu mount an even more ambitious attempt to maintain control over treaty relations.

CHAPTER THREE

Negotiating Time:
The Postponement Strategy

By the dawn of 1860, it seemed the bakufu had created a viable response to Western demands that Japan enter the international system. The tactics chosen by the bakufu, specifically its combination of foot-dragging negotiation and unilateral alteration of key provisions of the treaties, set the tone of early trade relations. By early 1860, however, Edo adopted an aggressive stance designed to adhere even more closely to its traditional strategy. The new goal was to negotiate a delay in the opening of further treaty ports, thereby strengthening its weakened physical boundaries.

The narrative of the years 1860 through 1862 reveals how the senior councillors, in this last period of their dominance over foreign affairs, negotiated their way to a success that ironically contained within it seeds of change for Japan's diplomatic culture. It also illustrates the extent to which the foreign representatives in Japan were willing to accommodate the bakufu in order to preserve the overall framework of treaty relations. The impetus for such agreement was spurred by the rise of terrorism, most notably against the architect of the isolation strategy himself, Ii Naosuke.

New Leaders, Old Strategy

Ii's policy of suppressing dissent inside and outside the bakufu, which had enabled him to make Yokohama rather than Kanagawa the Kantō treaty port, also precipitated his downfall. The direct antecedent of his demise was his 1858 conflict with the daimyō of Mito, Tokugawa Nariaki, over the shogunal succession crisis. This was exacerbated by his decision to sign the Ansei treaties without imperial approval. The subsequent "Ansei Purge" that Ii instituted the same year led to the arrest, exile, and execution of opponents of his strong-bakufu policy, regardless of their status. Nariaki, for example, despite being a blood relative of the shogun, was sentenced to house arrest in Mito, where he languished until his death in September 1860.[1] The ruthlessness of Ii's attack made him a target for radical anti-bakufu samurai. On the morning of March 24, 1860, in the heart of Edo, a few hundred yards from his own mansion, a group of Mito rōnin assassinated the great councillor outside the Sakurada Gate of Edo Castle.

The new leaders of the bakufu were Ii's own men and were committed to his goal of adapting, yet maintaining, Japan's traditional foreign policy. Unlike Ii, however, they favored direct negotiation, which was certainly less confrontational, though not more conciliatory, than the tactics employed by their late patron. More important, though, the senior councillors did not deviate from the overall bakufu strategy worked out in 1858.

Heading up this group immediately after Ii's murder were Kuze Hirochika and Andō Nobuyuki (later known as Nobumasa). Andō in particular had worked closely with Ii, being appointed as the bakufu's key intermediary with Mito domain in 1858, while Kuze was called back to service immediately after Ii's assassination. Under their leadership, new policies to defend Japan's boundaries now took center stage.

According to the Ansei treaties, Edo was to be opened for trade from January 1, 1862, onward, while Osaka was to open on January 1 the following year. Hyogo, located about twenty miles west of Osaka, was to open on the same day as Osaka and function as the port and settlement site for the central Kinai region. In addition, the town of Niigata was to have opened as a port on January 1, 1860. It, however, was located on the Japan Sea, was cursed with a shallow anchorage, and was far too isolated to play any significant role in trade. This, for the bakufu, made it a perfect port, but Townsend Harris had succeeded during his initial negotiations to include a provision in the treaty that another port could be substituted for it. Concerned less with Niigata than with Kanagawa or Osaka, the bakufu eventually agreed to search for a replacement site on the west coast of Japan.[2]

Edo's primary diplomatic goal, however, soon became to delay the opening of all four sites, which became known in Japanese as "postponement of the two ports and two cities" (*ryōto-ryōkō kaishi-kaikō enki*).

Though he had spent most of his negotiating energy on the Yokohama-Kanagawa issue, Harris had had an almost equally difficult time in getting the bakufu to agree to opening Osaka and Hyogo for trade. There were two main reasons for this, both inhering in the bakufu attempt to preserve key physical and ideological boundaries. The first was expressed by officials such as Iwase Tadanari, who feared losing control over trade if Westerners were allowed to mix directly with the powerful Osaka merchants and the daimyō who maintained warehouses and trading arrangements there.

Osaka once had been the economic center of the country, and still was a production hub in late Tokugawa times. It remained the repository for much of Japan's tax rice, which was sold on the market and converted from the silver standard maintained by the city's merchants to the gold standard in use in Edo. Although Osaka was under direct bakufu control, Iwase's pivotal memorandum of late December 1857 reflected the concern that Kinai merchants would be in a position to monopolize international exchange and use that as a basis for cornering domestic trade.[3] Weaning Edo from economic dependence on Osaka had been a bakufu goal since at least the 1780s, and Iwase was sensitive to any changes that could cause a resurgence of the Kinai area.

Yet even more troubling for the bakufu was the ideological implication of opening the region to international trade. Osaka and Hyogo were the gateways to Kyoto, the home since 794 of the imperial family and its court. Filled with imperial relatives and other nobles, known collectively as *kuge*, Kyoto had been politically dormant since the early days of the Tokugawa shogunate. Starting in the late eighteenth century, though, the intellectual movement known as *kokugaku* (national learning) slowly had been crafting a political ideology centered on the emperor in the hopes of reviving the Japanese polity.[4] Kokugaku scholars such as the philologist Motoori Norinaga rejected the traditional Tokugawa reliance on Confucian or Neo-Confucian texts from China as guides to political and social organization. Rather, they urged their disciples to return to Japan's own ancient political, social, and ethical traditions. These scholars believed that Japan's essence was concentrated in the person of the emperor, and some went so far as to consider the Tokugawa mere usurpers of imperial authority. By the mid-nineteenth century, as the West began trickling into Japan through the cracks in the bakufu's armor, the emperor was becoming the center of a growing anti-bakufu, anti-Western movement.

For the first time in living memory, moreover, the emperor himself addressed a political question. Kōmei, who had reigned since 1846, gave tacit support to the kokugaku school, and over time he increasingly voiced his own anti-Western beliefs, albeit within the confines of the Tokugawa-controlled court compound. Yet his support for the anti-Western movement emboldened some of the Kyoto aristocracy to begin forging political links with dissident samurai groups. Among them, a mid-level courtier named Iwakura Tomomi and his ally Sanjō Sanetomi would take the lead in organizing contact with mid-level samurai. This reactivation, so to speak, of the court complemented the more active political stance of those daimyō who, during the Opium War, had started to seek information on regional events and threats to both their own domains and Japan.[5] Kyoto's new activity confirmed some discontented daimyō in their belief that the court could be used to pressure the bakufu.

Even as these fault lines were developing, the shogunate's treaty negotiators during 1858, Inoue Kiyonao and Iwase, had been sensitive to the growing importance of Kyoto and its potentially catalytic role in linking domestic and foreign problems. The two had not only fought tenaciously against opening the areas closest to the imperial city, but had also succeeded in refusing Harris's demand that Kyoto itself be opened to trade, only grudgingly offering Osaka and Hyogo in its stead.[6] Iwase and Inoue chose to subordinate their fears of opening the Kinai region in exchange for treaty provisions that seemed to erect strong boundaries around Kyoto. Indeed, during the negotiations, Iwase had revealed the bakufu's fear of domestic unrest by expressing to Harris that "under no circumstances was war from abroad so much to be feared as intestine [*sic*] commotion."[7] Ii Naosuke ultimately reversed this conclusion (see chapter 2), fearing foreign war more, but Ii clearly believed he could eat his cake and have it, too, by ignoring and then controlling domestic opposition to treaty relations. What was incontestable was the sensitive role of Kyoto in national politics.

Despite Ii's signing of the treaties without Kyoto's blessing, the court was now inextricably intertwined in the treaty issue, especially as it continued to withhold its approval of the pacts. Ii's successors turned to vague plans floating about since 1858 for a coalition of some kind between the court and the bakufu. From this eventually came the policy of *kōbu-gattai* (court-bakufu unity), and a plan to arrange the marriage of the emperor's sister, Princess Kazunomiya, to the young shogun Iemochi. The court, however, steadfastly refused permission for the marriage until Edo promised to expel foreigners once and for all.[8]

The bakufu's response to the court was to try to postpone the opening of the remaining ports and cities mandated in the treaties. This plan was a natural progression from the boundary policy pursued in Yokohama by Ii and was not, therefore, a mere political expedient designed solely to mollify Kyoto. As part of a coherent strategy, indeed, postponement was nothing less than a demand to change the treaties and it eventually led to the collapse of Harris's treaty archetype.[9]

The Impact of Domestic Pressure

Andō and Kuze's task was made easier, and indeed more urgent, by the undeniable economic disruptions that had been occurring since the opening of trade in July 1859. The disruptions were the result of three interrelated factors: currency, exports, and fear. The complexity of currency exchange was an unforeseen problem and quickly became a major concern of the bakufu once trade commenced. Inoue and Iwase had of course negotiated with Harris over exchange rates, but the discussions did not have the political or symbolic urgency of the land issue. The two sides finally agreed to an equal exchange of coin, but this led to enormous problems.[10] The key difficulty lay in the different values of Japanese and Western coin and the seemingly arbitrary nature of the bakufu domestic pricing system.[11] In short, the Japanese silver coin, the *ichibu*, contained more silver per weight than the Mexican dollar, which Western traders used in China as well as Japan, thus making it more valuable. However, the weight-for-weight ratio mandated by the treaties resulted in three ichibu equaling one Mexican dollar, which meant that Japan was losing bullion in the exchange, even given the heavier weight of the foreign coin.

Moreover, the bakufu artificially maintained a 1:5 gold-to-silver domestic exchange ratio, while the West had a 1:15 ratio. As a result, almost as soon as the ports opened, sharp Western speculators exchanged their dollars for ichibu, then bought gold coins at one-third the world price and immediately exported them to the West for massive profits. In response, the bakufu tried various stratagems to staunch the gold flow, including issuing paper money and coining a new half-ichibu to be issued two to the dollar. Numerous Western complaints, primarily from Rutherford Alcock acting on behalf of British traders, forced the bakufu to revert to the 3–1 ichibu-dollar exchange during 1859 and 1860.

Between 1860 and June 1861, more than five million silver dollars worth of Japanese *koban* gold pieces had been exported from Yokohama and the equivalent amount of silver dollars injected into the Japanese economy.[12] Peter Frost concluded, however, that the true significance of the disruption caused by the currency trade was not the outflow of coin, but the destruction of the bakufu's bullion monopoly during the years 1859–1860 and its effects on domestic trade. In order to cope, Edo began debasing the value of gold and silver coin alike. The inevitable result was a rise in prices, abetted by counterfeit currency appearing at the same time.[13]

Commodity prices in at least part of the country were immediately affected. Harris informed Secretary of State Seward in May 1861 that consumer prices around Edo had risen 200 percent since July 1859.[14] While general unrest had not yet broken out, the bakufu was greatly concerned about increasing anti-Western and anti-Tokugawa sentiment because of the economic situation. Edo was worried in particular about the reaction of lower-ranking samurai, many of whom were already ill-disposed toward Westerners. These samurai, cut off from the land for centuries, were paid in fixed rice stipends that did not keep pace with rising consumer prices, and were therefore losing economic ground daily. The potential for revolt, a direct threat to regime stability, was of concern to key bakufu officials.[15]

The second cause of the early 1860s economic problems was rising export levels. Not until 1865 did Japan run a trade deficit, and indeed both Alcock and the British press constantly commented on the lack of imports by Japan during these years.[16] The sudden purchasing of consumer goods by merchants at Yokohama not only contributed to the rise in prices but also raised bakufu fears that there would be shortages in Edo's huge domestic market.

Edo contained at least half a million samurai, ranging from domainal lords to low-level clerks, all of whom were prohibited from engaging in trade and were therefore dependent on the Edo market for many of their needs. An additional half million commoners rounded out the population of the metropolis. These inhabitants of what was called the "low city" essentially formed the service sector for the samurai, and they, too, were dependent on the influx of goods from around the country.

In response to the economic disruption caused by foreign trade, a bakufu order of late April 1860 restricted the direct sale of five primary goods: raw silk, hair oil, clothing fabric, candle wax, and minor cereals. These items were to be consigned first to licensed Edo wholesalers, who would then distribute them for foreign trade to Yokohama merchants.[17] Even as other Japanese merchants worked with their Western counterparts to evade the restriction, Western diplomats complained that the order in effect placed some of the most valuable trade items under a tighter bakufu monopoly. For the bakufu, however, the problem was how to limit the amount of exports and thus maintain stable consumer prices by regulating supply in the domestic Edo market.

These currency and export problems contributed to a final cause of economic disruption: a general climate of fear. The bakufu, in addition to the five-goods order cited above, had begun to hoard rice in its Edo storehouses, and daimyō were doing the same. An atmosphere of unease was growing, feeding on the economic problems listed above. Moreover, the bakufu was ordering new taxes, further weakening the position of farmers and townspeople. Hoarding spread to merchants, and this worked in conjunction with the currency and export problems to raise prices further and to deepen the feelings of uncertainty swirling about Japan.

The bakufu's fears were stoked by the increasing strength of one voice over which it had little direct control, that of common opinion. Tokugawa Japan's vigorous world of woodblock prints and cheap broadsheets (*kawaraban*) had steadily commented on international issues since Perry's arrival nearly a decade previously. It now took aim at bakufu and foreigner alike. Unhindered by the need for diplomatic niceties, numerous prints engaged in a very different style of negotiation with imperialism than that undertaken by the government.

Such prints vividly illustrated the effects of Western intrusion into Japan, emphasizing both the dangers to the populace and the possibilities of a domestic response to foreigners. The currency chaos was a favorite theme, for example, being portrayed as a battle between anthropomorphized Japanese and native coin that jousted with each other, sporting arms and legs out of their metallic bodies. More disturbing, the potential for physical violence was openly portrayed. One print, for example, centered on a black garbed and hatted foreigner forced to his hands and knees by the blows of a mob made up of workers of traditional occupations, such as loan collector or litter bearer, all of whom supposedly saw their livelihood threatened by Westerners.[18]

With no public debate officially allowed, political commentary abounded in these mass-produced prints. They both reflected public opinion and helped shape it, consciously and openly transgressing the political and physical boundaries so laboriously created by the bakufu. Edo's response was to try to avoid a situation that would require the construction of further boundaries, for each new one required more resources, both tangible and intangible, from the overstretched government.

Broaching Postponement, 1860–1861

It was in response to these elite and commoner voices that the senior councillors crafted the postponement policy. It is unlikely that the bakufu ever intended to open Osaka or Hyogo to trade; it had only grudgingly agreed to open even a single street in Edo to temporarily visiting foreign merchants. A formal postponement for an indefinite period of time seemed not only to offer a neat solution to the economic and political problems facing the bakufu, but such a plan also was consonant with the goals of Edo's diplomatic strategy.

The senior councillors decided to negotiate in a two-stage process, first eliciting U.S. support for the plan and then making a formal request to Great Britain, by now the leading treaty power. Andō accordingly hinted to Harris the course the bakufu would pursue when, in late May 1860, he asked the American minister voluntarily to limit the export of silk, candle wax, and oil (three of the five restricted goods).

This was a turning point in Japanese–American relations, though it might not have seemed so at the time. Although this was less than a year after his Yokohama defeat, Harris, now dean of the diplomatic representatives in Japan, did not want to see the bakufu use the excuse of domestic unrest as a way to abrogate his treaty. Perhaps even surprised himself at his changing opinion, he immediately was sympathetic to the bakufu's plight.

In a letter to Washington dated August 1, Harris anticipated Andō's formal postponement request by asking for discretionary authority to close Edo to trade for one year should the British and French representatives agree to do so. He noted his fear that "indiscriminate admission of foreigners, at the time fixed by the Treaties, to the right of residence in this capital, will lead to the most deplorable consequences, and to a state of affairs fatal to the best interests of all."[19] He was beginning to understand the importance of preserving certain boundaries within Japan, as long as the American presence was accommodated to some degree. Harris's support would prove important for the bakufu and, indeed, would become more crucial in the coming months. More than that, however, Harris had taken the first steps toward forming a nascent American–Japanese front vis-à-vis the other treaty powers.

By the early 1860s, however, Great Britain bulked largest in Japanese eyes. Between 1860 and 1863, Britain's share of total Japanese trade jumped from 55 percent to more than 80 percent.[20] Under such conditions, London not only led the Western nations in their relations with Japan but also took center stage in bakufu conceptions of the international power hierarchy with which it had to contend. The United States and Harris might be useful in persuading the British to agree to postponement, but the key ingredient was Rutherford Alcock's acquiescence. Playing foreigner off against foreigner could work only if the most powerful of the Western ministers agreed to the scheme.

The second phase of the postponement plan thus commenced when, in late August 1860, at the British legation in the temple of Tōzenji, located near Shinagawa, Andō and fellow senior councillor Wakisaka Yasunori met Alcock.[21] The senior councillors understood that a mere request for postponement would not be persuasive. They instead gave the British minister details of price rises and the growth of antiforeign sentiment, and concluded with a request that the opening of Edo, Osaka, and Hyogo be postponed indefinitely as a way to "calm the people's hearts."

Alcock, however, had his own agenda. He had been growing increasingly dissatisfied with trading conditions in Japan. Far from the free trade mandated in the treaties, British merchants labored under numerous unofficial roadblocks, including unfair pricing, shady accounting practices, and lack of access to goods. In response, Alcock's answer to the problems enumerated by the senior councillors was simple: produce more, end government interference, expand trade, and let prices seek their natural level. This was a capsule summary of Britain's global economic strategy, a view that the Japanese could not have been expected to appreciate.

Alcock did, however, hold out one ray of hope to the Japanese, hinting that he would accept the postponement of opening Edo if all the other foreign representatives agreed.[22] Moreover, within Alcock's rebuttal was embedded a crucial suggestion, that the bakufu send an embassy to Europe to plead its case. Only four months before, the first Japanese embassy to the West had exchanged ratified treaties with U.S. President James Buchanan in Washington, D.C. Alcock no doubt wanted to secure a diplomatic triumph equal to Harris's, but, as we shall see, he soon conceived of the embassy in more radical cultural terms.

France proved to be equally unreceptive to the bakufu's entreaties. Despite French trading interests, Paris, much like London, saw Japan within the context of a larger global strategy. Much of that strategy, of course, focused on expanding French influence across the globe, but equally crucial, it sought to avoid exacerbating Anglo–French overseas tension. Paris's immediate concern was that it not get too involved where it did not have adequate force to use in pursuit of its objectives. In East Asia, the French naval presence did not even begin to rival that of Britain's, and thus French Minister Duchesne de Belle-court's instructions ordered him to work in concert with the British.

After contacting Bellecourt on August 26, the bakufu thus discovered that the French shared Alcock's opposition to postponement.[23] By temperament, Bellecourt was even less inclined than Alcock to undermine the treaty provisions and this neatly dovetailed with the British minister's initial suspicion of the postponement request. Nevertheless the upshot for the Japanese, though they did not know it, was that if they gained Alcock's acquiescence, French opposition would almost certainly cease as well.

In subsequent months, Harris's role naturally assumed increased importance for the bakufu. He met regularly with its leaders to review Japanese–Western relations and discuss postponement. His most significant suggestion to Andō came during a meeting on November 24. Harris, who had been lending Henry Heusken to the Germans to help draft a Prusso–Japanese commercial treaty, informed Andō that "it would be to your advantage to leave out of the Prussian treaty Hyogo, Osaka, etc.," although since Nagasaki, Hakodate, and Kanagawa had already opened, it was impossible not to include them as open ports.[24] Harris was suggesting that since Osaka and Hyogo were not yet opened, Prussia had no right to include them in its treaty. Though this was not a valid legal argument, Harris's logic was that only existing conditions could appropriately be transferred to new agreements. If the Japanese succeeded in omitting the two sites, they would in essence be presenting the other treaty nations with a fait accompli over the two ports and two cities. Both Harris and Andō seemed to believe the bakufu could then turn around and employ the most-favored-nation provision to put pressure on the other powers to agree to postponement.

For the next two months securing such a treaty with Prussia became the goal of the senior councillors. With the background influence of Harris, they succeeded in omitting any reference to the two ports and two cities in the new treaty, which was signed January 24, 1861. Putting subtle pressure on the British, they even informed Alcock of the change before the treaty was concluded.[25] Harris, whether he understood all the ramifications or not, was helping the bakufu maintain its boundaries with the West.

The Challenge of Terrorism, 1861–1862

As the bakufu, with Harris's help, began to maneuver the treaty powers toward postponement, its plans were thrown into disarray by a spiraling outbreak of terror. What had only been represented in art, in the public prints, now became reality. Ii Naosuke's assassination was an early page in this dark chapter of treaty relations, and showed that violence could strike at Japanese as well as Westerners. Even before then, once the treaty ports opened, it did not take long for disaffected samurai to lash out at the barbarians polluting their shores. In late August 1859, less than two months after the beginning of trade, two Russian sailors in Yokohama were set upon by a group of ruffians and murdered. They were buried on the land of Sōtoku Temple in Yokohama, being joined there in late February 1860 by two Dutch sea captains also cut down in the streets of the port.[26] In January 1860 Alcock's Japanese interpreter, Dankichi, was murdered outside the gate of the British legation at Tōzenji.

The most shocking act of terror, however, came in January 1861 and served as solemn proof of the bakufu's assertion that trade would lead to violence against foreigners. Henry Heusken, Harris's longtime secretary, had for months been helping the Prussians in their negotiations with the bakufu, and he unwisely returned home each day by the same route. On the night of January 15, only two weeks before completion of the treaty, Heusken was riding through the pitch-black, wooded, narrow streets of Shinagawa. Although accompanied by groomsmen and bakufu guard, he was set upon at a small bridge by an unknown number of men. Slashed across the torso, he managed to gallop past his attackers but soon collapsed. He was carried back to the Prussian mission, where he died the same night.

Heusken had arrived in Japan with Harris in 1856, and the two had lived isolated in Shimoda for more than a year and a half before setting foot in Edo. Because his native language was Dutch, the only Western language known to the Japanese, he had played an integral part in every aspect of Harris's negotiations with the bakufu. The most prominent Westerner murdered so far, the twenty-nine-year-old was also one of the foreigners most favorably disposed toward the Japanese. At this time, he had, among all the early diplomats, perhaps the greatest facility with the language and quite likely knew the most about Japan. His journal reveals an open and intelligent young man who was on his way to becoming the very first Japanologist; later young diplomats, such as Ernest Satow, merely followed in his footsteps.[27] Heusken was buried close to the U.S. legation in Edo, in the graveyard of Kōrinji, where he rests to this day.

Heusken's assassination shocked the diplomatic corps, as it was the first of their number and they realized that, living in Edo, they were as vulnerable as he had been. Led by Alcock, the Western representatives, with the notable exception of Harris, immediately withdrew to Yokohama in protest. In response to the violence the bakufu had repeatedly warned them about, the Western diplomatic corps, sans Harris, now saw Yokohama in a very different light from a year previously. The very spot they had so recently condemned as isolated and a violation of treaty agreements suddenly became a symbol of safety, harboring grateful diplomats. The meaning of boundaries, it seemed, was malleable according to the exigencies of the time.

Andō and Kuze realized the recent spate of murders, especially Heusken's, could jeopardize their plan for postponement. They worked quickly to retain Harris's good offices after Heusken's murder. Indeed, it appears the loss of his longtime companion convinced Harris of the veracity of the bakufu's warnings about the link between foreign trade and domestic instability. Harris, though he did not blame the bakufu for Heusken's assassination, did demand that the murderers be caught and that an indemnity be paid to Heusken's widowed mother, all of which was agreed to without demur.

On February 6, only three weeks after Heusken's demise, Andō met Harris again and showed him a draft of the postponement letter to the Western governments. The letter included a request for an unlimited delay, but the American urged Andō to set a more realistic time frame, such as seven years, until January 1, 1868. Despite the psychological shock of losing Heusken, Harris had not wavered in his decision to help the Japanese.

Once the bakufu informed Alcock that it was preparing to send an official letter from the shogun to the Western treaty powers requesting postponement, the British minister fleshed out his plans for a Japanese embassy. Alcock wanted the Japanese to see Britain's strengths firsthand, learn about its ceremonial customs, and visit with the ruling houses of Britain and its European neighbors. This was in part designed to correct any false impressions of the relative strengths of the Western nations the Japanese may have gained during their 1860 mission to the United States. Alcock told Andō that an embassy of high-ranking officials would offer the Japanese a unique chance to learn about the true bases of British national strength.[28] It was also the best way for Britain to wean Japan from its close relations with the United States, and to influence the bakufu as it undertook, in Alcock's words, a "reformation from above," shoring up its predominance in national politics.[29]

The official letter requesting postponement and the senior councillors' attachment were sent out to the treaty powers in May 1861. As Harris had suggested, the senior councillors' attached letter was sent to the foreign ministers of Russia, Portugal, and the United States, and also to the resident ministers in Japan of Great Britain, France, and Holland. Harris had calculated that the senior councillors' words would have a greater impact on Alcock, Bellecourt, and Jan K. de Wit than on their respective home governments, and the bakufu would need to win those three representatives over to its side to have any hope of success.

The letters were a Japanese attempt to interpret treaty relations within the context of the nature of Tokugawa rule and Japanese culture. The fault line running through the letters reveals the extent to which Tokugawa diplomatic culture was changing even as the bakufu attempted to gain Western approval of a policy designed to shore up its sagging defenses. The letters repeated the old excuses for postponement: high prices, domestic unrest, and the like. Yet Kuze and Andō, the signatories, clearly expressed their understanding that trade was inevitable and that the people of Japan had to be brought toward a modern understanding of the nature of international relations. Postponement, they argued, was a way "not to force [the people] in distress, but to enlighten [them] slowly."[30] The senior councillors did not fail to mention to all the treaty powers that the recently concluded Prussian treaty omitted reference to opening the two ports and two cities.

The dispatch of these letters left the bakufu hanging on the response of the treaty powers. Yet just the type of internal challenge to Edo's authority that the senior councillors feared soon threatened not just the postponement issue, but the entire framework of treaty relations. In the spring of 1861, as part of his attempt to gauge the bakufu's veracity regarding domestic conditions, Alcock set out on an extended journey throughout Japan after a vacation in Hong Kong. While his trip was less than momentous, the events following it were the most important in the short history of treaty relations. On the night of July 5, less than a day after Alcock's return to Edo, the British legation at Tōzenji was attacked by a band of Mito samurai.

Tōzenji was located near the border of Edo, not far from the Tōkaidō, in the vicinity of Shinagawa post station. Woods surrounded the temple, and a steep hill backed the compound. Alcock and the other Englishmen lived in the former priest's house behind the main hall, which overlooked a small pond. Shortly before midnight, several dozen rōnin evaded a bakufu guard of more than 150 samurai and penetrated the legation at three points. During fierce fighting at the front gate two bakufu guards were killed and ten were wounded. British marines fired their rifles while the Mito samurai attempted to hack through the defenders with their long swords. In the residence, attackers poured into the narrow hallways, aiming for Alcock's quarters. The Englishmen beat back the attackers in the darkness, shooting their rifles and even employing a whip. Of the Englishmen, Laurence

Oliphant, who had recently returned to Japan, and Nagasaki consul George Morrison were seriously wounded. Alcock himself narrowly escaped assassination. As he reported immediately to Lord John Russell, "the Legation looked as if it had been sacked after a serious conflict. Screens and mats were all spotted with blood, the former thrown down, broken, and torn; furniture and bedding all hacked, books even cut through by the sabres."[31] Nearly a century and a half later, Tōzenji's entrance pillars still bear sword cuts and bullet holes, offering mute testimony to the fury of the battle.

The Tōzenji attack could easily have derailed Anglo–Japanese relations, ending all hopes for accommodation on port postponement. Moreover, here was a classic excuse for Britain not only to refuse the bakufu's request, but also to pressure Edo into making more concessions designed to benefit British traders. Yet barely six weeks after the attack, Alcock reached agreement with Andō and Kuze that postponement should proceed. What accounted for the quick settlement of this major issue in the midst of a crisis in Anglo–Japanese relations?

There is no question that Alcock and London were outraged by the attack. Alcock wondered to Russell in the days after the skirmish whether the bakufu was able to protect foreigners in its midst, or whether it even wanted to do so. He made no attempt to hide his fury at the bakufu's impotence in protecting the legation, noting that English lives were "under the nominal protection only of a Government which has shown itself either treacherous or incapable."[32] Yet the senior councillors moved quickly, just as they had after Heusken's murder, to maintain their dialogue with the treaty powers.

After two weeks of hurried and unofficial meetings with Alcock, Andō and Kuze sat down for a long discussion with the British minister in mid-July. The two senior councillors blamed the attack on domestic instability from the rise in prices and the growing influence of the antiforeign group in Japan. The only way to protect foreigners, they urged, was to deal with the source of the problem: trade.[33]

Alcock pondered for several weeks over the senior councillors' claims and the situation in Japan. The problem facing him was geostrategic in nature, for if trade engendered unrest and unrest led to a political revolution, then Britain faced the possibility of losing all its Japan trade. More important, though, were the British to be kicked out of Japan the regional repercussions could be unthinkable. How could Britain protect its China position if this small country had defied the will of London? At another level, revolution in Japan meant general instability in the East Asian trading region. Again, the political effect on China and the potential for further French and Russian machinations were highly troubling. The only recourse seemed to be to support Edo's plan to keep the extra sites closed to foreigners.

The pivotal meetings occurred on August 14 and 15, between Alcock and Vice Admiral James Hope of the British China squadron, and Andō and Kuze.[34] Alcock played precisely into the councillors' game plan by averring that Britain was naturally the most interested of all the Western powers to maintain treaty rights. As such, the fate of the two ports-two cities issue likewise rested with Britain, for it was unlikely any other treaty power would oppose the British position. During this discussion, the Japanese explained the political importance of the emperor, and for the first time Alcock began to discern the relationships of the emperor, kuge, bakufu, and outer daimyō. Andō, for his part, exercised his growing understanding of great power relations when he requested British assistance in pressuring a Russian squadron to leave the island of Tsushima, in the Japan Sea, where it had docked and begun building some permanent facilities (see page 77).

Alcock did not agree to postponement at this meeting, but he had made up his mind by the next day, August 16. The fact that he chose not to employ the threat of force to deflect the bakufu's entreaties, despite having the commander of the British China squadron by his side during the meetings, underscores just how Japan fit into Britain's global strategy. Like Siam, Japan occupied in British thinking a crucial position as a stable buffer state close to Britain's major territorial interests. It was therefore antithetical to British strategy directly or indirectly to destabilize Japan or to use the military to extend trading rights, which might lead to territorial expansion. Years of service in China had impressed upon Alcock that country's overriding importance to Britain. Because of this preconception, he was willing to control his natural instinct to use force the way he had in China. He knew, of course, that he was abetting the Japanese in limiting trade and contact with the West, but that was a price that must be paid in order to keep the larger policy intact.

Writing Russell on August 16, Alcock called the situation in Japan a "crisis," but noted his satisfaction at the candid answers and explanations proffered by the bakufu. His thinking no doubt was influenced by the senior councillors' postponement letter of May, which he included for Russell and which seemed to lay to rest any fears that the bakufu did not understand that treaty relations were permanent. Alcock concluded by stating that two obvious policies were either to wage war or to surrender the British position entirely in Japan. "But if both those alternatives are rejected," he wrote, "none other is left but that offered by the Japanese Government,—to trust them, strengthen their hands by consenting to defer rights it might involve them in a civil war to insist upon."[35] Alcock, as did Harris before him, saw that the bakufu's boundaries were crucial to the entire structure of the Japanese state. Britain would respect those boundaries for the time being to maintain Anglo–Japanese trade relations. One month after Alcock penned this dispatch, Iwase Tadanari, the former foreign magistrate largely responsible for the treaty structure, died at the age of forty-four.

The mid-August meeting revealed the bases of accommodation between the Japanese and British diplomatic strategies. The goals of both could intersect without themselves being altered. Though some historians, such as Ishii Takashi, have seen the meeting as an Alcock success, it was equally a deft performance by Andō and Kuze.[36] They defused a crisis situation with very few concessions on their part and secured all they had pursued during a full year's worth of negotiations. Moreover, the two had convinced Alcock that postponement was vital to Japanese stability, and such stability could be secured only by the bakufu. Alcock was unable to conceive of any political alternative to the shogunate, and that made postponement necessary. At the same time, though, international events in the waters west of Japan also led Alcock to see the Japanese as potential partners in regional strategy.

The Tsushima Incident, 1861

The Japanese ability to adapt their diplomatic strategy in response to regional geopolitical pressures was shown by events on the island of Tsushima during much of 1861. The bakufu tactic of playing on British strategic concerns allowed Andō to use the events as a means of making Alcock an accessory in preserving Japan's physical boundaries. On the morning of March 13, 1861, a Russian warship, the *Posadnik*, had sailed into the inlet of Ozaki, on the island of Tsushima, and soon thereafter its captain demanded landing rights. Tsushima, which actually comprised two islands, was located approximately midway between Honshū and the Korean peninsula and had served as a conduit for Japanese foreign relations with Korea since prehistoric times. During the Tokugawa era, the daimyō of Tsushima, head of the Sō family, had served as an intermediary between the bakufu and the Korean government, providing Edo with intelligence that had come to Korea from Ming and Qing China. The Sō had also undertaken diplomatic missions, sometimes without Edo's knowledge, and facilitated trade between Japan, Korea, and China.[37] The last Korean embassy to Edo had come through Tsushima a half-century before, in 1811, but the island still served as the closest link to the continent.

The arrival of the *Posadnik* sent a shock wave rippling from Tsushima to Edo, reviving old bakufu fears. It was the Russians, after all, who had been the first threat to Japanese isolation, seven decades previously. The 1792 visit of Adam Laxman to Nagasaki and thence to Hokkaido had started a series of events culminating in the burning of northern Japanese villages by the Russians in 1806 and the capture of a Russian officer, Vasilii Golovnin, in 1811.[38] Even after a period of quiescence in Russo–Japanese relations, agents of the Tsar had reemerged in the months following Perry's arrival in 1853, and they had signed two supplementary treaties with the bakufu before finalizing a formal commercial treaty in 1858.

The opening of Yokohama, however, had revealed the limited trading interests of the Russians, who had almost no activity at the port. Their only real presence in Japan was in Hakodate, where a consul served primarily as a supercargo for passing Russian ships.[39] Initially, then, the Russians had seemed far less a concern than in earlier days, but the arrival of the *Posadnik* exposed the latent military threat from St. Petersburg. Equally important, it raised a host of questions for both Japan and Great Britain.

Russia had no de jure access to Tsushima, since the Ansei treaties mentioned nothing about the island. On that point, therefore, the bakufu was secure in its refusal of the Russian demand for landing rights. However, two deeper concerns underlay bakufu policy, one external and one internal. The external concern, of course, was the threat to Japan's boundaries, for if any foreign power took over Japanese territory, such holdings could be used as a base for future incursions. Since the Russians had already shown in the early 1800s their willingness to pillage Japanese land, their new desire to have a permanent foothold near the Japanese mainland was quite disturbing.

The bakufu's internal concern was that the Tsushima incident might raise the underlying question of Japanese territorial boundaries. Tsushima had occupied an anomalous position, being considered by Korea a vassal and by Edo a domain. Moreover, the Sō family had conducted its end of the Pusan trade relatively independently from Edo. To what degree was the bakufu in control of Tsushima, and was it truly a part of Japanese territory? It was again the Russians who brought up these troublesome questions, just as they had back in 1855 with respect to Japanese control over Hokkaidō, the Kuriles, and Sakhalin. Despite the potentially far-reaching consequences of its actions, the bakufu eventually chose to assert its control over Tsushima. In pursuit of this policy it received help from Great Britain.

Tensions rose immediately after the Russians dropped anchor. One week after their arrival Sō Yoshikazu, the daimyō, sent a strongly worded note to samurai and commoners alike throughout the islands, "admonishing against rash actions."[40] Domainal officials had heard of meetings taking place where fear of the Russians led to calls to drive them off the islands. Despite twice having informed Edo of the situation, the domain did not receive a response before a second Russian ship joined the *Posadnik* in early April. This was followed by the formal request of the *Posadnik*'s captain, Nikolai Birilev, for permission to build a landing area for Russian ships and to have provisions of timber and food made available.[41] No reply came from the domain, and growing frustrated at the lack of response, Birilev employed the time-honored tactic of raising the specter of British involvement, warning the domain that the British were on their way to Tsushima. In this way he hoped to force a meeting with Sō Yoshikazu, which the domainal officials refused.[42]

In mid-May, however, events threatened to spiral out of control. On May 13, the Russians sent out a survey boat from the *Posadnik* that attempted to make its way around to the eastern side of the island. Despite the temporary presence of one British warship and two bakufu warships, the *Kankō Maru* and *Denryū Maru,* purchased from the Dutch in 1855 and currently in the service of Saga domain, the Russians continued their surveying.[43] Eight days later, on May 21, hostilities erupted when a Russian survey boat tried to force its way through a picket of samurai and farmers. The two sides clashed and the Russians captured at least one samurai. According to initial domain reports, one farmer was killed, while the captured samurai soon committed suicide.[44] Domain officials now forcefully refused Russian demands for a landing site and provisions, a message the top aide of the Nagasaki magistrate repeated to Birilev on June 10.[45]

By mid-July, the bakufu involved itself directly in the crisis and decided to bypass the recalcitrant Russian captain. Foreign magistrate Muragaki Norimasa, vice ambassador on the 1860 mission to the United States, was sent to Hakodate where he requested the Russian consul, Goshkevitch, to order his ships away from Japanese territory.[46] Muragaki and later foreign magistrate Oguri Tadamasa fruitlessly argued with Goshkevitch in person and by letter throughout the summer of 1861.

By midsummer, however, the bakufu had decided radically to change its tactics, and to employ against the Russians the very threat Birilev had used against the Japanese: the presence of the British in Japanese waters. This was a risky move that could have backfired. It was an embarrassing admission of bakufu weakness, for Edo repeatedly had tried to expel the Russians for six months now. Worse yet, the British could easily take advantage of the situation and not only evict the Russians but also take over the island or demand some other reward. Tsushima was particularly attractive to the British, as George Lensen pointed out, since they were barred by the terms of their 1858 and 1860 treaties with China from establishing any naval stations between the Amur River and Korea. Under such conditions, the island offered a perfect base close to the continent.[47] Yet Andō and the senior councillors believed they saw an opportunity to employ the British to protect the interests of Edo and London alike.

The senior councillors were correct in their assumption. British naval policy in the region was guided by its overarching strategy of limited territorial entanglement. This, of course, extended to preventing territorial gains by other European maritime powers. Indeed, this was the type of situation envisioned by the admiralty as far back as 1854, when Admiral James Stirling had attempted to discern the bakufu's policy toward belligerent parties in its waters. Stirling's 1854 convention, signed while the Crimean War was being waged between Britain and Russia halfway around the globe, had sought to deny to any belligerent ships the use of Japanese ports. Although the actual convention wound up replicating the Perry treaty, due in no small measure to misinterpretation, British policy remained unchanged.[48]

Because of its location, Tsushima could be the greatest threat to British interests in Northeast Asia. An anti-British force could use it to create a bottleneck between British ports in southern China and ports in north China, and Manchuria. It could be used, as well, as a staging point for attacks against those southern British bases or for aggressive moves against either the Chinese or the Japanese. Both Tsushima and the Japanese mainland now appeared more than ever analogous to Siam in Southeast Asia. The British needed Tsushima neutral, and they also needed to keep Japan a stable maritime buffer between the Russians and the Chinese. All this was threatened by Birilev's jerry-built landing site. It was at this point that the Tsushima issue intersected with Edo's plan to postpone opening the two ports and two cities.

In mid-August 1861, when Andō was finalizing agreement with Alcock on postponement, it will be recalled that the commander of the British China squadron, Vice Admiral James Hope, had heard directly from the bakufu about the Tsushima situation. Hope, of course, had known of the Russian presence on the island from his own survey ships, but he now was informed for the first time on the extent of the Russian threat. The bakufu requested Hope's assistance in driving the Russians off the island. The British could have made their help a quid pro quo for not agreeing to postponement, but neither Alcock nor Hope took that route. Instead, Andō convinced the two officials that the Russians threatened Britain's trading position in Japan.[49]

This gambit was clearly in line with the bakufu's policy of playing foreign powers off one against another whenever feasible. From one point of view it even could be considered as an affirmation of the MFN clause of the 1858 treaties. Russia's position in Tsushima might gain for it an advantage that by its very nature could not be shared with the other treaty powers. This was in contravention of Japan's treaties with its other partners. Such a view was reflected in Alcock's advice to the bakufu, which urged Andō not merely to complain directly to St. Petersburg, but to request that each treaty power cooperate with Edo in opposing this move by the Russians, which was "not only contrary to the right of Japan, but the common interest of all."[50] More important, Japanese and British foreign policies worked in tandem, as both sides sought to protect their interests by protecting the treaty structure.

Admiral Hope quickly announced that he would sail to Tsushima to meet Birilev and deliver Edo's demand. Arriving on August 28 with two ships, he informed Birilev of his mission and left a letter of protest to the commander of Russian naval forces in the region, Commodore Likhachev. The British appearance dovetailed neatly with bakufu pressure on Hakodate consul Goshkevitch and Likhachev found himself with few options. On September 19, 1861, Birilev and the *Posadnik* withdrew from Tsushima, and within three days all remaining Russian ships were ordered back to Siberia. The outcome was immediately reported to the bakufu by Tsushima officials.[51]

As in the case of postponement, the Japanese and the British had found common ground in the Tsushima incident. Japan's strategy was to preserve its territorial boundaries and Britain now supported that very goal. There is nothing in the records of the period to indicate that the British were considering intervening in Tsushima before Andō requested Alcock's help, though it certainly would have been natural for them to do so. The significance of the episode was in the convergence of the global strategies of the two sides, and it underscored the importance to both of maintaining certain boundaries.

Settling Postponement, 1861–1862

Though the Tsushima incident raised the specter of grave threats, postponement remained the bakufu's main policy goal. In pursuit of this, the government sought to resolve any outstanding issues with its treaty partners. It tracked down at least half of those responsible for the July 1861 attack on the British legation, thus satisfying London's demands for punishment, and recompensed Heusken's mother for his murder, further cementing its relationship with Harris. More important, Andō and Kuze did not fail to organize the embassy to Europe for which Alcock had such high hopes.

The idea of an embassy was not quite as simple as it may have appeared to Alcock. Only one precedent existed, of course, the 1860 mission to the United States. The members of that mission were chosen with an eye to their political reliability. In other words, Andō and the senior councillors in 1860 had not wanted to send to the United States men who might look too carefully at what they saw.[52] The maritime edicts had kept Japanese from traveling abroad for more than two centuries in part as a way to protect the intellectual boundary that surrounded the bakufu's political authority. New forms of government, new ideas of politics, and new economic theories all posed a potentially grave threat to shogunal rule. Thus, despite the presence on the 1860 mission of Fukuzawa Yukichi, who was soon to become the greatest interpreter of the West to Japan, the bakufu was more than satisfied by the lack of any deep impression made on the ambassadors and their subordinates.

Planning for the 1862 mission not surprisingly mimicked that of the earlier one. After some debate within bakufu circles, Andō named Takeuchi Yasunori as envoy extraordinary and minister plenipotentiary. Takeuchi was serving both as foreign magistrate and finance magistrate, and he stood fairly high in bakufu councils, which undoubtedly pleased Alcock. Second in charge was Matsudaira Yasunao, foreign magistrate and Kanagawa magistrate, while chief inspector and inspector in charge of foreign affairs, Kōgyoku Takaaki (Kōrō), rounded out the embassy's leadership. Despite their ranks, these men were not particularly influential, nor were they the type of aggressive, inquisitive characters who would bring back innovative ideas that might seep into public discourse.

Yet beyond the safe bureaucrats chosen to lead the mission, the bakufu appointed a small constellation of Japan's future leaders, including Fukuzawa Yukichi, now given a second opportunity to encounter the West; Fukuchi Gen'ichirō, later a participant in the 1871 Iwakura Mission and one of Meiji Japan's most important journalists; and Matsuki Kōan, who would serve as Meiji foreign minister under the name Terajima Munenori.[53] In all, thirty-five young men were to travel with Takeuchi as attendants, secretaries, porters, and the like.

In his eagerness to maintain the momentum toward an agreement, Andō moved to dispatch the embassy even before London definitively agreed to postponement. In fact, just as Alcock was receiving a positive response from Lord John Russell, the embassy set sail from Shinagawa on the evening of January 21, 1862, heading southwest and reaching Paris a little more than two months later.

The bakufu's seeming success in foreign policy now reverberated back into domestic politics. On February 13, Mito rōnin, in an attempt to replicate their assassination of Ii Naosuke two years before, attacked and wounded Andō outside the Sakashita gate of Edo Castle. The violence offered further proof of the disconnect between the negotiated nature of Japan's foreign relations and the growing chaos in its internal affairs. Nothing less than the expulsion of all foreigners would satisfy the terrorists, but this was hardly an option for the bakufu. The best that the senior councillors could do was to maintain the agreement with the powers and hope that the strengthening of the physical boundary through this scheme might also brace the ideological boundary still under attack.

In a final meeting in mid-March, Kuze assured Alcock that the bakufu would be destroyed were the Europeans to press for the opening of any of the two ports or two cities.[54] No starker warning about the destabilizing effects of foreign affairs could be made, and the Englishman did not question this dramatic statement. Instead, Alcock wrote to Russell the following day, March 17, "that the Government of the Tycoon has real difficulties of no ordinary kind and actual dangers to contend with, threatening the dynasty and the existence of the Government, I am quite satisfied."[55] Six days later Alcock left Japan for London, taking along the chief bakufu interpreter, Moriyama Takichirō.

The Embassy in Europe: Negotiation and Observation, 1862

The Takeuchi embassy, meanwhile, had made its way around the globe, reaching Marseilles on April 3, 1862, and arriving in Paris four days later.[56] Reflecting Alcock's influence on the planning of the mission, the ambassadors spent a week resting and sightseeing before beginning preliminary negotiations. Staying at a central Paris hotel, they journeyed throughout the city and suburbs, and their travels were recorded regularly in French newspapers. Ten days after their arrival, they had a formal audience with Napoleon III during a visit to the Tuilleries. What struck the ambassadors most, it seemed, were the open and abundant expressions of French nationalism, from the flags they first saw at Marseilles to Napoleon's invocation of the "grandeur of the nation."[57]

With notable efficiency, however, Takeuchi smoothly moved to the main business of the embassy, opening talks with Foreign Minister Antoine-Eduoard Thouvenel on April 28. Takeuchi's original instructions were to ask for an unlimited postponement, but after initial forays with French diplomats, he formally requested a ten-year delay. Thouvenel's response confirmed the Japanese in their belief that Great Britain was the main player in European international politics, for the foreign minister declared that France could not make any decision without an Anglo–Japanese agreement first.[58] Nevertheless, Thouvenel indicated his general approval of postponement, though for no longer than three years. He also urged a lowering of the tariff on spirits to 5 percent, to help French wine exports. In addition, the French wanted the bakufu to end the ban on exports of raw silk and silkworm eggs, which could help them recover from the ravages of the *pebrine* silkworm disease.[59]

Thus apprised of London's key role, the ambassadors' interest in French culture and the "grandeur of the nation" quickly cooled. Takeuchi and the embassy left Paris the following day and piled onto Channel ferries, arriving in London on April 30. They immediately entered into another round of sightseeing, this one inspired by Alcock's desire to showcase Britain's cultural, economic, and political strengths. They viewed arsenals, schools, foundries, and museums, and attended numerous balls and meetings with British aristocrats, events that were well recorded in the London *Times*.[60]

Here, it seemed, was a potential threat to the bakufu's carefully-tended intellectual boundary; in fact, this was precisely Alcock's goal in urging Edo to let the embassy travel widely in Britain and on the Continent. Though desirous not to alienate the British minister, such a liberal mandate was a fine line for the senior councillors to tread. On the one hand, they indeed desired to learn about the West's strengths, as Andō had indicated in his conversations with Alcock. On the other hand, though, it was unclear whether they could control what their representatives saw while abroad, and even less the impression that would make. In pre-treaty days, at least, the bakufu could on the whole import only that information it desired. Now, it had to rely ever more on its age-old restriction on free travel for Japanese, a point on which the treaties remained silent. Unfettered public access, to foreign knowledge posed an incalculable threat and had to remain a bottled genie. As for those picked to go abroad, they had to be trustworthy in the first place and well watched in the second.

Andō indeed picked his men carefully, for despite their whirlwind of new experiences, none of the embassy's members began to compile a record of their observations that even remotely foreshadowed the massive undertaking of Kume Kunitake during the Iwakura Mission precisely a decade later. Only Fukuzawa Yukichi, who was soon to leave government service permanently, used his personal diary as the basis of his later bestseller, *Seiyō jijō (Things Western)*.[61] The presence of bakufu inspectors on the journey ensured that the younger members, in particular, did not stray too far from their narrow duties.

Burdened by sightseeing, the Japanese held no substantive meetings with the British until Alcock returned to London on May 30. He had stopped off in Paris en route, where in support of the Japanese goals, he convinced Napoleon III and Thouvenel of the necessity of a postponement longer than three years. Here too, perhaps, was a case of the Japanese employing barbarian against barbarian, as the British swept away any lingering French resistance to postponement.

There was little actual negotiating done in London, as accommodation had already been reached at the local level, back in Japan, and Russell deferred to Alcock's understanding with the Japanese. Alcock met the embassy a number of times in its London hotel to iron out the language of the agreement. The price the British demanded for postponement was a bakufu promise to end any unofficial restrictions on the sale of merchandise to foreigners, the hiring of labor, and the collection of illegal customs fees.[62] This, Alcock hoped, would finally assure the conduct of "free trade" in Japan as promised back in 1858.

On June 6, 1862, Russell and Takeuchi signed the London Protocol. By its terms, Edo, Osaka, and Hyogo were to be kept closed for an additional five years, until January 1, 1868. In return, the ambassadors promised to "strictly execute" the other provisions of the Ansei treaty, as well as "to suggest" to the shogun that the tariff on wines, spirits, and glassware be reduced to 5 percent.[63] The next day, Russell transmitted copies of the protocol to European ministers living in London, warning them that to try to open the ports according to the original timetable would threaten everyone's trade.[64]

A week later, the embassy left London for the Hague, then traveled to Russia and finally back to Paris, signing agreements similar to the London Protocol with all other treaty powers. They completed their work in Paris on October 2, 1862, and arrived back in Edo at the end of January 1863.

The London Protocol was the capstone of the bakufu's attempts to maintain key physical barriers toward the West, primarily by preventing the building of new settlements. It might be considered the highpoint of Tokugawa diplomacy, the more so as no one at the time could foretell whether future settlements ever would be opened. It was a dramatic reaffirmation of the negotiated nature of the Japanese–Western relationship as well as of the diplomatic astuteness of the senior councillors. Andō and Kuze, accidental leaders, drew together all the straws of their strategy, worked with Alcock and the other representatives, dispatched an embassy, and convinced Western governments of the necessity of postponement.

At the same time, however, it is vital to recognize that the Japanese benefited from international conditions beyond their control. First, the United States had plunged itself into a fratricidal Civil War, and President Lincoln had other concerns than to insist on treaty rights in Japan; this allowed Harris to work with the bakufu in flexibly maintaining the treaty structure he had negotiated. More crucial for the Japanese, China remained the cornerstone of Great Britain's Asian policy and London was in no mood to force the issue of trade in Japan.

Within the last five years, Britain had fought two wars with China, and it was not looking to spill more blood. Lord Palmerston, prime minister from 1855 to 1865, except for a brief spell in 1858–1859, had suffered much public criticism and had undergone panels of inquiry in Parliament due to his use of force to protect British interests in China. Although he had been upheld at the polls after the British bombardment of Canton and the burning of the Summer Palace in 1860, Palmerston was aware that, in both Parliament and the country in general, the use of force was unpopular and its morality, especially against "less civilized" lands, was doubted.[65] When Kuze stated that forcing the opening of the ports would lead to civil war, Alcock interpreted the comment to mean that Britain could enforce the treaties only through arms, and that was the last thing Palmerston and Russell wanted to hear. Finally, one can speculate that London was willing to postpone the opening of a mere four sites in Japan since just a year and half earlier it had secured, albeit through force, the opening to trade of eleven more cities in China, some of them in the interior.

In the final analysis, the London Protocol closed the first phase of Japanese–Western treaty relations. In the five years since Harris had signed his commercial treaty in 1858, the bakufu actively worked within the framework of the treaties to protect its interests and Japanese sovereignty as best as it could. Edo had negotiated on two levels, domestically and with its treaty partners. The bakufu moved to quell or respond to domestic dissent by new tactics such as postponement, while it co-opted the Westerners into respecting the particular political, physical, and ideological boundaries it chose to defend. These parallel negotiations reinforced each other and allowed the bakufu to operate in a space between two diametrically opposed parties.

Nevertheless, the legacy of the policy that led to the London Protocol was more ambiguous. On the one hand, the very arguments Edo used in favor of postponement revealed the extent to which it was willing to entertain Western concepts of international relations even while attempting to maintain its traditional worldview. On the other, the bakufu's success now led its domestic opponents to redouble their efforts to destabilize both internal and external politics, while the treaty powers henceforth were to become increasingly resistant to granting Japan any more leeway in fulfilling its international agreements.

CHAPTER FOUR

The Limits of Negotiation: Expulsion and Gunboats

The Tokugawa bakufu's defense of its diplomatic culture found its apotheosis in the 1862 London Protocol. Yet the succeeding years saw direct challenges to Edo's strategy of negotiation, resulting in imperial calls for the expulsion of foreigners and in military clashes between outer domains and the Westerners. Caught in the middle, the bakufu found its strategy temporarily strengthened but weakened in the long-term.

The success of the London Protocol ironically led to a breakdown of the unique combination of circumstances that allowed for its birth. In both the center and the periphery of the Japanese state, the daily operation of treaty relations was fraught with difficulty due to persistent instability and challenges to the status quo. The first blow to the community of interests forged since 1858 was the sudden disappearance of the first generation of actors on both the Japanese and Western sides.

A Change in Actors

In Japan, the fate of the bakufu's diplomatic strategy now rested in the hands of a new group of leaders. Since 1860 and the assassination of Ii Naosuke, the key policymakers had not been those who had crafted the negotiating strategy. Rather, Ii's successors, Andō Nobumasa and Kuze Hirochika, still hewed closely to Ii's policy, and indeed, they pushed Ii's agenda even further than he had (see chapter 3). Domestic politics, however, claimed both men by 1862. Andō, as noted earlier, was seriously wounded in the Sakashita Gate incident of February, but he managed to maintain a role in the negotiations with Rutherford Alcock. He soon fell victim, however, to the continuing political struggle between reformist daimyō and bakufu policymakers that had first exploded over the shogunal succession issue of 1858. After Ii's assassination, the reformist clique slowly succeeded in taking over bakufu policy making. Andō, closely identified with Ii, was forced to resign in early May 1862 by pressure exerted on the court from this resurgent reformist party headed by the Satsuma domain. He was followed in retirement two months later by Kuze.

In their place, Satsuma installed a new triumvirate of reformist leaders in Edo. Hitotsubashi Keiki, son of Mito's Tokugawa Nariaki, was the shogunal candidate of the reformist party back in 1858 and now became shogunal guardian. Matsudaira Shungaku (Keiei) of Fukui became *seiji sōsai,* the equivalent of regent. Finally, Matsudaira Katamori of Aizu became *Kyoto shugo,* effectively superseding the Kyoto deputy as the main bakufu official in the imperial capital.[1] These three immediately clashed with their domestic critics within the bakufu as well as with radical anti-bakufu figures in the far western domain of Chōshū. Being extraordinary appointees to the bakufu bureaucracy, they focused primarily on domestic political issues, initially leaving day-to-day management of foreign relations in the hands of the senior councillors Mizuno Tadakiyo, who would serve until 1866, and Itakura Katsukiyo, who remained in his post for two years, until 1864.

Meanwhile, on the Western side, Japan lost its closest ally. Townsend Harris, who had lived in Japan since 1856, had requested in late 1861 to be relieved of his post. On April 26, 1862, a few weeks before Andō's resignation, Harris presented his order of replacement to the shogun. Long having given up his journal, Harris left no record of his thoughts as he prepared to leave Japan, but he must have been gratified that he had so recently played a major role in preserving the fruits of his labor. His replacement, Robert Pruyn, arrived in Edo four days later, on April 30, 1862, and took up his duties on May 17.[2]

During these months Alcock was also out of Japan, back home to negotiate the London Protocol. After leaving Edo on March 23, 1862, he did not return for nearly two years, until March 2, 1864.

The legation was run in his absence by Alcock's chargé d'affaires, Edward St. John Neale, who did not have as extensive service in Asia as Alcock. On June 24, French Minister Duchesne de Bellecourt announced his recall, though he was actually to stay on for almost another two years, until April 1864. Bellecourt and Dutch Minister Jan K. de Wit were now the senior Western representatives in Japan, but neither had influence or military power equivalent to Neale, so they continued to play secondary roles. Before long, all these actors would be forced to respond to ever-escalating acts of violence.

Terrorism and the Namamugi Incident, 1862–1863

The negotiated relationship struck between the bakufu and its treaty partners was subjected to severe strain in 1862. The first challenge came even as the Takeuchi mission was still in Europe. A second assault on the British legation at Tōzenji occurred on the night of June 26, the lunar year anniversary of the first attack. This time, despite a bakufu guard of more than five hundred samurai, infiltrators managed to kill two British marines guarding the compound, though they failed to penetrate the legation itself. British demands, when they came, were surprisingly restrained, for Foreign Secretary Lord John Russell's mid-September instructions essentially called for a £10,000 indemnity for each murdered sailor and stronger security at the legation.[3] This was a great deal of money, to be sure, but nothing like the numerous demands made by Alcock a year previously. It was perhaps the case that Russell, having just met with the bakufu's representatives, was willing to give Edo the benefit of the doubt.

Six weeks later, however, there occurred an event that shocked the foreign community and galvanized British anger. On September 14, four English riders heading east on the Tōkaidō encountered the three-hundred-man train of Shimazu Hisamitsu, who was the father of the Satsuma daimyō and was the effective head of the domain. Hisamitsu was on his way back to Kyoto from Edo after his successful maneuver to install Hitotsubashi Keiki, Matsudaira Katamori, and Matsudaira Keiei in their new top bakufu positions.

The British party consisted of three residents of Yokohama and a visiting merchant from Shanghai, twenty-eight-year-old Charles L. Richardson. At the small village of Namamugi, located between Kanagawa and Kawasaki post stations, the riders came up on the end of the

Satsuma procession. Although the British turned their horses off the road as gestured by the samurai, several of Hisamitsu's retainers suddenly drew their swords and attacked the party. The only woman in the group, a Mrs. Borradaile, escaped the violence, but the three men were set upon. The Yokohama merchants, William Clark and William Marshall, both were seriously wounded, but they managed to gallop back to Yokohama. Richardson, however, was left behind and was cut down from his horse. He was attacked again while seeking shelter and bled to death on the road. When the news reached Yokohama, the foreign community demanded an immediate reprisal and organized a posse to bring Hisamitsu to justice. Chargé d'affaires Neale wisely defused the mob and prevented them from sallying forth en masse, but a crisis had now been reached.

For Neale, the attack was more than simply the murder of a British merchant, however gruesome and unfortunate. It represented a threat to free passage along the Tōkaidō within the boundaries permitted by the treaties. It appeared that a pillar of the entire treaty structure now hung in the balance. London's policy was predicated on maintaining amicable relations with Japan, but such a challenge to the treaties could bring about a radical change in British strategy, leading even to military intervention. For the bakufu, the Namamugi Incident, as it came to be known, was precisely the kind of breach in the physical barrier between Japanese and Westerners that it had long feared. Richardson's murder raised the issue of security to a new high, and provided Edo with an excuse to try to rebuild, perhaps even strengthen, the boundaries inside the country.

Regardless of the tension felt by all parties, events moved slowly. Neale's dispatch recounting the murder did not arrive in London until October, and Russell's response reached Edo only in late December. The bakufu took advantage of the space given to it by the measured pace of communications and attempted to negotiate its way out of the crisis. Even as rumors of attacks on the Yokohama settlement by rōnin stirred up Westerners, the bakufu dispatched Kanagawa magistrate Abe Masato to assure Neale of his countrymen's safety. Neale, in fact, held numerous meetings with foreign magistrates in the months after the attack. Edo further attempted to mollify Neale by informing him that twenty-four guardhouses were to be built along the Tōkaidō between Kawasaki and Hodogaya, spanning the length of Kanagawa and ostensibly protecting Westerners within the range of free travel permitted them by the treaties.[4] Implicitly, of course, these same guardhouses could also control Western movement near Yokohama, through intimidation or harassment.

In late December, Russell's instructions regarding the Richardson murder reached Edo. The demands this time were substantial: Neale was to obtain £100,000 sterling and a formal apology from the bakufu, while Satsuma was to be held responsible for a £25,000 indemnity and the trial and execution of the chief perpetrators of the attack.[5] Moreover, Neale was ordered to use ships of the China Squadron to carry out reprisal or blockade against either party should the demands be refused.

Despite the harshness of the stated demands, a growing understanding of Japanese domestic politics influenced British policy. Russell's instructions explicitly stated:

> The distinction between the Government and the Daimios [*sic*] is one that must be kept in view. The Prince of Satsuma is said by one of the Japanese Ministers to be a powerful Daimio, who could not be easily coerced by the Japanese Government. . . . Her Majesty's Government have made full allowance for the inability of the Tycoon's Ministers to control the powerful Daimios.[6]

Russell no doubt was influenced by Alcock, who was still on home leave and who continued to digest the political information imparted to him the previous year by Andō and Kuze (see chapter 3). Indeed, Alcock now was penning his two-volume memoirs, in which he recounted his thoughts on viewing the corpses of those believed to be the initial Tōzenji attackers back in the spring of 1862: "I could not help musing on the strange state of uncertainty in which we were left as to the actual position of the Government in this Country and its relations with its subjects and great feudatory princes."[7]

Both sides worked to defuse the crisis as 1863 dawned. In concern for the safety of their traders in Japan, Western representatives allowed themselves to be co-opted into helping the bakufu reassert its control over the interactions between natives and foreigners. In mid-January, the bakufu sent Neale a copy of an order restricting all daimyō to a secondary road within Kanagawa, thereby prohibiting their use of the Tōkaidō. This order appeared to assure safe travel along the road for foreigners. While this was one goal for the bakufu, the gesture, a seeming about-face from Ii Naosuke's policy, just as equally helped ensure that Westerners would have no chance to encounter any other important political actor in Japan.

Moreover, the new restriction order carried no political cost, for in mid-October 1862 the bakufu had revised the centuries-old "alternate attendance" (*sankin kōtai*) requirement. This arrangement, begun in the first decades of Tokugawa rule, mandated that daimyō live half the year in Edo and the other half in their home domains. The staggered attendance schedule kept the lords busy shuttling across the Tōkaidō and the other main roads in Japan, and was a serious drain on daimyō coffers.[8] As a result of the policy change, the streets of Edo emptied as daimyō gratefully fled to their domains. This all but ended the possibility for future altercations between lords and Western residents on the Tōkaidō. Neale, of course, was unaware of the domestic context or the bakufu's political goal. Greatly impressed with Edo's effort, he wrote Russell that "the abandonment . . . of the sole great high road of Japan leading from Yedo to Nagasaki is undoubtedly a strong and gratifying proof of the Sincerity of the Government."[9]

Remaining unresolved was any agreement between London and Edo over how to settle Japan's response to the Richardson murder. Even though Neale relayed London's demands for reparations to the foreign magistrates on March 14, 1863, six months after the attack, he did not yet believe that a crisis was at hand. This was despite yet a third assault on the hapless British legation, in which a new, as-yet unoccupied, compound was torched by arson. Regardless of the pressures, Neale kept a cool head and a long-term view of the situation.

In an important dispatch to Russell just nine days after the fire, he wrote, "There is no reason why our relations with Japan, accompanied by all its regrettable episodes, should not be viewed by the same light as our early intercourse with other Asiatic states. . . . Viewed as a whole, our relations with this country present no serious cause for discouragement." He went on to recount that since 1859, the total volume of trade had increased three-fold, and exports now topped one million pounds sterling. Moreover, Neale stressed to London the deleterious effect of treaty relations on Japanese domestic politics, implicitly urging a less belligerent British tone: "The Tycoon and his Government, as an undeniable fact, have fallen into national discredit by assenting to the much-dreaded renewal of intercourse with Western people, *though indeed this assent was obtained under irresistible pressure*."[10] Such a nuanced view was not shared in London.

Japanese Resistance and British Response

London's express authorization for the use of force to secure its demands was a direct threat to the negotiated nature of Anglo–Japanese relations. The bakufu was caught in a double bind. On the one hand, it could not admit responsibility for Satsuma's independent action (the attack on Richardson) and it did not want to give such an impression by paying the demanded indemnity. On the other hand, it had neither the strength nor will to punish Satsuma or to force it to pay its share of the indemnity.

Similarly, any use of force by Britain posed a danger to Edo on two fronts. First, the treaty powers could consider such an action as a precedent to be followed in other places in Japan and in other situations where the bakufu was unable to conform to Western demands. Second, a Western attack would embolden domestic critics of the bakufu who charged that Edo could no longer fulfill its traditional foreign affairs role. The bakufu chose to rest its hopes for a peaceful resolution of the crisis on its tactic of negotiation, whereby it might ameliorate the British demands.

Despite Edo's refusal to respond directly to the demands, Neale nevertheless made a crucial recommendation on March 29, urging London that any punitive action taken be aimed solely at Satsuma, thereby keeping hostilities far from Edo.[11] As the man on the spot in the pre-telegraphic age, he was in a position to ensure that his views translated into action. Neale's understanding of the reality of Japanese domestic politics and his desire to avoid long-term damage to the treaty structure led to this measured proposal. Even as he wrote London, however, he learned that the shogun, breaking all tradition, had left for Kyoto for an audience with the emperor at the end of March 1863. He had been preceded there by Hitotsubashi Keiki and Matsudaira Katamori. These departures left few key policymakers in Edo, thus complicating attempts to resolve the crisis and revealing the lack of resources at the bakufu's disposal.

The vacuum in Edo forced Neale to threaten the bakufu openly in the first week of April. In a letter to the foreign magistrates, he warned that Britain's Namamugi demands must be replied to in a "categorical character" within twenty days, otherwise the British fleet would undertake "such measures" as necessary to obtain the reparation.[12] Even after delivering this threat, though, Neale met constantly with foreign magistrates Takemoto Masaaki and Takemoto Masao and was persuaded to make no fewer than five extensions in his twenty-day deadline, pushing it forward into mid-June.[13]

Neale's leniency was explained in part by the successful bakufu attempt to employ the United States as a mediator between the two nations. In mid-April, foreign magistrate Muragaki Norimasa, leader of the 1860 mission to the United States, met with U.S. Minister to Japan Robert Pruyn and formally asked him to intercede with Neale over the "inflexible" Namamugi deadline. The request was fully in keeping with Article II of the 1858 treaty, which called on the United States to exercise its good offices in "such matters of difference as may arise between the Government of Japan and any European power."

The bakufu had already invoked this part of the treaty back in 1859, when it urged Townsend Harris to garner European approval of Yokohama as the main treaty port (see chapter 2). This time, Muragaki tempted Pruyn with visions of an agreement establishing bonded warehouses in Yokohama, a long-held U.S. goal.[14] Pruyn in fact did negotiate with Neale, helping to secure the various extensions, and he reported back to Washington that Tokugawa diplomats "attributed the successful result of their application entirely to my mediation."[15] Whether the bakufu actually felt this way cannot be discerned, but its policy undeniably reflected the traditional tactic of using barbarian to control barbarian; moreover, it made Pruyn a de facto supporter of bakufu policy.

Ultimately, Pruyn's intercession with Neale failed to prevent a British attack on Satsuma, but an exploration of events surrounding Britain's intervention shows that the bombardment had little effect on the formal treaty structure. Neale and the bakufu had reached agreement for payment of the Namamugi indemnity in seven installments over a series of days in mid-June. When the first date, the eighteenth, broke with news from the Japanese that the bakufu would yet again delay, Neale felt he had no choice but to order the British squadron, now headed by Admiral Augustus Kuper, to take action, though Kuper made no immediate moves.

On the final deadline night of June 24, however, the bakufu dramatically paid its bill. Ogasawara Nagamichi, a new member of the senior councillors, appeared without notice at the consulate in Yokohama bearing the entire amount of £100,000, plus the £10,000 demanded for the second Tōzenji attack. A contemporary British print showed the consulate's Japanese and Chinese servants counting out the stacks of silver coin by lantern light, with bakufu officials in the background talking easily to the British diplomats.[16] Neale immediately ordered Kuper, who apparently had no tactical plan ready in any case, to stand down. Ogasawara thus had broken a bakufu deadlock over paying the indemnity and had avoided an open breach with the Westerners. But he had done so only because he was about to challenge the entire treaty structure by relaying a shogunal order to expel all foreigners and close the treaty ports.

Before examining the crisis of the expulsion order, the Namamugi Incident should be put into context. Ogasawara's indemnity payment of June 24 ended the bakufu's role in the incident. Meanwhile, the British had received no satisfaction from Satsuma, so Kuper's flotilla finally embarked for the domain capital of Kagoshima on August 6, nearly one year after Richardson's murder. A one-day engagement ensued on August 14, with both sides suffering heavy losses. Most of Kagoshima's shore batteries were destroyed, along with an unspecified number of buildings. About midway through the engagement, a shot from shore hit Admiral Kuper's flagship *Euryalus* dead center, killing the ship's commanding and first officers. In all, the British suffered eighteen killed and fifty wounded.[17] Neale claimed that up to fifteen hundred Satsuma soldiers were killed and the better part of Kagoshima destroyed. The British squadron immediately repaired to Yokohama and undertook no further hostilities against Satsuma.

Uproar ensued in Britain when news broke of the bombardment. The government's decision to use force was critiqued and the loss of British life was lamented. The Prime Minister, Viscount Palmerston, and Foreign Secretary Russell were strongly questioned in Parliament, and a motion was introduced to repudiate the attack. Public criticism excoriated the government as well; the *Times* argued that

> a list of 11 killed and 39 wounded is a long one, considering that our antagonist was not the Tycoon himself, but only one of his lawless subjects. Nor is this the whole cost of our petty victory, for among the 11 killed are the names of two Captains, Gosling and Wilmot—a sacrifice of superior officers which would have been considerable even for such actions as that of the Nile.[18]

Nonetheless, the Namamugi affair had very little effect on treaty relations per se, though it added to an atmosphere of tension between

Japanese and Westerners. From Russell down to Neale, the British discriminated between the shogunate and Satsuma and attempted to treat the bakufu as leniently as possible. The size of the indemnity, it is true, was large, while that of Satsuma's was small, but Russell believed the bakufu could afford to pay more than could a single domain. There is no evidence that British officials considered this an extraordinary crisis or that treaty relations were threatened. Finally, public outrage in Britain confirmed for Russell the dangers of undertaking military operations in Japan except in the most dire of circumstances. Being forced to defend his actions over a one-day naval engagement convinced him that Japan could not become another China, the object of sustained military attention.

Inside Japan, the British action raised the question of the national character of the Tokugawa government. It emboldened Satsuma reformers to press on with modernization policies and open relations with the British. The Namamugi Incident, therefore, became a domestic problem, one that eventually would impact foreign affairs, but not for another half-decade. In contrast, the events leading up to the Shimonoseki bombardment of September 1864 reveal the increasing difficulty the bakufu faced in maintaining the boundaries it considered vital to its own survival.

Weakened Boundaries and the Shimonoseki Incident, 1863

From 1863 on, the narrative of treaty relations becomes more complicated. Multiple domestic actors now struggled to make their voices heard, while policy differences among the Western powers, and even between countrymen, increased. As a result, new challenges to the treaty structure emerged, set in motion by the court, which demanded the expulsion of all foreigners, the bakufu, which sought to modify this decree, and the domain of Chōshū, which unilaterally enforced the expulsion order by attacking foreign shipping in western Japan. Though each of these interconnected developments in its own way was an attempt to shore up the physical boundaries of Japan, the result was to put Edo's diplomatic strategy under severe strain.

The sojourn of the top echelon of bakufu policymakers in Kyoto from February through April 1863, during the height of the Namamugi crisis, reflected a bakufu attempt to reassert its monopoly over foreign policy-making.[19] The court had learned in the previous months that it could influence foreign policy by exploiting the growing rifts within the Satsuma-supported bakufu triumvirate of Hitotsubashi Keiki, Matsudaira Keiei, and Matsudaira Katamori, as well as between those three and the senior councillors. Acting on its xenophobic hatred of Westerners, the court, supported by Chōshū radicals, dispatched the courtier Sanjō Sanetomi to Edo in December 1862 to demand the expulsion of all foreigners. Within one month, the bakufu had agreed to close all the treaty ports.

Keiki, in de facto charge of the shogunate, based his policies on the Satsuma-backed court-bakufu alliance. Thus, when he received the December demand to expel the foreigners, he instinctively sought to preserve his relationship with Kyoto, and readily agreed to the decree. In the manner of the day, however, the imperial order was phrased vaguely enough to leave considerable leeway to the bakufu in terms of actual implementation. Yet foreign affairs remained the preserve of the senior councillors, now led by Ogasawara Nagamichi, and they did not agree with Keiki's political calculation that the court posed a more serious threat than the foreigners did. The result was a widening split between the councillors and the Keiki leadership.

This breach reflected in part the growing power of Ogasawara. Born in 1822, he was the eldest son and heir of the fudai lord of Karatsu, in northwestern Kyūshū. Joining the senior councillors in November 1862, he was given the foreign affairs portfolio, thus briefly eclipsing the foreign magistrates. Ogasawara was opposed to both the expulsion order, once it was adopted, as well as to court interference in bakufu policy-making, and he immediately began to consider how to circumvent the order, in contravention of Keiki's wishes. Keiki, in the meantime, came under increasing pressure from Kyoto nobles, themselves influenced by antiforeign elements in Chōshū.[20] Once Shimazu Hisamitsu, leader of Satsuma, withdrew his support from Keiki's attempts to preserve the alliance among the bakufu, the court, and some of the great lords, Keiki was left alone. The result was his decision to set June 25 as the date for expulsion, hoping thereby to mollify the court.

The senior councillors, however, were still unwilling to force the issue with the West, arguing that such an act would bring war and national calamity. Ogasawara, thus, used the opportunity provided by Keiki's continuing focus on domestic politics to begin diluting the expulsion decree. His first act was to ignore the finalized nature of the order, instead simply presenting Western representatives with a request to begin talks on closing the treaty ports. This was the message delivered on June 24 to Neale concurrent with the payment of the Namamugi indemnity.

Ogasawara was playing for time, hoping to convince Keiki to change his mind, but not daring to oppose him outright. His halfway proposal, nonetheless, was perceived by the foreign diplomats as an illegal and strategic assault on the treaty structure. Neale indignantly wrote the bakufu that the expulsion edict was unheard of in all diplomatic relations and was "a declaration of war" by Japan against the treaty powers.[21] The Western representatives immediately and jointly rejected Ogasawara's request and promised to defend themselves against any "forcible attempt" to expel Westerners in Japan.[22]

Yet the allies, as they now began to call themselves, made it clear that they would use force only in the case of the ports actually being closed. The very fact that the Western representatives disavowed a "first-strike" policy gave the bakufu latitude in deciding how to proceed with the issue of port closing. Yet the bakufu was now only one part of the equation, and domestic political elements would push both Edo and the treaty powers into uncharted territory.

On June 25, 1863, the date Keiki set for expulsion and the day the Western powers refused to enter into talks about port closing, batteries of the Chōshū domain in western Japan opened fire on an American ship, and in the next days they targeted French and Dutch vessels. Chōshū had recently come under the control of zealous anti-Western samurai who hoped not only to drive the barbarians across the sea, but to strike a blow against the bakufu, as well, in the name of imperial authority. Western reprisals temporarily silenced the batteries, but the domain soon rebuilt them, preventing any ships from getting through the Shimonoseki Straits. The straits passed between the western tip of Honshū and the northern coast of Kyūshū at the entrance to the Inland Sea, and offered direct passage to Osaka from ports on the Asian mainland.

The situation was highly volatile and confused, but did not immediately spin out of control.[23] Much of the confusion came from infighting among bakufu cliques, specifically Keiki and the senior councillors. For example, the very day the U.S. minister learned of Edo's desire to discuss port closing, he nonetheless was visited by one of the Kanagawa magistrates, who informed him that the bakufu would not attempt to enforce the policy it had just announced. Pruyn chose to believe the senior councillors and immediately wrote to Washington that "the government at Yedo . . . honestly intend to preserve peaceful relations, and is fully aware of the extreme folly of attempting to carry the Kioto decrees into effect."[24]

On July 2, less than a week after the Chōshū attack, junior councillor Sakai Tadamasu met with Neale and Bellecourt to inform them the expulsion order was no longer in effect, yet he never revealed that the specifics of the order had come from the bakufu itself, in the person of Hitotsubashi Keiki. Sakai went so far as to arrange for British steamers to transport bakufu troops to Osaka for a possible showdown with the court over accepting the treaties, which still had not been ratified by the increasingly anti-Western emperor.[25] Such an agreement exposed the deep split inside the bakufu. Ogasawara and the senior councillors were willing to collaborate with the treaty powers to defend Edo's traditional strategy even if that meant threatening civil war in Japan; Keiki, however, felt that the claims of domestic stability overrode the potential for conflict with the West.

Unaware of the politics roiling inside Edo Castle, Neale at no time considered relations between Britain and the bakufu to be at a breaking point. More than a month after the supposed closing of the straits, he downplayed the significance of Chōshū's actions in a letter to Russell, assuring him that trade was uninterrupted. Neale, though professing public outrage over the expulsion edict, had already received further information from the French that the bakufu did not intend to carry it out, and he thus took pains to explain to Russell the "conflicting facts and perplexing circumstances" that attended the whirlwind of events.[26]

Trade, of course, remained the raison d'être of the West in Japan, and London's concern over trade levels is easy to understand. At this remove, it is difficult to judge accurately the amount of trade, at least in monetary terms, due to poor record keeping and inaccurate affixation of prices. Neale assured Russell in mid-September that trade had more than doubled to £675,000 ($3.5 million) in the first half of 1863.[27] Yet other figures painted a more complex picture. British consular reports from February 1864 showed a year-on-year decline of nearly 43 percent in silk exports from Yokohama during 1863.[28] A modestly growing tea export level and general rises in both imports and exports counterbalanced this. Any decline in silk shipments, however, would have a widespread effect on Yokohama, which handled more than 86 percent of Japan's total exports, of which silk accounted for 83.6 percent.[29]

Based on the best available monetary figures, then, the economic effects of the closing of the straits were unclear. More important, though, Western diplomats did not believe that relations were at a critical juncture, as evidenced by Neale's several letters to London. Yet the bakufu was caught between domestic and foreign pressure, and was split internally, as well. Its weakened leadership sought to extricate itself by proposing a plan fraught with symbolism: the closing of Yokohama.

The Ultimate Boundary: Closing Yokohama

The question of boundaries was now an open issue, for both the court and Chōshū had acted to expel the treaty powers. The bakufu had blunted Kyoto's demand but felt constrained to align its policy in general with these powerful domestic voices. The result, once total expulsion had been dropped, was a plan to close Yokohama, the largest and most important treaty port.

From one perspective, closing Yokohama could be considered a logical development of the bakufu's post-1858 strategy. Edo had created the port as a physical boundary between Westerners present in Japan and the Japanese, and had forced the treaty powers to accept it despite its questionable legitimacy (see chapter 2). Moreover, it had remained the primary port due to a further negotiation that delayed the opening of other trading sites. Closing it would likely put Westerners back where they had been for more than two and a half centuries, Nagasaki.

Yet Yokohama was failing as a boundary, and that made its closure all the more appealing to the bakufu. By 1863, as noted above, trade with Britain alone had grown substantially, from £325,000 in 1861 to £675,000 two years later. The number of Western ships visiting Yokohama increased from a bit more than 100 in 1860 to 170 in 1863, while the permanent population at the port reached three hundred residents.[30] Moreover, Yokohama was growing in size. By 1863, the swampy land due south of the original site was being drained and built up with warehouses and other structures.

A further threat to Japanese attempts to maintain the limited size of Yokohama emerged with the stationing of French and British troops near the port in the summer of 1863. No amount of communication between the bakufu and Western representatives could disguise the fact that attacks on foreigners had been increasing in intensity since the 1861 sack of the British legation. Rutherford Alcock had landed British marines after that first assault, and the Chōshū shelling of Western ships forced Neale and Bellecourt to demand a limited joint force to ensure the safety of their countrymen.

Senior councillor Sakai Tadamasu, part of the "caretaker" bakufu during Keiki's absence in Kyoto, met with Bellecourt and Neale in late June, and on July 3, Edo gave its consent to the presence of French and British garrisons in Yokohama, calculating that accepting a small number of troops now would prevent the dispatch of a larger contingent later. That same week the French landed 250 troops from the Chasseur d'Afrique, who took up position on the Bluff overlooking the foreign settlement.[31] The British presence took a bit longer to be felt. Temporary detachments served until January 22, 1864, when HMS *Vulcan* landed 1,500 Royal Marines of the 20th Regiment, who had previously been based in Hong Kong.

The British and French limited their troops to defensive functions. Neale, and later Alcock, did not use the forces as the opening wedge in a campaign to take over more territory, for that was clearly antithetical to their entire policy. Indeed, Neale had to justify to London his stationing of troops in Japan, assuring Russell that "they were required with no prospect of aggressive or hostile undertaking, but as a precautionary measure."[32] The specter of Kagoshima still lay over British policy.

Despite the limited and defensive nature of their presence, the troops were a direct affront to the bakufu and a potential challenge to its authority. Ironically, they were sent to protect Yokohama, and it was Yokohama that was supposed to represent a bakufu-constructed barrier between Japan and the West. The problem, clearly, was Yokohama itself.

Equally worrisome was the increasing public attention given to Yokohama. Far from demarcating a barrier between Japanese and Westerners, the port was now openly portrayed in Japanese popular media as a mixing place, a harbinger of a new multicultural and multiethnic world. As the historian Ishizuka Hiromichi has asked, was Yokohama a Japanese city or not? In fact, he avers, it must be understood primarily as part of the network of British imperial cities in East Asia, and indeed, one of the three largest, along with Hong Kong and Shanghai. These three sites formed a qualitatively different type of urban space, reaching a critical density in which both the foreign and native parts intertwined and fed off each other.[33]

Social and cultural openness pervaded Yokohama. While the large Edo licensed monopolies may have held the lion's share of trade in the port, numerous merchants from different parts of the country set up shop, exchanged information, and eagerly absorbed news that rarely reached their native areas.[34] The merchants particularly reveled in the weak social bonds of the new city. The traditional social networks that tied them in their native regions did not exist in Yokohama, and they thus had much more freedom to interact and create relationships not beholden to established patterns.[35]

The unanticipated novelty of the port was perhaps best captured in a three-volume work titled *Yokohama kaikō kenbun shi (Things Seen and Heard at the Open Port of Yokohama)* published in 1862 by the noted ukiyo-e artist Hashimoto Sadahide. Sadahide was one of the most prolific artists of bakumatsu Japan, known in particular for his pictures of Yokohama and its foreign citizens. By the first year of Meiji (1868), he was the foremost producer of Yokohama-related prints.[36]

Sadahide's booklets were, in essence, a guide to life in Yokohama, comprising ink drawings interspersed with text. Such collections were increasingly popular after 1859, with eight publications on Yokohama alone appearing between 1860 and 1868.[37] Sadahide saw his booklets as an extension of the exchanges taking place in Yokohama, for to him the port was above all a place of international encounter. It acted as a magnet inside Japan, as he noted that "there is no end to the numbers of people who, having heard stories in the interior of our country, travel for one or two nights to come see Yokohama."[38]

Central to Sadahide's depiction of treaty port life are images of intermixing and mobility, encased in a tour of the city. Thus, a print titled "The Entrance to 2-chome on Kaigan Street" shows a plethora of treaty port inhabitants: a foreign family out for a stroll; Japanese on their way from their daily bath; numerous merchants; and a Chinese and a couple from Colombo, newly arrived in the port (see page 105). Symbolically, in this and other prints, Sadahide centers in the picture the open guard gates of the ward. Such gates were always open during the day and closed at night, but his pictorial representation is one of official barriers that in reality posed no hindrance to common intercourse.

Sadahide, and other artists like him, spread a message directly opposed to the bakufu's strategy. They portrayed Yokohama as open, not closed; it was growing in size and population, and now foreign troops occupied Japanese territory to guard it. With pressure mounting from the court to carry out the expulsion order, closing Yokohama seemed the best alternative, as well as a means to end the rift between Keiki and the senior councilors over foreign relations. The new plan was confirmed by the court on October 24, 1863, and transmitted to the foreign representatives the following day. Aware of how the plan would be received, however, the bakufu merely presented the Western diplomats with a request to discuss the closing of Yokohama, as they similarly had done with the ill-fated expulsion order of that June.[39]

Diplomatic Interlude: The Ikeda Mission, 1863–1864

The four Western ministers immediately rejected the bakufu's attempts to negotiate the closing of Yokohama.[40] Caught between Scylla and Charybdis, Edo drew inspiration from the previous year's London Protocol, betting that another embassy to the West, led this time by

"The Entrance to Kaigan dōri, 2-chome" in the Yokohama foreign settlement. From Hashimoto Sadahide, *Yokohama kaikō kenbun shi* (1862).

foreign magistrate Ikeda Nagaaki, would secure Western support to shut the port. Despite much historical obloquy, the Ikeda mission was not a last-minute, poorly planned expedition.[41] Rather, it revealed the codification of bakumatsu diplomacy, including its weaknesses. In essence, the planning for the Ikeda embassy minutely followed that accorded the 1862 Takeuchi mission, showing that bakufu leaders believed that following a like recipe would bring like results.

As it did in the postponement issue, the bakufu decided to single out one treaty power with which to work. This time it settled on France, for Edo and Bellecourt were already negotiating over reparations for the murder of a French officer, a Lieutenant Camus, in October 1863. Bellecourt, anxious lest the murder of a French national be treated as less significant than that of a Briton (Richardson the year previously), had already demanded an indemnity and suggested that Edo send a mission to France to pay it. At a mid-November meeting with Bellecourt, Ikeda proposed discussing the closing of Yokohama, but was rebuffed.

Although the chances to obtain a closure of Yokohama looked bleak, the bakufu redoubled its efforts, believing that the Camus affair afforded an entrée into negotiations. During late-November meetings with bakufu officials, the French minister continued to push the idea of an embassy, though he would not entertain ideas of closing Yokohama.[42] Despite the qualms of his superiors in Paris, Bellecourt detailed legation interpreter M. Bleckman to handle much of the actual negotiations over what he assumed would be a simple indemnity embassy. At the end of the month, the bakufu announced that it had decided to send a high-ranking mission to Europe and America and appointed Ikeda, foreign magistrate Kawazu Sukekuni, and inspector Kawada Hiroshi as its heads. They ambitiously planned to visit France, Great Britain, Holland, Russia, Portugal, Spain, and the United States.

With the French at last promising to receive this latest embassy, the bakufu drafted letters to Great Britain's Queen Victoria and Foreign Secretary Russell, explaining that Ikeda would be coming to England to discuss closing Yokohama. Similarly, the senior councillors prepared a letter from the shogun to Napoleon III, avowing their friendship and asking that the ambassadors be heard in their request. In addition, the bakufu attempted to maneuver Bellecourt into a position similar to Alcock's in 1862, by asking him and Bleckman to accompany the embassy to France and represent their interests.

Yet the weakness of this plan soon became evident. Ikeda and his colleagues worried that the bakufu had failed to secure an agreement over Yokohama before their dispatch. Simply sailing an embassy around the world was no assurance of success, and the three men were not sanguine about their chances for obtaining French consent to close the port. While still in Japan, in mid-January 1864, they baldly expressed their fears in a letter to the senior councillors, writing that "it is doubtful that foreign countries would agree" to the permanent closing of Yokohama, and suggesting a more limited time frame of five to ten years. The councillors' response to Ikeda and his partners was a simple confirmation of the order to seek a permanent closure.[43] A final letter from Ikeda on January 24, "reflecting on the difficulty of obtaining success in this mission," made it clear that the ambassadors understood that without first securing French support in Japan, there would be little hope in sending them abroad.[44]

Thus, up to the date when Ikeda and his party of twenty-one set sail from Shinagawa on February 6, the bakufu had followed almost to the letter the script from the first successful mission to Europe, complete with intimations of the government's weakness and protestations that continued trade at Yokohama would cause grave difficulties. In comparison to 1862, however, this time not one Western representative in Japan, including that of the presumed major negotiating partner (France), had agreed to the bakufu plan. The significance of the Ikeda mission was not that obtaining the closure of Yokohama was impossible, but that bakufu diplomats had learned only one lesson too well, and they applied it too rigidly. Agreement had to be reached first at the local level, and only then could successful negotiations take place on the foreign stage.

With no prior agreement, the Ikeda mission gloomily entered Paris in April 1864.[45] Suffice it to note that Ikeda and his colleagues, for all their pessimism, did not easily abandon their goal, meeting with Drouyn de Lhuys, the French foreign minister, five times over five weeks in May and June. Ikeda's attempt to gain goodwill by offering compensation for the murder of Lieutenant Camus carried little weight. Moreover, the French now demanded an indemnity for the Chōshū attack on a French vessel back in June 1863. The French were most interested, however, in removing any Japanese restrictions on the export of silkworms and eggs, faced as they were with the continuing *pebrine* disease. Closure was brusquely refused.

In the end, Ikeda signed what became known as the Paris Convention. A short, and short-lived, agreement, it contained an indemnity for the Shimonoseki attack ($140,000); a bakufu pledge to maintain freedom of passage in the Straits of Shimonoseki, with French help if necessary; and a lowering of tariffs on certain French products.[46] Yokohama was to remain open. Ikeda felt strong enough only to refuse a French demand that its citizens in Japan be allowed to travel in the Kanagawa region beyond the twenty-five-mile (ten-ri) limit established under the 1858 treaties, as well as to reject an Italian request to sign a commercial treaty. The ambassadors understood, however, that they would get no further with the other countries they intended to visit, so they cancelled their remaining itinerary. After signing the Paris Convention on June 20, 1864, Ikeda and the embassy left the city the same day to begin the journey home.

It was at this point that the Ikeda mission merged into the still-unresolved problem of Chōshū's closure of the Shimonoseki Straits. The catalyst for the merging of the two issues was the British minister, Rutherford Alcock. In essence, the bakufu's basic strategy had not changed, but Alcock, the most powerful Western diplomat in Japan, no longer supported negotiation as the primary pattern of relations.

Constructing the Attack on Shimonoseki, 1864

The flaw at the heart of the Japanese–Western treaty relationship was exposed in the pressures of 1863 and 1864. Ironically, the flaw was the very condition that made the relationship unique: its reliance on negotiation, which often meant restraint and a focus on solving issues bilaterally or multilaterally. In reality, this relationship based on negotiation emerged from a combination of geopolitical concerns, local conditions, and, most important, agreed upon norms of interaction between Japan and the treaty powers. This combination often worked to block actions that could upset the balance upheld by negotiation, but it was vulnerable to any actor who firmly decided to ignore those norms.

The fragility of this reliance on restraint was most vividly illustrated by Alcock's manufacturing of a crisis over Shimonoseki in 1864. The affair provides a salutary lesson in the limits of diplomatic intercourse and a reminder of the powerful effect that committed individuals can have on much larger groups and structures.

In the months following the June 1863 closing of the Shimonoseki Straits, a period when Alcock was in Great Britain, Western representatives in Japan and their home governments were far from convinced that a crisis was at hand. Although Chōshū had effectively sealed off the Shimonoseki passage, thus threatening to end trade from Nagasaki through the Inland Sea up to Osaka, it was not apparent that the closure initially had any great effect on commerce. For example, British chargé d'affaires Neale, submitting his consular report for 1862 and the first half of 1863, noted the "astonishing degree of progress which . . . trade has reached during the very period when the situation of affairs has been more menacing and alarming than at any previous period." He underlined this point in a little-disguised swipe at Alcock, extolling "a steadily progressing and prosperous trade . . . ignored or altogether overlooked as it may be in Europe by those who are anxious or interested in the events of a threatening character."[47]

Neale's reports resonated with Russell, who was still wary of military involvement in Japan after putting out the domestic brushfires caused by the Kagoshima bombardment in August. Russell, now consumed by affairs in Europe, such as the Schleswig-Holstein Crisis of 1863 and the 1864 Danish War, desperately desired to avoid future clashes with the Japanese, which could have spillover effects on other British relationships in Asia. He unveiled a powerful weapon in this regard in early 1864, when he allowed British diplomats proactively to restrict or prohibit British vessels from entering Japan's inland waters and seas. This Order in Council was essentially a legal means to avoid confrontation with Chōshū, and it underlined Russell's cautious and nonbelligerent attitude. In reporting the new order to Neale, Russell commended him for his low-key policy, stating that Whitehall was "prepared to make full allowance for the peculiar nature of the Japanese government. In short, the employment of measures of coercion or retaliation could only be warranted by the necessity of prompt interference for the protection of the lives and property of British subjects."[48]

Neale had only a few weeks left in which to maintain this nonconfrontational policy, for Alcock was already on his way back to Japan. On March 1, 1864, Neale sent his final dispatch to Russell, in which he stressed the pacific nature of Anglo–Japanese relations: "Trade is steadily flourishing [and] the general results are satisfactory beyond all expectation. The passage of the Inland Sea [Shimonoseki] remains obstructed by the Prince of Choshiu [*sic*] . . . but I am not aware of any detriment sustained to our commerce or navigation."[49] Alcock landed at Yokohama the following day.

Alcock renewed his residence in Japan simmering over what he considered to be the bakufu's double-dealing in its dispatch of the Ikeda mission to Europe. He had met the mission when both parties' ships docked in Shanghai and immediately perceived the mission's goal to be, in essence, a repudiation of his carefully crafted London Protocol. Alcock had built the Protocol around maintaining trade at the open ports of Yokohama, Nagasaki, and Hakodate. Now the bakufu wanted to close the most important of the three, Yokohama. Disregarding Neale's opinion of relations, as well as those of the senior councillors who were attempting to assure him that trade would continue, Alcock concluded that the treaty structure was mortally imperiled.

Less than a month after his arrival, he sent a long, aggressive dispatch to London, claiming that relations were at a "crisis." Belittling the steadily growing trade, he zeroed in on the original expulsion order of June 1863, overlooking the mountain of evidence that it was considered a dead letter by the bakufu. He wrote Russell that "the time has gone by irrevocably for concessions contrary to the spirit and intent of existing Treaties."[50] Within two weeks he had concluded that, as in China, the use of British force was required to save the entire structure. He urged Russell to action, asserting that "there will be no improvement until measures of a hostile and coercive character are resorted to . . . [the Japanese] will then learn to respect such rights, as the lesser of two evils, if for no better or higher reason."[51]

By early May, Alcock was close to panicking: "Something must be done to stop this underhand plotting for our final expulsion and the rupture of all friendly relations, or the end will surely come."[52] His hand was restrained for the time being only by the pre-telegraphic nature of international relations, when roundtrip communications with Europe could take up to five months.

Yet even Alcock's position was more subtle, and confused, than it appeared on the surface. Consciously or not, it was designed to maintain the overall framework of treaty relations. He was bound by Russell's decision that Britain would not attack its duly ratified treaty partner, the bakufu, and therefore he could contemplate the use of force only on rebel domains with which Britain had no formal treaty rights, and even then only when no other option remained. Whether this policy would raise problems for the bakufu's domestic control was either not understood or cared about by Alcock and London.

In his early May dispatch, Alcock affirmed his understanding of Russell's policy, arguing that he was calling for an attack solely on Chōshū, and that if carried out, "the Tycoon cannot regard such proceedings as an act of war against his own Government."[53] In the next sentence, however, without pausing to explain the logic of his position, Alcock declared that such an attack nonetheless would be a clear lesson to the shogunate not to oppose the West. This was despite strong circumstantial evidence that at least certain members of the bakufu would welcome an attack on Chōshū as a way to further reduce that domain's power.[54] To Alcock, obviously, British foreign relations ultimately rested on force, either as sanction or deterrent. That such action could cause the collapse of the very norms he had helped create in the early 1860s seemed overshadowed by the threat he perceived.

Alcock's new position was not shared by the rest of the treaty powers, and he had to spend the spring and summer of 1864 cajoling his fellow Western representatives into forging a plan for hostile action. The French had lost their longtime representative, Bellecourt, and were now represented by Léon Roches.[55] New to the country, and still learning about Japanese domestic politics, Roches continued Bellecourt's policy of cooperation with Britain, though he would soon pursue an independent French policy in Japan. Further, the Paris Convention had laid the basis for Western action by committing the bakufu to opening the Shimonoseki Straits by the autumn of 1864; failure to comply would force France to take matters into its own hands.

For their part, the U.S. diplomats knew their concerns were low on the list of priorities for Washington, which was in the middle of the bloody Civil War. Pruyn, however, threw what weight he had behind the bakufu, urging Alcock to scale back planned hostilities. He wrote the British minister in mid-May that any attack on Chōshū must be carried out so as not to provoke war with Edo and must have the goal of strengthening the shogun.[56] The Dutch, also represented by a new minister, Dirk de Graeff van Polsbroek, were content to follow the lead of the other Western nations and simply remain a member of the allies.

Alcock was thus given a great deal of latitude by the weaknesses of his fellow diplomats and the strength of the military force he could call upon. Even so, his belligerence did not extend to undermining every aspect of the Japanese–Western relationship. Unlike in China, where large British forces were slowly expanding their control over key Chinese ports and coastal areas, the British minister elucidated what might be termed the Alcock Doctrine, which followed in large part London's global strategy. The doctrine, embodied in a joint four-power declaration of July 22, 1864, reaffirmed the limited engagement policy of the West.

Key among the provisions was a joint pledge "not to ask for nor accept any concession of territory, nor exclusive advantages whatever, either in the open ports or elsewhere in Japan." In a later clause the four powers swore to "abstain from all interference in the jurisdiction of the Japanese authorities over their own people, as well as from all intervention between the contending parties in the country."[57] This was the origin of the neutrality policy later followed by the powers during the fighting and upheaval of the Meiji Restoration. This statement of relative temperance mollified the Americans, French, and Dutch. By late August, Alcock had their agreement to move on Chōshū.

The British minister, however, had not convinced his own superiors of the necessity for action. His main argument rested on a recent slowdown in silk exports from Yokohama, although even he had to admit that tea and cotton exports remained at previous levels.[58] But this information came too little, too late for Russell, who sent a firm command to Alcock on July 26, 1864, that "Her Majesty's Government *positively enjoin* you not to undertake any military operations whatever in the interior of Japan; and they would indeed regret the adoption of any measures of hostilities against the Japanese Government or Princes." Russell did not buy Alcock's argument that domains could be attacked short of outright hostilities on their part, nor did he believe that Great Britain had run out of options other than the use of naval force. The Foreign Secretary concluded his dispatch by ordering Alcock to exercise his power to prohibit British ships from attempting to pass through the Shimonoseki Straits.[59]

When Alcock's panicked dispatches of early May reached London, Russell took the extraordinary step of recalling the minister for consultation and strongly questioned his reading of the situation in Japan.[60] Again, on August 18, Russell repeated his admonitions not to undertake hostilities against Chōshū, and he ordered Alcock to concentrate instead on defending the foreign settlement at Yokohama, should such a course become necessary.[61] As we shall see, Russell's instructions reached Alcock too late.

As important as the jockeying between Alcock and Russell was the role of the bakufu as it attempted to maintain some control over the resolution of the Chōshū problem. The bakufu's leadership vacuum continued to hamstring policy. Ogasawara Nagamichi was forced to resign in July 1863 due to his role in paying the Namamugi indemnity, and decision-making power returned primarily to the senior councillors Mizuno Tadakiyo, Itakura Katsukiyo, and Inoue Masanao.[62] Mizuno and Itakura in particular were opposed to a renewed effort by bakufu hard-liners to close Yokohama, and they were supported by the senior foreign magistrate at the time, Takemoto Masao, and junior councillor Sakai Tadamasu, who had close ties to the old Ii–Andō clique.

Nonetheless, the shogunate had not been quiescent during the months in which Alcock was forging his policy, and it maintained constant contact with Western representatives. A key, if unstated, goal was to convince the West of the bakufu's continued authority over all Japanese territory, even if in reality Edo had no ability to control the outer domains. Accordingly, on June 30, 1864, the senior councillors sent a note to the British, French, and American ministers, with a request that "for the time being, we ask you to leave to us how to handle the treatment for Chōshū's attack" on foreign shipping.[63] Although this was an implicit admission that the bakufu was unable immediately to punish Chōshū, it was also an attempt to reaffirm Edo's position as the national government, at least in relation to foreign affairs. The bakufu's case was bolstered in late August when the domain of Aizu, a close ally of the Tokugawa, joined forces with Satsuma to repulse a move by Chōshū troops to take control of the imperial palace in what was known as the Forbidden Gate Incident.

By mid-August 1864, Takemoto, in particular, understood Alcock's determination to punish Chōshū, and he altered bakufu policy out of a desire to prevent an open breach between Edo and the West. His position had been previously strengthened at upper levels, starting with the appointment of Abe Masato to the senior councillors in late July 1864. Abe and Takemoto took charge of maintaining relations with the Westerners and adopted a policy of limiting the fallout from any Western action.

By this time, the Western attack appeared to be a foregone conclusion, and the bakufu representatives now focused instead on maintaining the overall balance of treaty relations and pretending that there was still an active role for negotiations. Accordingly, less than two weeks after Abe's appointment, Takemoto met with Alcock to assure him that the shogun was "sensible of the assistance he would derive from [Western] operations against Chōshū." This message was repeated to Pruyn, who relayed it to Washington.[64]

Takemoto took a slightly different tack during a meeting with Léon Roches on August 17. Acknowledging that the bakufu was unable to punish Chōshū, he expressed a new fear, namely, that Britain would use an attack on Chōshū as an excuse to occupy Japanese territory. If Roches would clearly state that the allies had no such goal, continued Takemoto, then the shogun "would tacitly give his agreement to the [Alcock] plan to punish Chōshū."[65] Roches was able to confirm the substance of the July 22 four-power memorandum that was earlier relayed by Alcock, and thus allay Takemoto's fears.

Despite these attempts to bring the two sides together, Japanese domestic politics intruded yet again. The Ikeda mission returned from France on August 23, carrying with it the Paris Convention. As noted earlier, Ikeda had agreed to the opening of the Shimonoseki Straits, with French help if necessary. This was unacceptable to the bakufu, not the least because it opened the possibility that France, or other treaty powers, could dictate to Edo when to use force against other Japanese. The day after Ikeda's return, the bakufu unilaterally disavowed the Convention and placed Ikeda and all the members of his embassy under house arrest.

The straits issue remained frustratingly murky for all involved. Alcock now knew that the bakufu had dropped its plan to close Yokohama; this, after all, was the goal of the Ikeda mission, and such a provision appeared nowhere in the Paris Convention. The catalyst, therefore, for his own plan to punish the bakufu (by bombarding Chōshū) had disappeared. Roches, for his part, first had to inform Paris, then wait for instructions, before responding to the bakufu's disavowal of the Convention.

For the bakufu, things were now coming to a pass with Chōshū. On August 24, the day it disavowed the Convention, Edo received permission from the imperial court to punish Chōshū as a rebel domain. The court agreed to this as the penalty for the Forbidden Gate Incident as well as for Chōshū's 1863 attacks on Western shipping. Despite the support of Kyoto, though, the bakufu was not yet militarily prepared to attack, and the Westerners might beat it to the punch.

In this swirl of events, Alcock's burning desire for action won out. Without waiting for Russell's latest instructions, which would order him not to engage in military activities, he sailed for Shimonoseki with seventeen ships in late August, one of them American and three of them French, and commenced bombardment on September 5. During a period of three days, the allied flotilla destroyed Shimonoseki's batteries and landed troops to carry off Chōshū's remaining cannon. Pictures of the landing showed hordes of British sailors celebrating at Chōshū's puny gunmounts. Unlike the Kagoshima bombing of the previous year, loss of life among both Japanese and Westerners was limited. Immediately after the engagement, Alcock and his flotilla returned to Yokohama. Chōshū was left unoccupied and the straits unguarded.

Once Alcock's expedition actually made ready to sail, the bakufu made one last attempt to assert its authority. On the morning of September 5, as the bombardment was set to begin, Edo urgently sought a final postponement of the attack, yet inexplicably coupled the request with an announcement that another embassy would be sent to Europe to seek the closing of Yokohama.[66] This revelation of continued infighting at Edo Castle was not the best way to get Alcock to change his mind. Finally, as operations were finishing, the bakufu sent yet another message, reporting that it had ordered the punishment of Chōshū, in conjunction with the imperial order, and requesting an immediate withdrawal of the allied armada. Less than a month after the Western bombardment, the bakufu launched its first campaign against Chōshū, which proved to be a military success.

The events of 1862 through 1864 revealed the limits of negotiation in Japanese–Western treaty relations. In particular, negotiation faltered at the moment of its greatest need, during a crisis, not least due to a lack of strong bakufu leadership, which led to vacillation and numerous ill-conceived plans. By the time of the Shimonoseki affair, top bakufu officials had dramatically changed their understanding of negotiation.

Whereas in Ii Naosuke's day negotiation encompassed ideas of resistance, by 1864 the bakufu saw even its own acquiescence to the Western use of force as a type of negotiation. Thus, when Takemoto Masao at least twice indicated to Western diplomats that Edo would not necessarily be averse to an attack on Chōshū, the bakufu showed just how far it was willing to change its tactics to preserve its role in dealing with the West. Takemoto was forced into this corner by the bakufu's failure to separate the Yokohama and Chōshū problems.

If the failure to delink Chōshū and Yokohama was the bakufu's fault, however, Alcock's determination to use force was the decisive element. Alcock saw the Chōshū and Yokohama issues as part of a larger threat. Although Edo disavowed the expulsion order numerous times, the repeated resurrection of the Yokohama plan, no matter how halfhearted, gave ammunition to his fears, as did the bakufu nullification of the Paris agreement reached by Ikeda.

From his dispatches the end appears inevitable, even though Alcock was not supported in his decision by his interim replacement (Neale), by at least one of his peers initially (Pruyn), and by his superior (Russell). No matter what action the bakufu took, short of a direct attack on Chōshū, Alcock had made up his mind, reflecting a temperament molded by, and more suited to, conditions on the China coast. The question was, to what extent did the Shimonoseki bombardment represent a Western challenge to the treaty structure?

The result of the bombardment appeared on the surface to be a complete victory for Alcock: the Straits were opened, never to be closed again, and Chōshū radicals lost control of the domain, which then adopted a policy of importing Western technology. Documents turned over by Chōshū also gave grounds to prove Alcock's long-standing suspicion that the bakufu had played a direct role in crafting the expulsion order of 1863. This in turn allowed him to impose a massive $3 million indemnity on the bakufu, which was designed to cover the whole expulsion-plus-Shimonoseki affair.

Yet even these results were less straightforward than they initially appeared. First, while it is true that the silk trade recovered, the figures quoted earlier showed that the closing of the straits did not have a major effect on overall trade. Second, bombardment was not an immediate panacea, for as late as mid-October, Alcock and Roches were complaining to Edo that silk was still being held back by officials in Yokohama.[67] Third, Alcock promised the bakufu that two-thirds of the 1864 indemnity would be waived should Edo allow Shimonoseki or another port on the Inland Sea to be opened to trade. Moreover, the Americans soon moved to waive their portion of the indemnity, thereby maintaining their quasi-independent policy toward Japan. In the end, the bakufu chose not to accept Alcock's offer, reaffirming instead its long-standing strategy of limiting ports, as well as the doctrine of keeping foreign trade out of the hands of the domains, in this case Chōshū.

Finally, Alcock himself did not reap the accolades from his policy; Russell's recall remained in effect, and Alcock left Japan on Christmas Eve, 1864, but not before writing several very long letters to London defending his actions.[68] Russell's terse responses indicated his attitude toward Alcock, but he was forced eventually to report the Queen's support of Alcock's policy. Russell, however, did not return Alcock to Japan, instead posting him to China.

In the end, though the treaty structure survived both the Kagoshima and Shimonoseki episodes, bakufu strategy had been seriously challenged. The events of 1862 through 1864 showed that Edo's diplomatic policy was becoming less viable in the changing conditions in Japan. The strains of repeated attempts at conflict resolution, and the failure to prevent the Western use of force, would now lead some bakufu officials to begin rethinking their relations with the West, a reflection of the hidden changes in their diplomatic culture.

CHAPTER FIVE

New Horizons:
Tariffs and Translations

The early 1860s had shown the limits of the Tokugawa strategy of negotiation. That strategy had failed both to control the anti-Western actions of Satsuma and Chōshū and to prevent the Western use of force in Japan. The bakufu's unsuccessful attempt to close Yokohama as a substitute for expelling foreigners served only to highlight that treaty relations were now a permanent feature of Japan's international life. More worrisome for Edo was that strategic failures could not but have profound reverberations. Like a chink in armor admitting the tip of a spear, the weaknesses in bakufu strategy resulted in a hesitant metamorphosis in the culture of Tokugawa diplomacy. Unlike earlier adaptations, such as Hotta Masayoshi's decision to seek imperial approval of the treaties, later changes reflected a conscious decision by certain policymakers to engage the world in new ways.

Conscious or not, this reorientation was neither planned nor part of a unified policy. It manifested itself in seemingly unconnected ways and yet at a pace concurrent with the events related in chapter 4. Two areas in which this metamorphosis can be traced are the question of tariff reform and Japan's growing base of knowledge about the world. The one economic and the other intellectual, they unintentionally served as the bridge between Tokugawa and Meiji Japan.

The Politics of Tariff Revision, 1862–1866

The issue of tariff reform provides a useful angle from which to examine the changes taking place in late bakumatsu foreign policy and the transformation of the bakufu's worldview. Tariffs were an integral part of foreign trade, imposed by governments as a way to garner revenue, protect native industries, or, if set low enough, lead to more trade. Their smooth collection required a transparent customs department, accurate bookkeeping, and an adequate physical infrastructure of customs houses and warehouses at open ports.

As recounted in the introduction in this book, trade in East Asia was a part of the larger hierarchically ordered tribute system employed by Chinese emperors, Japanese shoguns, and Korean kings as confirmation of their political status. In Japan, as elsewhere in this system, trade was conducted in part under the guise of tribute exchange, but the shogun also granted monopoly rights for favored daimyō and merchants to exchange goods with visiting embassies, all the while trying to reserve the main amount of trade for himself.[1] Most of the foreign goods thus received made their way into a closed trading system inside Japan, with trading monopolies granted to favored Osaka and Edo merchants who operated in more-or-less tightly regulated markets. The demands of "free" foreign trade, no longer conducted within a traditional political context, presented the bakufu with serious challenges to its entire economic system. Tariffs became one symbol of the struggle to maintain government control over trade and relations alike.

The 1858 treaties established tariff schedules for both imports and exports, as was common in trading relations among nations of the West. Though the specific mechanism of tariff duties was unfamiliar to the bakufu, the idea of collecting taxes on trade fit nicely with the long-standing remuneration it received from tribute with Korea, Hokkaidō, the Ryūkyūs, and the monopoly Nagasaki trade of the Dutch and Chinese. In any case, the concept of tariffs did not seem to arouse in either the government or the people any great emotion. Not until the Meiji period did the issue of tariff reform become invested with a political significance tied to a growing nationalist backlash against the "unequal" aspect of the treaties (see chapter 6). From such a perspective, Japan did not fully throw off the yoke of the treaties until 1911, when it regained full tariff autonomy.[2]

To later observers, the changes in tariff rates during the 1860s appeared as another symbol of bakufu weakness and the loss of Japanese sovereignty. Such authors focused their attention on the 1866 Edo Convention, which set a uniformly low tariff rate, as simply the result of a diplomatic "crisis" during the previous summer.[3] In the last years of the Tokugawa regime, however, bakufu leaders did not consider tariff reform a major problem; indeed, they seized upon it as a way to blunt more threatening Western demands. Yet, in the end, unbidden by the bakufu, tariff reform suggested and even mandated a new type of foreign relations for Japan.

Free Trade and Tariffs in the West

The tariff question, of course, extended far beyond merely East Asia. It encompassed key issues related to the entire structure of nineteenth-century global trade. By the middle of that century, the leading industrializing countries were expanding their export activities with one another. Growing urban populations in Western Europe and North America eagerly absorbed a host of mass-produced goods, both luxuries and daily necessities.[4] Great Britain held a predominant position as the "world's workshop," and the decade of the 1860s was the high tide of the British Free Trade movement.

Free trade was the core of Britain's economic strategy, a key element in the intellectual and policy framework for the expansion of British global influence through capitalism. Since the 1850s Britain had been moving ever closer to tariff-free trade, which was the logical endpoint of its commercial policy. The push for free trade was self-serving, in that British manufacturers had a comparative advantage second to none, particularly in textiles, iron, and glass. In any tariff-free regime British traders would thus benefit the most, producing salable goods at the lowest cost, and obviating any need for tariff-based income. Moreover, it is important to underscore that Britain did not limit its free-trade policy to underdeveloped countries; rather, it sought to incorporate its European and American trading partners equally into a global free-trade scheme. A landmark in this movement was the 1860 Anglo–French Treaty of Commerce, which marked a trade revolution lowering tariffs around the globe.[5]

The 1860 Anglo–French agreement was known as the Cobden Treaty, so named for its main proponent, free trade apostle Richard

Cobden. It was, in fact, the culmination of a decades-long process stretching back to 1825, led by the Board of Trade, an official government organ. The board arranged, for example, for the Foreign Office to send various free trade materials to all diplomatic heads of missions in both 1851 and 1861, the goal being to proselytize countries around the globe. It steadily reduced duties and by 1860 had all but abolished protective tariffs.[6]

The 1860 Anglo–French treaty was the capstone of this process. It lowered French duties on English coal and manufactures to less than 30 percent, and substantially reduced British duties levied on French wines and brandy. The results seemed to confirm the wisdom of Britain's economic policy, for in the decade after the treaty was signed, British exports to France more than doubled.[7] This success with France, which traditionally had one of the highest tariff rates in Europe, spurred British attempts under Prime Minister William Gladstone later in the 1860s to reduce the number of tariffed goods from 419 to 48, the rates of only 15 of which were considered substantial.[8] Thus, a major plank of British foreign trade policy during the 1850s and 1860s was the expansion of free trade with all its partners. In such a view, perhaps, the 1860 Anglo–French treaty could also be seen as comprising "unequal" aspects.

Other major Western trading nations attempted to mimic the British move away from tariffs, though not as thoroughly or consistently. French wine manufacturers, for example, buoyed by the success of their increased exports to Britain, successfully petitioned Paris to push for lowered tariffs on French spirits around the globe. Further, as the *pebrine* disease steadily decimated French silkworm stocks, Paris desperately sought to lower the export duties on silkworms and their eggs levied by foreign, mainly Asian, countries.

Across the Atlantic, the United States during this period was undergoing a seesaw movement in tariff rates, due in part to the havoc of civil war. While Townsend Harris was preparing for negotiations in Edo, the 1857 Act was passed, which made the U.S. tariff the lowest among all free-trade nations. Yet, by the time Harris was helping the bakufu convince Britain to postpone the opening of the two ports and two cities, the 1861 Morill Tariff Act instigated a decade-long rise in rates, setting average duties at 18.8 percent, with general duties doubling from 5 to 10 percent. By 1869, average U.S. duties stood at 47 percent. The following year, however, a massive tariff reduction began, immediately making 130 articles duty free, and reducing all manufacturing duties to 10 percent by 1872.[9]

Japanese Tariffs in Regional Perspective

It is within this international context that the history of Japanese tariffs must be understood. It should be stressed that the Japanese tariff was not only significantly different from the Chinese, but it also was not entirely disadvantageous. The bakufu knew of tariff schedules from its copy of the 1855 Anglo–Siam agreement, as well as from Harris's Siamese treaty. To Edo, the money from Western trade was a bonus to that already paid by the licensed monopolies. Most important, tariffs seemed to be unconnected to the strategy of maintaining the treaty ports as a physical boundary between Japanese and Westerners. Not for half a decade would the bakufu see a connection between tariffs and those concerns.

In fact, the issue of tariff schedules did not even arise until after the Iwase–Harris treaty was completed on February 23, 1858. The entire issue was settled in one day, February 25, and the schedules were appended to the treaty. Unlike the acrimonious debate over the number and location of treaty ports, the tariff issue did not greatly concern Iwase Tadanari, Japan's main negotiator. Once Harris broached the question, Iwase proposed a general duty (on both imports and exports) of 12.5 percent. Harris, for his part, quickly surrendered the fanciful hope of having no export duty at all, and accepted a general rate of 5 percent. However, as he reported later that summer, "the articles regulating trade and tariffs were left almost entirely to me, the Japanese saying they were so much in the dark, that they could not exercise any judgement in the matter."[10] With Iwase's agreement, Harris divided imports into four classes.[11] As the main tariffed group included some of the West's major products, the 20 percent tariff set by Harris was not inordinately low.

As with the treaty itself, the tariff schedule was copied in all of Edo's future agreements, with one exception: in the 1858 Elgin treaty, British diplomats pushed through a 5 percent duty for their country's cotton and woolen manufactures. This still left certain textile goods as well as a host of other items subject to the 20 percent rate. Neither Harris nor any other European negotiator questioned the right of the Japanese government to supervise and collect tariffs—under the watchful eye of European consuls, of course. This was the arrangement already in place in Siam.

The Japanese situation, however, was dramatically different from the Chinese, where the foreign-managed Inspectorate of Customs collected the Qing Court's tariffs. Since the late eighteenth century, Great Britain in particular had struggled to force the Qing into creating a stable tariff system. A theoretical 20 percent across-the-board tariff was irregularly supplemented or undermined, depending on the location and Chinese official, by corruption and other such activities. One of the main goals of Lord George Macartney's 1793 embassy was to garner a settled tariff for the trade Britain hoped to conduct.

Not until the 1842 Treaty of Nanjing, however, did Britain obtain legal sanction, imposed by force, for establishing a regulated tariff system at the newly opened ports. Manipulations adversely affecting trade continued, however, so that by the mid-1850s only Shanghai had become a major trading spot. Either local antipathy and violence toward the foreigner or the complexities of doing business kept Canton, Fuzhou, Ninbo, and Xiamen (Amoy) from developing into trading entrepôts. As a partial remedy, Britain persuaded the Qing Court to establish an Inspectorate of Customs in 1854 and appoint Westerners to run it. This set up was not entirely deleterious to the Qing, for the customs officials managed to bring steady revenue into the treasury, but it clearly was a major infringement on Chinese sovereignty.[12]

Only with the punitive 1858 Tianjin (Tientsin) Treaty did the Chinese tariff system take its final form, setting a uniform tariff rate of 5 percent at all trading ports. The revamped system was strengthened by London's newly secured right to send its ships far into Chinese interior waterways, thereby expanding British trade and bypassing the corrupt internal transportation system, which was a source of much pecuniary gain to numerous Chinese officials.

The Tokugawa bakufu endured nothing like this foreign control over its international trade. The Ansei treaties placed Japan in a structural position analogous to Siam. Edo maintained control over the entire customs framework, employed its own officials, and garnered 20 percent duties on some of Europe's key exports. Whereas bakufu officials complained repeatedly in early trading years about fiscal instability arising from the inequitable exchange rates, they showed little, if any, distress over the tariff situation. More significantly, since Edo depended on a land tax for the vast majority of its income, tariffs could be used for purposes other than economic. Within half a decade of the establishment of trade, the bakufu began strategically to employ graduated tariff reform as a way to achieve political objectives.

Tariffs and the London Protocol, 1862

The first indication that tariffs could be sacrificed to political goals came in the final stages of negotiating the 1862 London Protocol. Andō Nobumasa, Kuze Hirochika, and Rutherford Alcock had not raised the issue during their various negotiations. The two senior councillors obviously knew that Western resistance to postponement was weakening and correspondingly felt no need to make unnecessary gestures. Alcock, for his part, had received no concrete instructions regarding economic issues from London to guide him during those negotiations.

The French in Paris had first proposed the idea of tariff revision in the spring of 1862 (see chapter 4). During discussions in mid-April, Foreign Minister Antoine-Edouard Thouvenel suddenly inserted a demand that the import duty on French wines and spirits be reduced to 5 percent from the current thirty-five. The Japanese delegation, headed by Takeuchi Yasunori, had not received any instructions regarding tariff revision, but it did not have to make a unilateral decision anyway, because talks halted once Thouvenel revealed that Paris would agree to postponement only if the British and Dutch also assented.[13] The scene then switched to London, to which Alcock had already returned. On his way back, however, he had stopped in Paris to discuss the postponement issue with Thouvenel, and there he learned of the French tariff proposal.

Once in London, the Japanese ambassadors found Alcock's willingness to argue for postponement was at the last minute influenced by a plan to adopt and expand the French call for reduced tariffs. During a meeting on the evening of June 5, Alcock explained that London wished a duty reduction not solely in spirits, but also on pane glass, which would be reduced to 5 percent from the current twenty. Alcock, however, was not demanding the reduction, but merely asking that the bakufu consider the issue once the embassy returned home.[14]

Takeuchi quickly agreed to the proposal, and the following day met with Russell at the Foreign Office to sign the London Protocol. The penultimate paragraph in the protocol stated that the ambassadors "engage to suggest to the Tycoon and his Ministers to evince their goodwill to the nations of Europe . . . by reducing the duties on wines and spirits imported into Japan, and by permitting glassware to be inserted in the list of articles on which an import duty of 5 per cent is levied."[15] This arrangement suited both sides and preserved for the Japanese the current tariff schedule. Moreover, Takeuchi had acquiesced only at the last minute to ensure fruition of the overall goal of postponement. Tariff reduction would proceed, but at a level and pace determined by the Japanese government in concert with its trading partners.

That the issue was viewed in Edo as a political one is shown by an analysis of the London Protocol done by the foreign affairs magistrates in November 1862. Takemoto Masao, head of the magistrates, argued that "if the bakufu were to decide to lower the duties now, this would furnish [the Westerners] with evidence that our government does desire lasting friendship and does not seek to restrict trade. It would help to still the clamor of opinion. . . . We think it best, therefore, that the bakufu should make no difficulties."[16] The senior councillors rejected Takemoto's advice to lower tariffs immediately, but they did accept his opinion that tariff reduction could be used tactically to achieve political goals, as evidenced by Takeuchi's success in London. More important, even in the absence of clear political ends, the bakufu from this point adopted Takeuchi's approach of flexible response and measured tariff concessions to maintain control over the treaty structure. The Americans would be the first to put this new policy to the test.

The American Tariff Gambit, 1862–1864

Even before the London Protocol was transmitted to Western representatives in Japan, Edo attempted to raise the duty on certain imported tea-packaging items. This request collided with one by the new U.S. minister, Robert Pruyn, to secure the abolition of duties on all Japanese exports as well as on imports of tea-related items.

To outline the situation, green tea, although accounting at the time for only about 11 percent of Japan's total traded goods, was the major export to the United States. It initially was sent as bales of loose leaves to China, where it was properly packed for transoceanic shipment. By the early 1860s, Japanese tea producers had begun to import from China the various packing materials, such as boxes, pans, and foil; this allowed them to prepare the tea themselves for export. The foreign importers of these items, however, paid no duty, so while Edo's licensed tea exporters had to pay high prices for the packing goods, the bakufu was missing a chance to increase its revenues by taxing the importers. Accordingly, in August 1861 the bakufu proposed that imported tea-packaging materials be levied a 20 percent duty.[17] The issue languished, however, lost in the buildup to the Takeuchi Mission, until the following year when Pruyn turned the request on its head.

One of Pruyn's main goals was to force the bakufu into building bonded warehouses at the treaty ports, and the tea duty issue was a convenient way to approach it. Bonded warehouses were storage buildings where foreign merchants could deposit their imported goods, duty free, until a sale was arranged; if no sale was forthcoming, the goods could be reshipped home with no duty penalty.

The Ansei treaties did not provide for such warehouses, requiring instead that merchants pay duties on goods as they were offloaded, regardless of whether they were later sold. The British had maneuvered around this system by arranging to have their merchants pay the duty to each port's consul. The consul would hold the money until a sale was completed, then pay the duty (based on the final sale price) to the Japanese customs magistrates. Pruyn hoped to secure a similar situation for U.S. merchants during the interim, while waiting for the bakufu to erect the bonded warehouses.[18]

The U.S. minister presented a much more wide-ranging proposal, however, to the foreign affairs magistrates in late June 1862, recommending that all tea-packing materials be imported duty-free. Pruyn's main worry was that the Japanese aimed at a total tariff of 25 percent on tea and tea-related items, which would make the cost of tea too high for American importers. He assured the Japanese that maintaining the current 5 percent rate on tea alone would ensure that trade would grow steadily.[19] Due in part to the internal political upheavals in the bakufu and the problems posed by the Richardson affair, Edo did not respond to Pruyn's suggestion, fearing, apparently, that this was just the first wedge in a campaign to make duty-free all items not covered specifically by the treaties.[20]

Frustrated in his first attempt, Pruyn could not raise the issue again until early December with Takemoto and Inoue Kiyonao, who had returned to duty as foreign magistrate. This time he proposed not only that all tea-packing materials be left duty-free but also that tariffs be abolished on all Japanese goods bought by Western merchants for export.[21] Though the new request likely was a negotiating tactic to get the bakufu to take up his tea scheme, Pruyn in fact received no response, leading him to inform Inoue that the United States would not automatically follow the London Protocol if it did not make progress on its own tariff-related issues.

In response to Pruyn's threat and not wanting to lose the goodwill of the Americans, Inoue and Takemoto entered into four months of negotiation and concluded a draft of a tariff reduction treaty on March 19, 1863. Its provisions included establishing bonded warehouses, maintaining the duty-free status of tea-packing materials and processed tea, and limiting to 5 percent the import duty on a limited number of other goods.[22] The foreign magistrates saw this last set of reductions, add-ons during the negotiations, as the price to be paid for maintaining the Japanese-American "special relationship" first forged with Townsend Harris.

Despite having a complete draft, though, Edo managed to delay its signing for more than ten months. During the upheavals of the Namamugi and Shimonoseki incidents, the bakufu steadfastly refused Pruyn's repeated demands to formalize the convention. In part, Edo took this stance because Pruyn continued to push for abolition of the export duty on all Japanese goods, and Inoue and Takemoto wanted to make sure they had buried this idea before signing the full agreement.

More important, though, the bakufu hesitated over building the large bonded warehouses, even though it had agreed to do so in the draft. At one level it worried about the expense of the construction project, for the Tokugawa treasury had been running low for years, strained by sending delegations abroad, coping with inflation, paying indemnities to the West, and supporting reconstruction projects across Japan.

At a deeper level, however, Edo was concerned by reports describing the warehouse system in Europe, which were submitted by members of the 1862 embassy. Because of their size and efficiency, the bonded warehouses there increased trade substantially. More warehouse space in Japan would mean more trade and more traders, thus enlarging the foreign presence.[23] Wary of expanding Yokohama more than it already was growing on its own, the foreign magistrates kept Pruyn on tenterhooks throughout the summer and autumn of 1863.

Fidelity to the overall bakufu diplomatic strategy, however, soon brought about a reconsideration of the tariff issue. Edo's change of heart was directly connected with its planning in the summer of 1864 for the ill-fated Ikeda embassy to Europe to secure the closing of Yokohama (as recounted in chapter 4). Foreign magistrate Takemoto Masao had argued two years previously that tariffs could be used to gain political goals, and the senior councillors knew Pruyn had kept the French and British informed of his negotiations. With French officials pushing for a mission to Paris, however, the goal of closing Yokohama clearly outweighed any considerations over tariff rates. Further impetus was provided by French Minister Duchesne de Bellecourt, who again proposed a reduction on wine tariffs during September 1863.[24] As arrangements for the Ikeda embassy continued on to the end of the year, the bakufu renewed negotiations with Pruyn.

Pruyn answered one bakufu concern in mid-October, agreeing to postpone the provisions regarding the bonded warehouses until the summer of 1864, although the revised import duties would go into effect once the convention was signed.[25] The foreign magistrates interpreted this to mean that the actual signing of the provisions regarding the warehouses would be postponed, and on January 23, 1864, they informed Pruyn that they would finalize the convention. Edo also informed the U.S. minister that it wished to discuss tariff revision concurrently with France and Britain; its new plan was to conclude a tariff reduction pact and offer it to those countries as an enticement to close Yokohama.[26]

The two sides reached agreement on January 25, and the final document reflected one of the bakufu's key aims: none of the convention's four articles compelled the Japanese government to establish bonded warehouses. Article I enumerated duty-free items, all related to the preparation and packing of tea, and Article II listed imports to be levied a 5 percent duty.[27] The convention was to come into effect on February 8, 1864. The enumerated goods in Article II were compiled with England and France in mind. They included a reduction in duties on glass and glassware, as requested by Alcock during final negotiations on the London Protocol, and wines and spirits, as requested by Thouvenel at the same time.

The day following final agreement, Edo informed Bellecourt and Neale of the reduction in duties.[28] The convention was formally signed between Pruyn and the bakufu on January 30. On February 4, the eve of Ikeda's departure for France, Edo announced the reduction in tariffs on wines and spirits to 5 percent and further added that the duty on *articles Parisien* (primarily clocks and crystal) would also be lowered to 5 to 6 percent from twenty percent.[29]

Ultimately, the Japanese tariff reduction policy failed in its main goal, to bring about the closing of Yokohama. Edo had but three things to show for its efforts. It had delayed for two years any substantial reductions first proposed by France and Great Britain in 1862. It also had defeated two worrisome demands by the Americans, namely that Japanese exports all be made duty-free and that the bakufu build large bonded warehouses. Finally, the bakufu negotiators had balanced all their concessions almost equally in the interests of the Americans, French, and British. With each Western treaty partner reasonably satisfied by the revisions, they did not for the time being seek greater concessions.

The Americans had started the ball rolling with a specific set of proposals back in 1862. By the time he left Japan in April 1865, however, Pruyn could not know that the negotiations he had initiated eventually would help lead to radical changes not only in the bakufu's economic strategy but also in its entire diplomatic culture.

The 1866 Tariff Convention

On its face, the final act of tariff revision appears to reveal a sudden, major surrender of sovereignty by the bakufu. It is more accurate, however, to see the 1866 Tariff Convention, which was also known as the Edo Convention, as the ultimate stage of a half-decade-long process, and not a precipitous diplomatic collapse by the bakufu.[30] For nearly a year and a half after the 1864 tariff reductions, the Western treaty powers made no new demands. Yet with the coming to Japan of the new British minister, Harry Parkes, the tariff issue became entwined with unrelated problems between Japan and the treaty nations.

Parkes had arrived in Yokohama in early July 1865.[31] He was an old China-hand, like Alcock before him, and had been sent from there to steady British policy after Alcock's bombardment of Shimonoseki. Like Alcock, he was under instructions not to antagonize Anglo–Japanese relations, and Alcock's recall afforded a salutary lesson in challenging Russell's will. New to the complex situation in Japan, though, Parkes was ignorant of the balance of interests built between the bakufu and the treaty powers during the past years.

He did not, or did not want to, see that negotiation was still the bedrock of Japanese–Western relations, even in its weakened state. Most appallingly, in his eyes, was that the court had never formally approved the 1858 treaties, though that had had no bearing on actual trade relations. What it did provide, though, was an entrée for new British pressure on the bakufu. Parkes had successfully used force, or the threat of force, numerous times while in China, and saw no reason a similar policy of intimidation could not be employed in Japan. His problem was that there were no urgent issues clouding treaty relations.

Within three months of his arrival, however, Parkes created just such a sense of crisis over imperial ratification, thereby allowing himself to craft a new set of petitions. His three key demands were imperial approval of the 1858 treaties, the opening Osaka and Hyogo to trade on January 1, 1866, and more tariff reductions. As a sweetener to his abrupt pronouncement, Parkes informed the bakufu that, were his three wishes to be granted, he would make good on Alcock's 1864 offer to waive two-thirds of the $3 million Shimonoseki indemnity.

In his approach, Parkes also adopted a major tactical change that he thought would restrict the bakufu's maneuvering room. He threatened to open negotiations directly with the imperial court and backed this up by browbeating the French, American, and Dutch ministers into accompanying him to Osaka, in a small armada, to meet with the shogun. By this means, Parkes, like Alcock before him, turned a unilateral British plan into a joint Western policy. The upshot was a tactical bakufu concession in November 1865, as well as a resolution of the lingering court-bakufu impasse. Parkes and the other ministers met in Osaka primarily with senior councillor Abe Masato, who accepted that the bakufu needed to secure imperial ratification of the treaties. Abe soon enlisted Hitotsubashi Keiki to press upon Kyoto the necessity of finally approving the Ansei pacts.

For his temerity, Abe was stripped of his rank and position by the court itself, an unheard of act and one that presaged a growing imperial role in domestic politics. The ideological supremacy of the shogun was again called into question by spillover from foreign affairs. In order to maintain domestic peace while it attempted to deal with Parkes's offensive, the bakufu acceded to Abe's punishment, and went so far as to dispatch Ogasawara Nagamichi to Kyoto to submit the shogun's resignation. The court refused the offer, seeing it as a symbolic gesture on the part of Tokugawa Iemochi, but finally was provoked into approving the treaties the bakufu had signed nearly a decade before.[32]

Ogasawara and fellow senior councillor Honjō Munehide, like Abe, supported existing treaty relations, and thus were not opposed to Parkes's demand that the court recognize the treaties. What was of grave concern, however, was Parkes's proposal to open Osaka and Hyogo ahead of the schedule set forth in the London Protocol, which mandated that both sites remain closed to trade until 1868. The senior councillors still viewed the treaty ports as the main physical boundary between Japan and Westerners, and to commence trading ahead of schedule at the new sites would be to thin out the bakufu's defenses and to foreclose the possibility of negotiating further delays in their opening. The court, of course, wanted to keep Osaka closed permanently, but the immediate problem for the bakufu was to defeat this latest Western demand, and then deal with Osaka when the time came. Edo, therefore, quickly informed the Western representatives that the long-delayed imperial approval of the treaties had been given. In place of opening Osaka, however, the senior councillors stated that they were willing to discuss another round of tariff revision back in Edo.

This tactic by Ogasawara and Honjō left Parkes with a dilemma: whether to accept what had been given, or carry out his threat to negotiate directly with the court. Parkes thought the emperor a useful bargaining tool, but never seriously considered breaking off relations with Britain's duly ratified treaty partner, nor was it likely that London would have allowed him to do so. Having strict instructions from Russell not to undertake any military actions, a legacy of the Alcock years, Parkes decided that success in two out of three demands was acceptable and he and the other diplomats retired to Edo. Tariffs were thus on the table again, with Edo hoping that a successful sacrifice of the current tariff rates would defuse the Western demand to open Hyogo and Osaka early. That, in turn, would prevent the possibility of a breach between the court and bakufu over opening Osaka.

Yet Western pressure continued even as the bakufu formulated its tactics. At least three times during late 1865 alone, Parkes and the other Western representatives demanded that the two locations be opened immediately; this they repeated even after apparently surrendering the idea by returning to Edo in the first place.[33]

Attached to each of the Western demands, however, was the proposal to discuss lowering the tariff, and bakufu officials back in Edo concentrated on this lifeline. They were helped in shifting the focus to economic matters by the temporary U.S. minister, A. L. C. Portman, Robert Pruyn's replacement, who on November 30 informed the bakufu that he and the other representatives were "returning to Edo and awaited the quick appointment of officials to discuss tariff revision."[34] The U.S. minister had already given up on attaining the early opening of Hyogo and Osaka. By the end of January 1866, Parkes, too, had been disabused of the notion. Mizuno Tadakiyo and Honjō steadfastly pushed the tariff agenda, and the issue of Hyogo and Osaka dropped by the wayside.

Yet the bakufu now considered further tariff reduction in a new light. As early as November 1865, when the shogun ordered Honjō to Osaka to deal with Parkes's demands, the senior councillors had begun to see that lower tariffs could expand the volume of foreign trade. The extra income from more trade would offset the lower level of tariffs and thus help replenish the bakufu treasury. Though still in its nascent stages, this was a radical transformation in the thinking of certain senior councillors. No doubt growing concerns over the fiscal strength of the bakufu occasioned it, but such a view ran directly counter to official thinking about the necessity of limiting trade as much as possible. Regime stability clearly was of a higher order than trade levels, though there was as yet no serious thought over how to disentangle the two, when they had been linked in bakufu policy since 1858. The simple fact was, that domestic and foreign events were beginning to overtake the ability of the senior councillors to respond, even as they entered into multiple negotiations. Foreign magistrate Oguri Tadamasa was ordered to meet further with Parkes, who by now had proposed a uniform 5 percent import and export duty, identical to the one he had known in China. But Oguri was more receptive to an alternative plan put forth by French Minister Léon Roches, whose policy disagreements with the overbearing Parkes were heating up.

Despite the bakufu's unilateral nullification of the 1864 Paris Convention (as recounted in chapter 4), Roches had not broken off relations with Edo. In fact, the French had made no response to the nullification, perhaps being mollified by the opening of the Shimonoseki Straits through allied force. Of more consequence, though, Roches and his superiors were concluding that the British-led allied policy was less and less advantageous to France. In particular, they were concerned that if relations continued to be influenced by force, that force would almost certainly be British, thus maintaining London's de facto leadership of the treaty powers. The French would over time lose the status they held under a treaty structure based on negotiations between ostensibly equal treaty partners. Roches thus turned increasingly to unilateral negotiations with Edo. He spent 1865 building a closer French–bakufu relationship, including setting up the Yokosuka shipyards and ironworks and garnering the funds for establishing a joint Franco–Japanese trading company.[35]

In early 1866, Roches proposed to make Yokohama a free port, which was essentially the same suggestion made two years previously to Ikeda Nagaaki by Foreign Minister Thouvenel in Paris. To attract the bakufu this time, Roches explained the domestic economic benefits that would accrue under such a plan. He noted that the bakufu, by abolishing import duties, could tax Japanese merchants at the point of entry to Japanese cities; this would allow Edo to set whatever tax rates it desired. The alternative, he stressed, was dealing with Western merchants who, supported by their consuls, continually would seek to evade the port duties.[36]

Oguri adopted Roches's view of import levies, while hoping to maintain the current level of export duties. This proposal, however, opened a major breach between Roches and Parkes, and Oguri fruitlessly tried to gain the Englishman's approval during early 1866.[37] Parkes immediately understood that the Oguri–Roches plan would make British imports more expensive at the final point of sale and likely lead to reduced demand by Japanese consumers. Moreover, the British merchant community had been pressing him, in lieu of establishing completely free trade, to create in Japan a Chinese-style inspectorate of customs, run by foreigners.

Ultimately, the senior councillors would sacrifice the Oguri–Roches plan in a final gamble to keep British support in the coming months. Now it was the turn of foreign affairs to help the bakufu's domestic situation. Edo was in the throes of planning for another military expedition against Chōshū, which it hoped would solve the problem of the rebellious domain once and for all, thus strengthening bakufu authority. It therefore desperately needed funds and hoped to delay payment on the latter half of the 1864 Shimonoseki indemnity. Not wanting to lose the goodwill of the British at this pivotal moment, the senior councillors could hardly oppose Parkes's 5 percent tariff proposal. Sensing the advantage, Parkes now included two new and radical demands: that trading in the ports be completely open to all Japanese and that Japanese be allowed freely to travel abroad. The latter demand, in particular, would ostensibly mark the death-knell of the maritime edicts established over two centuries before.

Here again was clear proof of the inextricable connection between domestic and foreign politics. The bakufu was about to gamble its power in a showdown with Chōshū. Were it to lose the support of the British, the outcome might be disaster. The senior councillors knew that Parkes's demands were a direct assault on the core of its diplomatic strategy, which would efface the physical and ideological boundaries central to the bakufu's authority. Yet the trade-off seemed unavoidable. Tariffs were now a lynchpin to political survival.

Negotiations proceeded quickly and the bakufu reached final agreement with Parkes over the Edo Convention on June 25.[38] Nonetheless, the tariff provisions were not as far-reaching as they might initially have seemed, for they were primarily extensions of the 1864 agreements. As a general statement, the bakufu reaffirmed its commitment under the 1862 London Protocol to remove any remaining unofficial restrictions on trade, such as interference in purchasing goods or shady accounting practices. Regarding tariff rates, a standard 5 percent duty was levied on nonenumerated imports and exports, to come into effect July 1, 1867. The prohibition on opium importation was maintained, as was the prohibition on exporting rice, wheat, and barley. The highest specific duty was on raw silk.[39]

To observers, it was the nontariff portions of the convention that seemed truly radical. Article 4 provided for the establishment of free bonded warehouses; the bakufu thus acceded to the demand first voiced by Robert Pruyn in 1862. Finally, and most radically, Article 10 allowed all Japanese unhindered passage abroad, ending a two-century restriction on overseas travel.

As always in treaty negotiations, however, things were not as clear-cut as they seemed. The bakufu wrote into the convention crucial safeguards that would weaken the impact of Articles 4 and 10. Most important, Article 7 preserved bakufu control over the landing and shipping of cargo and the hiring of boats and servants, and it empowered the governor of each open port to negotiate with foreign consuls the resolution of any problems involving these issues. Moreover, Edo was given the right to revise duties on tea and silk after two years, in consultation with the British, thus injecting a degree of tariff autonomy on Japan's two main exports. Finally, and most important, the bakufu and its local officials reserved the right to decide which Japanese could go abroad and which would be refused, regardless of the intent of Article 10. The result was that domestic port affairs and emigration mechanisms remained firmly in Edo's hands, as they had since 1859.

Parkes knew that, ultimately, he could do nothing to ensure enforcement of the bakufu promises to remove the remaining restrictions on trade and allow overseas travel. Acknowledging that the agreement was on paper only, he wrote the Foreign Secretary, Earl Clarendon, that "in giving the Japanese credit for these timely concessions to the progressive spirit of their countrymen, I am not insensible to the proneness of this Government to avoid the execution of engagements which conflict with a traditional policy."[40]

Free trade, nominally established by the 1862 London Protocol, was reasserted in 1866, but Parkes understood the bakufu still held a tight rein over treaty port interactions. The bakufu had answered foreign demands for lower tariffs, thereby pacifying the Westerners and easing Japanese–Western tensions. Nonetheless, it had negotiated away the theoretical justification for two of its central diplomatic props. The principle of free passage abroad was, perhaps for the first time in Japanese history, clearly affirmed, while the conceit that the shogun ordered the and foreign realms alike was increasingly impossible to sustain.

Despite facing these new challenges, the bakufu opened its fateful Summer War against Chōshū three weeks after signing the Edo Convention. Yet even as it sought to reassert its domestic authority and to preserve a coherent view of the world, the intellectual boundary established by the Tokugawa founders was receding under a deluge of new knowledge about the world.

Widening the World: Translations and Barbarian Books to 1868

In historical retrospect, the Ansei treaties formed one bridge between early-modern and modern Japan, as they created and ordered a structural relationship between that nation and its Western treaty partners. Yet the treaty regime was just one aspect of the totality of Japanese–

Western relations, albeit the most visible. Equally important, Japanese knowledge of the outside world formed a similar link both between historical eras in Japan and between Japan and its treaty partners.

This "knowledge base" was not a static body of information. It continually grew and linked various actors, from bakufu officials to intellectual groups, from artists to Yokohama international merchants. Nor was this body of knowledge about things Western isolated from treaty relations, for it influenced the evolution of both Japanese foreign and domestic policy, and those two, in turn, interacted upon each other. The existence and development of this knowledge base, from an historical perspective, lies at the intersection of Tokugawa and Meiji Japan, altering the former and helping to gestate the latter. And at its heart lay the practice of translating barbarian books.[41]

The Tokugawa bakufu, of course, was not ignorant of the outside world. Edo required both Dutch and Chinese traders in Nagasaki to furnish reports on conditions in Europe and Asia (see chapter 1). In addition to these formal reports, the bakufu ordered and received Dutch and Chinese books on international affairs, with many of the Chinese ones being translations of European works. Equally important was the official patronage given to "Dutch studies" (*rangaku*) by the bakufu starting with Tokugawa Yoshimune, the eighth shogun, who ruled from 1716 to 1745. The names of intellectual pioneers arising from this movement, such as Sugita Genpaku and Maeno Ryōtaku, dot Japanese history.[42]

By the nineteenth century, the bakufu regularized, even bureaucratized, and expanded its gathering of global information. Fear of Russian expeditions to Japan, as well as the British *Phaeton*'s entry into Nagasaki in 1808, spurred the bakufu formally to begin long-term intelligence gathering. Starting in 1809, the shogunate commissioned members of the Astronomical Bureau (*tenmonkata*) to translate Western maps and atlases. In 1811 it formalized their work, establishing within the bureau a department for the translation of barbarian books, called the *bansho wage goyō*.

The need for accurate global information became even more apparent in the 1840s, during the Opium War. Major Chinese works, by authors such as Lin Zexu (Tse-hsū) and Wei Yuan, were brought into Japan, there avidly read by bakufu officials.[43] By the mid-1850s, the foreign threat was racing toward Japan, though Commodore Perry reached Edo Bay before the shogunate could reform its information analysis department. In 1855, however, a year after signing Perry's

Treaty of Amity, the bakufu created the *Yōgakusho,* or Institute for Western Studies, which superceded the Astronomical Bureau. In Novem-vember of the following year, the institute was renamed the *Bansho shirabesho,* or Institute for the Study of Barbarian Books, a title that lasted until the early 1860s, when the name changed twice more, to *Yōgaku shirabesho* (Institute for the Study of Western Books) and fi-nally to *Kaiseijo* (Institute for Development) in 1863.[44]

The personnel of the institute found themselves at the nexus of scholarship and policy formation. From the beginning, the bakufu conceived of the institute as a source of expertise for its new corps of foreign affairs specialists. Its first director was the Confucian scholar Koga Kin'ichirō. He led a team that included Tsutsui Masanori, the official who had negotiated and signed the 1855 Russo–Japanese Treaty of Amity, as well as Iwase Tadanari, Mizuno Tadanori, and Kawaji Toshiaki. Each of these men had been appointed by Abe Masahiro in 1854 to serve as "officials responsible for the reception of foreign countries" (*ikoku ōsetsu gakari*), and they formed the first group of foreign magistrates in 1858 (as related in chapter 2). Until 1857 Abe, as head of the senior councillors, supervised the entire operation.[45]

By the late 1850s, a new group of younger scholars, men who would have a major impact on the evolution of Japan's foreign and domestic policies in the coming decades, joined the translators in Ku-danshita, on the outskirts of Edo Palace. This class included Tsuda Mamichi, Katō Hiroyuki, Kanda Hiroyuki, Yanagawa Shunsan, and Nishi Amane. The arrival of these younger scholars was paralleled by the increase in the number of books imported from abroad, and the translators expanded their horizons beyond geography and atlases to works on philosophy, history, and law. The bakufu soon realized the value of direct exposure to the outside world and sent some of its most promising young scholars abroad to study.

These activities reflected a hidden change in Edo's diplomatic culture. On the surface the traditional boundaries remained, but to a small de-gree, to be sure, the bakufu found itself reaching outside those carefully maintained boundaries, even if only to figure out how to make them stronger. As with tariffs, self-interest slowly was leading certain Tokugawa officials to a new understanding of Japan's relation to the rest of the world.

However, the institute's works were not chosen merely as part of an intellectual program. Under the guidance of the senior councillors, the institute increasingly focused on issues directly related to the conduct of foreign affairs. A good example is the translation of English grammars. Due to the long-standing trade relations between Japan and Holland, the bakufu's main translators until the late 1850s were all specialists in the Dutch language. Certain families in Nagasaki held hereditary translator positions through which they maintained contact with the Dutch traders on Dejima during the centuries of Tokugawa rule.

Once Perry arrived, however—and even more, once the treaty ports opened—the Japanese quickly discovered that Holland was a minor international power, and that most of the foreigners it dealt with spoke English. Fukuzawa Yukichi, for one, recalled his "bitter disappointment" during a visit to Yokohama in 1859 when he discovered that his years of studying Dutch were all for naught, for "as certain as day, English was to be the most useful language of the future."[46]

Just as Fukuzawa set about learning English, so too did the institute's translators. Between 1862 and 1865, they produced no fewer than five English grammars and dictionaries, including a pocket dictionary.[47] Their interest was neither academic nor economic, but rather was motivated in large part by the twenty-first article of the 1858 Anglo–Japanese treaty, which stated that all communications from Great Britain to the bakufu would be in English. The treaty had provided a five-year moratorium during which Dutch and Japanese versions of official communications would be attached to the British documents. This five-year period was to permit the training of English-speaking bakufu officials. The institute was the place where the English-language textbooks so crucial to the maintenance of treaty relations would be produced.

Some of the most important work undertaken by the institute was in the field of international law, which had a direct bearing on the negotiations that were continuously being pursued with the treaty powers. The Chinese had been the first in East Asia to grapple with the demands of Western international law and the peculiar problem of translating completely foreign concepts. The imperial Commissioner Lin Zexu first attempted to translate Emeric Vattel's *Law of Nations* in the days immediately preceding the Opium War in 1839, when he sought to suppress the importation of opium. The first complete translation of a legal handbook, however, was of Henry Wheaton's *Elements of International Law* (1836) by the missionary William A. P. Martin in 1864.[48]

The following year, the bakufu institute reprinted the Chinese edition of Wheaton, just a year after its appearance in China. It circulated widely in Japan, even though it was not translated into the vernacular until 1868, under the title *Bankoku kōhō*. Institute head Matsumoto Ryōjun personally presented a copy of the Chinese version to the shogun, Tokugawa Iemochi, in late April 1866, where it was undoubtedly read by Hitotsubashi Keiki, who was soon to become shogun himself.[49]

Wheaton's book introduced key legal concepts such as national sovereignty, alliances, and international comity. Many of the issues raised by Wheaton, such as consular jurisdiction and neutrality, were already a part of Japanese international life, if not lexicon, due to treaty relations. Yet the book was the first extensive, coherent explanation of how all these practices fit together, stressing the rights and obligations owed by nations to their diplomatic partners.

Of particular importance to the future course of treaty relations were the sections of *Elements of International Law* dealing with extraterritoriality. Wheaton argued that extraterritoriality was subordinate to the overarching "independence of the State as to its judicial power." It exists only "by special compact between the two States," and thus was not a natural right reserved for Western countries. Yet, he argued, more modern nations could extend their judicial mechanisms to less advanced polities for the purposes of facilitating international trade and intercourse.[50] Translation would thus lay bare Western conceptions of the link between domestic political structure and foreign relations.

Such ideas were not introduced into Japanese thought without difficulty, nor was the translation process a simple, unreflective activity. The concepts of sovereignty, public law, and rights all were either new or had distinct connotations in Tokugawa usage.[51] Nonetheless, even as the translators struggled to provide correlative meaning to these Western ideas, they were broadening the intellectual horizon of the educated few that were in a position to read or discuss these works.

If the idea of individual rights vis-à-vis the state caused cognitive difficulties, the international concept of equality between nations large and small was easier to absorb, due in large part to Japan's recent international history. The impact of ideas such as these on civil and criminal law, and their connection with the legislative authority of modern states, would continue to have great impact on the younger scholars of the institute. While the bakufu was not yet, nor ever would be, ready to change the bases of its power so radically as to mirror Western states, it was nonetheless the efforts of its translators that first introduced into Japan such transformative ideas.

Working at the institute also led to various intellectual paths for its

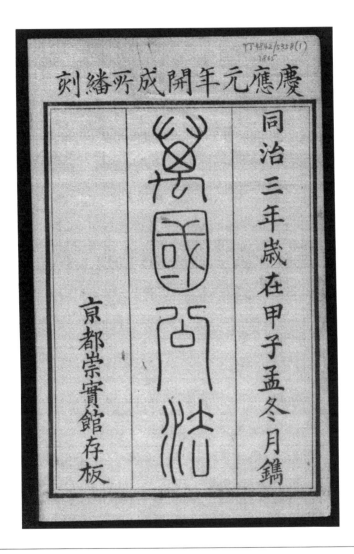

Title page of *Bankoku kōhō* (1865). Courtesy of the Harvard-Yenching Library.

younger scholars, paths that ultimately would lead some of them to become leading lights of Meiji Japan. It was while at the institute, for example, that Nishi Amane began to write his own opus, also titled *Bankoku kōhō*. Nishi had accompanied fellow institute member Tsuda Mamichi to Holland for a study assignment during 1862–1864. There he had taken classes with the legal theorist Simon Vissering and later combined his notes from Vissering's lectures with references from Wheaton's study to produce his book.[52] The impact of his work for the bakufu on Nishi's intellectual development cannot be overstated, a pattern that repeated itself with his colleagues (see chapter 6).

The output of the institute was impressive, and over the years it began to fill out most of the bases of a comprehensive library and research collection. Indeed, a century after the fall of the bakufu, more than 3,600 books collected or translated by the institute were found in Japan's National Diet Library.[53] Yet the scholars of the institute were not the only translators of Western books during the 1850s and 1860s. Though not housed under one roof, or supported by the bakufu, numerous scholars expanded the intellectual horizon of Japanese high and low. These works were treasuries of information, although the amount of errors was also alarmingly high. The 1853 *Bankoku kairo no ki (A record of the sea routes to foreign countries)*, for example, was a five-volume treatise on each major geographic region of the world, while the *Bankoku chiri bunzu* of 1856, by Kondō Kenzan, was the first popularly published world atlas. Otsuki Bankei's *Bankoku shishō chimei fu* of 1857 listed all the countries in the world, together with their capitals, and outlined the hemispheres and major islands. Another important work was the *Bankoku seihyō* of 1860, a collaborative effort between Fukuzawa Yukichi and Okamotoyaku Hakkei. This book, a translation of a Dutch statistical handbook for the years 1845–1854, was filled with political, military, and economic information.

By the late 1860s the work of scholars both public and private had helped change dramatically the Japanese leadership's view of the world. While there was still great fear of, and ill feeling toward, Westerners on the part of a great many Japanese, many of those in charge of official relations had a better grasp of the nature of the Western style of international relations, and they began to see Japan within a larger international context. Thus did the last major boundary of the bakufu's traditional diplomatic culture, the intellectual, crumble from within.

The result was a steady, though tardy, emergence of a new culture, one that at least began to conceive of the benefits of tearing down the long-standing Tokugawa barriers protecting Japan.

Nishi Amane, a leader in this effort, was an adviser to Hitotsubashi Keiki, who became shogun in 1867. Keiki, now known as Tokugawa Yoshinobu, had once strove mightily to expel the barbarians. Now, half a decade later, influenced in part by the labors of the institute's translators, he wrote to the court that

> treaties are the basis of international relations. If there were to be no permanent and lasting rules, the large would in the end overcome the small, the weak would be dominated by the strong. . . . A country's very existence depends on the observance of treaties. . . . If we alone, at such a time, cling to outworn customs and refrain from international relations of a kind common to all countries, our action will be in conflict with the natural order of things.[54]

Yoshinobu's challenge was to reconcile his new understanding of foreign affairs with the pressure put on him by the bakufu's domestic opponents, those who leaped into the breach in the Tokugawa's boundaries and took advantage of Edo's weakness. In the end, it would prove to be an impossible task for him.

Treaty Relations and the Fall of the Bakufu

Whether or not one views the work of the institute as a harbinger of modernization, historical irony attended its labors. Even as top leaders in the bakufu began to grope toward a new understanding of the Japanese polity and the international system, their power was irreversibly fading, frittered away by these very leaders in a futile attempt to maintain the domestic balance of power between Edo and the outer domains.

The 1866 Summer War against Chōshū, the planning for which compelled the bakufu to accept the tariff concessions enumerated in the first part of this chapter, was a disastrous defeat for Edo. More important than the military reverses at the hands of the Chōshū forces, the failure of the expedition meant the effective end of Tokugawa authority in Japan.[55] The fruitless attempt to chastise Chōshū brought about a rapprochement between that domain and Satsuma, thereby uniting the two most powerful opponents of the Tokugawa.

It also unified other bakufu opponents, restored the influence in Kyoto of staunch anti-Edo nobles such as Iwakura Tomomi, and caused various moderate daimyō, such as Yamanouchi Yōdō of Tosa, to begin proposing methods of returning power to the emperor.

Such were the deteriorating conditions facing Hitotsubashi Keiki when, as Tokugawa Yoshinobu, he became the fifteenth shogun on January 10, 1867, succeeding Iemochi, who had died during the Summer War. Yoshinobu was a reformer steeped in the pro-imperial ideology of his birth clan, the Tokugawa of Mito. Although Yoshinobu partisans, such as the industrialist Shibusawa Eiichi, spent much of the Meiji period trying to burnish the last shogun's pro-emperor tendencies, it is clear that Yoshinobu desperately desired to maintain the Tokugawa role in Japan. He understood that the structure of the bakufu would have to be changed radically if it were to retain anything like its power of the previous two centuries.[56]

Foreign affairs played a major role in the last shogun's plans. His outreach to the West is well known and will be but briefly touched upon here.[57] Of all the top-level bakufu officials during the last years of the shogunate, Yoshinobu had gradually come to perhaps the most expansive view of international relations, a far cry from his early days of supporting the 1863 imperial expulsion order. He now understood that Japan had to build up its national strength by emulating Western patterns of domestic and international activity.[58]

This view translated into extensive contacts with foreign representatives in Japan. He met with Léon Roches in March 1867, just two months after becoming shogun, to discuss continued French financial support for the shogunate and to hear Roches's political advice regarding bakufu–daimyō relations.[59] The following month he met with Harry Parkes to sound out British support for his new policy of strengthening bakufu–Western ties.

These were also the months of Franco–British competition for influence in Japan, during which Roches moved ever closer to the bakufu while Parkes kept a more circumspect distance.[60] Perhaps fatal for Yoshinobu's hopes was the fact that, despite Roches's preference for the bakufu, the Alcock doctrine was still in effect, thus preventing any joint Western support of the Tokugawa. It is arguable whether the neutrality policy was in reality a dead letter, since British merchants sold Satsuma and Chōshū weapons and legation interpreter Ernest Satow barely concealed his anti-bakufu attitude. Yoshinobu consequently could expect no unilateral French help and no allied effort, military or otherwise, to support his reform plans.[61]

Domestically, of course, the machinations of mid-level samurai in Satsuma and Chōshū, such as Ōkubo Toshimichi and Saigo Takamori, and the accelerating deterioration of the Tokugawa bases of support, robbed Yoshinobu of any realistic chance of constructing a new political system incorporating the emperor and the most powerful outer lords. In less than a year, he had tendered his resignation to the new sixteen-year-old emperor, Mutsuhito. This time the resignation was accepted, and on January 3, 1868, Satsuma and Chōshū took control of the imperial palace in Kyoto in a coup designed to cut Yoshinobu off from the emperor. The new "imperial forces" then abolished the nearly seven-hundred-year-old office of shogun.

The months immediately following Yoshinobu's resignation were a time of great political (not to mention social) uncertainty. The former shogun actively sought to forge a system in which the Tokugawa would be primus inter pares, albeit subordinate to the emperor, and he continued to try to enlist the Western treaty powers to his side.[62] His attempts, however, were too late to do much good, for the balance of domestic politics had tilted beyond recovery. Thus, because of its proximity to the Summer War and the collapse of Tokugawa power, the 1866 Tariff Convention marked the end of the evolution of bakufu diplomatic strategy.

Two events after Yoshinobu's resignation signaled all but the end of Edo's activity under the Ansei treaties. On January 10, just a week after stepping down as shogun, Yoshinobu met with the British, French, American, and Dutch representatives at Osaka Castle. Here he informed them of his resignation and made a last-ditch attempt to gain their support in the struggles yet to come. He then recounted his own view of the bakufu's actions vis-à-vis the West, repeating an earlier message of his from late November 1867. More important, he sought to subtly rewrite recent events and shape the historical memory of his times:

> We know well that it is impossible to say that we have treated foreign relations perfectly . . . but happily now, the opening of the country is settled. The Tycoon has not failed to fulfill any part of the treaties, and he entirely understands the importance of foreign affairs. . . . We sincerely desire that, in view of our friendship, you will give us your sympathy and support.[63]

What was revealed by Yoshinobu's protestation was the existence of an altered diplomatic culture. From the goals of isolation pursued by Ii Naosuke through the adaptations of Andō Nobumasa and Abe Masato, the bakufu had time and again made tactical concessions to protect the culture that animated its actions. In the end, the weight of these changes combined to cause the collapse of the strategy it so tenaciously pursued. It is clear, though, that the bakufu dealt each step of the way with the West through careful analysis and reasoned decision. Western and domestic pressure may have presented a Gordian knot, but Edo consistently hewed to its policy, making changes only when it felt it had to, or when its thinking evolved due to the very relations it was trying to manage. And even at the very end, the bakufu championed its original view of trade relations.

On January 1, 1868, just two days before the Satsuma–Chōshū takeover of the imperial palace, Hyogo and Osaka opened for trade as mandated in the 1862 London Protocol. Domestic opposition to having foreigners live and trade in the "sacred precincts" of Kyoto had not abated, and the site designated by Iwase Tadanari and Townsend Harris back in 1858 for the Hyogo port remained empty on that day. Instead, about ten miles to the west, on a narrow, swampy strip of land isolated by the Rokkō mountains to the north and the Uda River to the east, the small hamlet of Kobe welcomed its first foreign merchants.

There was much Western resignation at this replication of the Yokohama opening a decade before. As the London *Times* wryly remarked, "it is difficult for any one who knows the Japanese to believe that any trading of much consequence will be carried on with them, at any rate for a long time to come."[64] The bakufu, its vision consistent, ended its treaty relations as it had begun, by carrying out its own interpretation of them.

Rethinking Negotiation: Moving toward Revision

The beginning of the Meiji era gave little hint of the radical changes for which it ultimately became known. The new imperial leaders, an amalgam of daimyō, samurai, and court nobles, did not take power in January 1868 by fundamentally transforming Japanese society and culture. Also, although stripped of authority, the Tokugawa still controlled a quarter of the land in Japan, and their direct military retainers far outnumbered the imperial troops. With the survival of its embryonic regime unsettled, the new government undertook policies that were less like reforms than actions to clarify and strengthen its own power. These moves were ad hoc, at best, combining the irreconcilable goals of erecting a stable central government and attempting to maintain the traditional semiautonomous nature of the domains.[1]

Asserting Authority: The Meiji Takeover of Foreign Relations, 1868

On one point the government was clear, quickly claiming the right to conduct foreign affairs. Despite Tokugawa Yoshinobu's postresignation meeting with foreign diplomats, the Tokugawa quietly abdicated their foreign affairs role just as they had their domestic power. From January 1868 onward, the Meiji government arrogated authority in foreign relations to itself, ignoring continued American and French hopes for a revival of the Tokugawa.[2] Yet the Meiji leaders could not be assured of continued Western support, for the still-surviving 1864 Alcock neutrality doctrine ensured that the treaty powers would formally support whichever side gained or asserted authority over foreign affairs, as long as it did not threaten the foreign presence. Firm control of foreign relations, then, was one of the prizes attendant on final domestic political and military victory. With civil war looming in early 1868, it was no surprise that the top Meiji leaders concerned themselves intimately with diplomacy.

Unlike the Tokugawa, those who had overthrown the bakufu had not had long-term contact with Westerners or extensive experience in negotiating treaty relations. They came to power with no distinct diplomatic culture of their own; rather, they were animated by an uneasy combination of pragmatism and ideology. The Western attacks on Kagoshima in 1863 and Shimonoseki the following year had pushed men such as Ōkubo Toshimichi of Satsuma and Kido Kōin of Chōshū to temper their anti-Western rhetoric and indeed form ties with British diplomats such as Ernest Satow or leading merchants such as Nagasaki's Thomas Glover.

Half a decade later, after replacing the bakufu, members of the Meiji government did not yet have a diplomatic strategy equal in complexity to that of the Tokugawa. Not surprisingly, their first moves were patterned closely after the traditional bakufu strategy of maintaining key boundaries between Japan and the outer world. This posture, of course, best fitted what might be identified as their inherent diplomatic culture, in essence a continuing desire to keep Japan, ideologically now under the control of the emperor, independent of foreigners.

The leaders of the Meiji government, chief among them Sanjō Sanetomi, Iwakura Tomomi, Ōkubo, and Kido, knew they had toppled the bakufu in part by taking advantage of the strains caused by the arrival of the West. Yet now in power, they understood that foreign affairs just as easily could be their undoing. Though domestic issues were paramount, the new government could not hope to remain in power without at the least the neutrality, if not the overt support, of the treaty powers. The realities of trying to control Japan, then, weakened their anti-Western line, though it did not undermine their cloaking themselves in the newly rediscovered authority of the emperor. The trick was to sunder the link between the emperor and anti-Westernism, a connection they themselves had made the centerpiece of their rise to power.

Accordingly, on February 8, 1868, just a month after the public announcement of the Restoration, Higashikuze Michitomi, one of the top court nobles in the new regime, met with leading Western representatives to announce that the new government would exercise supreme control in Japan's domestic and foreign affairs.[3] This meeting was followed two days later by a letter from the imperial government stating that it would "faithfully execute all foreign treaties."[4] The same day, February 10, the Foreign Affairs Department was established as one of the first seven governmental offices, proof of the importance the new leadership placed on treaty relations. Higashikuze was appointed one of five commissioners for foreign affairs, along with Sanjō Sanetomi and Date Munenari, the daimyō of Uwajima.

Trade continued despite the uncertain political situation, and Westerners now found themselves dealing with the new government in the port areas, where the Tokugawa had all but abandoned their position. By late February, the court was issuing orders regarding the protection of Yokohama residents on the main roads of Japan.[5] For the Meiji leaders this created a sensitive problem since most of their support came from antiforeign samurai disenchanted with the concessionlike tactics of the Tokugawa; yet they now took up where the bakufu had left off. Although the new leaders had shown reverence for the court, they were in danger of flouting the second half of the famous refrain, *sonnō jōi* ("Revere the Emperor, Expel the Barbarian").[6]

Ironically, it was they who now had to assure the safety of foreigners in their midst, not to mention facilitate the trade that was still bringing economic disruption to rural Japanese. In the early months of their rule it seemed that lower-samurai elements could rise up at any time against the new rulers, who no longer championed the purity of the imperial land. Almost immediately, the Meiji leaders were put to the test and felt the first wave of Western pressure so familiar to the Tokugawa.

Having pledged to uphold the treaties, the new leaders were constrained to honor the opening of the Kinai ports, despite their proximity to Kyoto. The issue of opening Kobe and Osaka had helped poison relations between the bakufu and the court during the last years of Tokugawa rule, and Ōkubo and his confederates had used it as a way to isolate Tokugawa Yoshinobu from potential supporters in Kyoto.

Now Ōkubo and Iwakura found themselves forced to adhere to Yoshinobu's policy to open Kobe or face the wrath of the treaty powers.

Although Kobe clearly did not rival Yokohama in economic importance, Western diplomatic representatives valued it for being closer to the heart of Japanese domestic politics then roiling in Kyoto and Osaka. The fact that Kobe was not Hyogo, at least as initially defined by Iwase Tadanari and Townsend Harris back in 1858, raised nary a ripple on the surface of relations, for Western diplomats were well used to such changes in the treaties. British Minister Harry Parkes and French Minister Léon Roches took satisfaction simply that another crisis was averted and that they had secured a foothold so close to the imperial capital. They soon would discover that propinquity to the emperor carried its own risks.

On February 4, 1868, the entire Western diplomatic community was at Kobe to celebrate the near-completion of the foreign settlement. The day ironically brought an even greater crisis than had the port never opened. As the festivities wound down, a detachment of Bizen (Okayama) samurai serving as imperial troops apparently skirmished with some French sailors. The samurai, all carrying rifles, suddenly opened fire on the assembled Westerners.[7] Though no one was killed, the assault was the first major attack on foreigners since the murders of two British officers in Kamakura four years before.

The attack thrust the new government into its first encounter with crisis diplomacy. Within five days, Western representatives sent a collective note to Higashikuze, who had become the primary contact with the treaty powers, demanding capital punishment for the officer in charge of the Bizen troops, as well as a written apology from the emperor's government. The diplomats made clear that any failure to uphold the treaties and to ensure the safety of foreigners would be laid at the government's doorstep, writing that it was "only by the prompt and signal punishment of this offence that the commission of such lawless violence can be prevented in the future and friendly relations be preserved between the governments."[8]

Iwakura, Ōkubo, and the other leaders had learned well from the Tokugawa failure to give satisfaction for such attacks. Ōkubo, moreover, hailed from Satsuma, the first locale in Japan to face Western naval bombardment due to the domain's refusal to answer for the Richardson murder. The government thus lost no time in arresting the leader of the Bizen detachment, a samurai named Taki Zenzaburō. After three weeks of negotiation with Parkes and his colleagues, the imperial government ordered Taki to commit *seppuku* (ritual suicide).[9] His elaborately staged execution on March 2 was witnessed by British diplomatic representatives, and it formed the basis for A. B. Mitford's famous account of "hara-kiri," which was first published the following year in *Cornhill Magazine* and later in his *Tales of Old Japan*.[10]

The new government was to get no quick respite from foreign emergencies, however, for a new crisis soon erupted. On March 8, 1868, just days after Taki's ritual suicide, a party of French sailors whose ship had moored in Sakai, south of the newly opened Osaka, was attacked by a group of samurai from the domain of Tosa. Chased through the streets back to their launch, eleven of the French sailors were cut down on the quay, some in their boat. The news made it back to Shanghai within ten days and to Europe by the end of April.

This was the greatest loss of life yet suffered by the treaty powers in Japan. It not only threatened peaceful relations between Japan and the West but also directly challenged the authority and competency of the Meiji government. It was an even more bitter pill for the French, for they had tacitly supported the bakufu until Yoshinobu's surrender of power, and now found themselves embroiled in a crisis with a government they barely tolerated. Perhaps aware of the dangers, Meiji officials quickly arrested twenty Tosa samurai as the perpetrators of the slaughter, overriding Tosa charges that the French had brought the attack upon themselves by their "barbaric" behavior in the port.[11]

Capital punishment was, in the minds of the French, the only proper response to this crime. The first of Roches's conditions for reparations thus demanded the beheading of the Tosa samurai "in the presence of Japanese officials and French sailors at the spot where the violence occurred," that is, the beach at Sakai.[12] Such a punishment, as Roches knew, would brand the Tosa soldiers as common criminals, for samurai were still allowed to commit seppuku, and only commoners were beheaded. Moreover, dragging them back to the scene of the crime and executing them at the beach would further compound their disgrace.

Two days of negotiation between Roches and Higashikuze resulted in a compromise. To mollify the French, the Tosa twenty were to die; to placate samurai feeling as much as possible, they would be allowed to commit seppuku. In a symbolic concession to Japanese feelings, the ceremony would take place at a temple in Kobe, albeit in front of the French minister and top French naval officials in Japan.[13]

With agreement reached, the suicides were scheduled for March 16. One by one, in order of rank and age, the Tosa samurai disemboweled themselves. As the eleventh man took his own life, however, Roches halted the ceremony, begging clemency for the remaining nine. Despite the standing imperial order of suicide, these last were sentenced to internal exile in Tosa, saved by Roches's particular notions of Christian charity and Western punishment.[14]

Through its quick responses, the imperial government had headed off a potentially disastrous encounter with the West. But the Kobe and Sakai attacks were further proof of the continued domestic dissent that threatened to undercut the government's authority over foreign affairs. The leaders realized they would need a more dramatic demonstration of their control over internal elements and their desire to have pacific relations with the West. Iwakura decided on the most symbolic gesture possible: opening up to Western representatives the inner sanctum of Japan, Kyoto and its emperor.

Western diplomats personally had met the Tokugawa shogun on only a handful of occasions during their ten-year relationship. For adherents to the imperial cause, it was anathema even to consider allowing a barbarian into the sacred presence. Undeterred, Iwakura pushed ahead with the audience, aware of its importance and the fact that it fit the international realities facing the government. The meeting would serve to assert the new ideology in Japan, that of imperial authority over domestic and foreign affairs alike. Yet, in that it accepted the need to treat directly with the West, it reflected a new culture coming into being.

In late March, French Minister Roches and British Minister Parkes and their parties arrived in the imperial capital for the first formal visit to that city by Western diplomats. The centerpiece of this precedent-setting encounter was an audience with the young emperor, Mutsuhito, who was to confirm for the Westerners that Japan was fully under his control. Roches was given the honor of first audience on March 23. In a scene reminiscent of Harris's first meeting with the shogun Iesada back in 1857, the French minister entered a reception hall where the emperor was surrounded by key advisers and hidden behind a screen. Despite its epoch-making nature, the official diary of the emperor noted laconically only that the French minister came before the sovereign and recorded the brief speech given by Meiji and the slightly longer one by Roches.[15]

Apart from Iwakura's goals, the audiences were symbolic another way, as well, for they exposed the real feelings of nonelite Japanese toward foreigners. As Parkes rode to the imperial palace the same day for his meeting, a disgruntled rōnin brutally attacked his procession. Parkes for a second time barely escaped injury, though his groom and a number of men in his party were wounded. Undeterred, he completed the audience three days later and, duly impressed with the ceremony in his honor, reported to Foreign Secretary Lord Edward Stanley that the emperor "has now for the first time, placed himself in communication with the outer world. . . . The etiquette observed upon the occasion conformed as closely as circumstances would admit to that which obtains at European Courts."[16] Iwakura had made a successful statement that the emperor would engage the West and would work to form a viable relationship with foreigners.

Politically, however, Parkes was still bound by the Alcock neutrality doctrine. With civil war brewing, he and the other representatives issued orders to their citizens that Tokugawa Yoshinobu and the emperor were to be considered equal belligerents, and thus not to be supported either way, despite the treaty powers' acceptance of imperial control over Japan's foreign relations.

The Meiji leaders thus were caught between domestic and foreign pressure, just as the bakufu had been. Despite their assertion of imperial authority and the attempt to recast the nature of Japan's relations with the treaty powers, it was clear that further attacks like the ones in early 1868 could bring down Western wrath. However, being seen as kowtowing to foreigners could embolden anti-imperial forces. Throughout the year, Ōkubo, Saigō, and Kido were preoccupied with defeating Tokugawa resistance and, having expeditiously handled the Kobe and Sakai incidents, temporarily let foreign relations assume a secondary importance (other than ensuring that Westerners observed their neutrality policy). Yet by the end of that year, foreign affairs again erupted into view, pushing the Meiji leaders to question their assumptions about international relations and spurring the emergence of a new worldview.[17]

New International Ideas and Diplomatic Missteps, 1868–1869

Sanjō, Ōkubo, Iwakura, and the other leaders quickly discovered, like the Tokugawa before them, that the Western international system operated according to its own set of norms. Though they had abandoned their early stance advocating expulsion, they had not dropped the idea of maintaining the bakufu's boundaries between Japanese and Westerners. Yet this policy, identical in many ways to the long-standing Tokugawa strategy, was challenged initially by the opening of Kobe and Osaka, and more so by the expansion of the treaty structure within Japan.

The new leaders soon came to understand that once a state entered into treaty relations with one country, it was all but impossible to avoid further pacts. The Western treaty system they had entered was an outgrowth of the European nation-state experience, itself influenced by the geopolitical conditions on the European continent where numerous autonomous bodies were contiguously arranged. European states considered it natural to sign treaties with many neighbors, for they could not avoid continuous economic, political, and social relations.

Moreover, a treaty system or structure that encompassed all these oft-times competing states, and that provided both norms of conduct and the mechanisms to ensure compliance with the system, was a natural outgrowth of the increasingly complex relations developing on the continent. For larger powers, such as Britain or Russia, a treaty structure designed to their liking could help preserve their privileges and position; for smaller powers, being enrolled in a treaty system meant protection against powerful neighbors and the chance to participate in major political and economic exchanges. This was the dynamic tension animating and preserving the Vienna system throughout the nineteenth century.[18]

The situation in Asia, however, was historically and culturally quite different. Japan was an archipelago, which up to the 1850s independently chose the limits of its foreign relations with noncontiguous political entities. After Perry, the Tokugawa had accepted signing the initial Ansei treaties with a limited number of European states that regularly acted in East Asia, either on sea or land.

Yet the nature of the European treaty system, which reflected the nature of Europe's economic life, led in East Asia to the creation of links between states that did not have an obvious economic or political relationship. States in Europe could not choose isolation because all polities participated in the same interlocked system of international agreements. This pattern spread to Asia, and thus, after the initial five treaties, the Tokugawa found themselves concluding agreements with minor European powers such as Portugal (1860), Belgium (1866), and Denmark (1867), pacts that the Meiji government honored with the original five Ansei signatories.[19]

Following the incidents of March 1868, diplomatic affairs quieted down. Starting in November, however, the Meiji leaders felt constrained to sign four additional treaties within the space of a year. The first two pacts, both in that month, were concluded with Spain and with the joint kingdom of Sweden and Norway. These were in essence nothing more than continuations of Tokugawa-era treaties, as Higashikuze Michitomi simply adopted the template of existing agreements, substituted the emperor for the shogun in the text, and with no government debate, signed them on his own authority.[20] They were thus all but bakufu instruments.[21] Yet the Swedish treaty failed to include a provision for a consul, which Higashikuze did not seem to understand would cause problems in controlling Swedish citizens in Japan, who were not bound by Japanese law. In addition, he accepted the regular Tokugawa commitment to shoulder the expense of building a legation for treaty partners, further proof that this agreement was merely a bakufu pact signed by a new domestic power.

After nearly a year of running port affairs, officials in Tokyo, as Edo had been renamed in September 1868, were beginning to understand the problems once faced by the bakufu.[22] Neither side was satisfied with the treaty regime, not that either ever had been. Western representatives continued to grouse about the lack of stable coinage exchange, and argued that obstinate Japanese officials and unfair charges marred the bonded warehouse system established under the 1866 Tariff Convention. On the Japanese side, Tokyo desired to resign all the bakufu treaties, replacing the shogun's name with the emperor's. Nonetheless, the Meiji leaders initially hewed to the bakufu's traditional strategy of tolerating Westerners yet steadily working for their continued isolation and eventual expulsion.

By the end of the first year of Meiji, the civil war in Japan had all but been decided in favor of the new government, and the Western powers ended their neutrality policy by recognizing the emperor as the lawful political authority. This recognition allowed the Meiji leaders to resume normal diplomacy, now having the full support of the treaty powers. This, in turn, meant resuming the long history of negotiating with the West.[23]

In early 1869, the Foreign Office, the *Gaikokukan,* took the first steps to imprint the new government's stamp on treaty relations. At the end of January, it sent an order to the administrators of all the open ports and cities requesting reports on how trading mechanisms were working. Any recommendations would be used to make changes in the treaties after a preparatory Foreign Office conference.[24] Four days after dispatching this order, Higashikuze sent notes to foreign representatives requesting revision of the treaties, noting that due to "the unprecedented reforms [lately undertaken], the Treaties we have signed with you have become unjust in name and reality."[25] Though Higashikuze's primary goal seemed to be altering the names on the treaties, the January 31 order hinted at broader revision goals. He hesitantly was groping toward a new foreign policy, in which revision would lead to greater control over foreigners. It seems premature, though, to see in this February 4 note to Western representatives the true start of the treaty revision movement.

Given the Foreign Office's desire to examine the administrative structure of the trading ports, Tokyo's experience in concluding its next treaty only highlighted the inflexible nature of the West. Higashikuze had been in talks with the Prussian minister, Max August Scipio von Brandt, regarding a treaty with the North German Confederation, which would supersede the Japanese–Prussian treaty of 1861. When he sent the diplomats the circular note regarding revision, Higashikuze also asked von Brandt to postpone signing their proposed treaty in order to revise it.[26]

Von Brandt ignored the plea and forced Higashikuze to conclude the treaty on February 20, 1869. Moreover, the German gave the Meiji leaders yet another taste of the united Western front that had challenged the Tokugawa, replying that "when other countries agree to negotiations over revision, then we will, also."[27] Three weeks later, on March 15, the Meiji Supreme Executive Council officially ordered the Foreign Office to prepare for treaty revision, although again no specifics were cited. Part of this momentum may have come from the timetable included in the treaties, through which either party could call for renegotiation after July 1872.

The Swedish treaty, von Brandt's arrogance, and a vague Japanese desire for revision were some of the mounting foreign issues confronting the Meiji leaders in the spring of 1869. Part and parcel of these concerns was the leaders' desire to understand the international system and Japan's place in it. In these early days, their thinking did not differ substantially from that shown by Tokugawa Yoshinobu at the end of his rule, namely, that Japan was part of an international structure and could not act as though in a vacuum. However, their thoughts soon would evolve, with the expanded access to foreign information and the slow impact of years of translating foreign materials. This general momentum was pushed forward by the existence within the Meiji bureaucracy of many of the bakufu's former leading international specialists, particularly those from the Institute for the Study of Barbarian Books.

Within the top echelon of leaders, Iwakura Tomomi left the clearest, and one of the earliest, statements about the new leadership's understanding of the nature of treaty relations and the types of reform that Japan needed.

In late March 1869, less than a month after von Brandt's curt dismissal of Higashikuze's request for postponement, Iwakura sent a long memorandum to Sanjō Sanetomi that dealt at length with foreign affairs.[28] This letter, more than any other early Meiji document, marked the intellectual beginning of revision.

Iwakura's dissatisfaction was not with the existence of treaty relations per se, but rather with the specific treaties inherited from the Tokugawa. Drawing together the strands of Tokyo's experience during the past months, he prescribed a dual policy of securing public approval of treaty relations, while at the same time renegotiating the pacts: "When the Tokugawa opened relations with foreign countries, [it was not addressed] whether this was good for the country or bad; after all, three or four Great and Senior Councillors concluded the treaties based on their fear of the foreign threat; they gained a day's peace, but among their numerous failures were deceiving the Imperial Court and lying to the people." However, he continued, treaties themselves are based on natural law, and thus "the good and bad [of treaties] must be decided based on reason, then when one wants to rely on military force, war can be decisively embarked upon."

Iwakura finally turned to specific grievances and outlined a nascent revision policy:

We must defend our imperial country's independence by revising the trade treaties we recently concluded with Great Britain, France, Holland, America, and other countries. Currently, foreign countries' troops have landed in our ports, and when resident foreigners break our law, they are punished by their countries' officials. It can be said that this is our country's greatest shame.[29]

Iwakura had articulated two distinct grievances, each being the concern of different aspects of international law. The first, the basing of troops in Japan, he viewed as a matter of pure force, and thus unjust even if supported by those tenets of international law that covered the temporary protection of a state's citizens in foreign lands. Western troops had been in Japan for nearly half a decade and, though reduced in number, showed no signs of leaving. Iwakura was setting forth an argument that Western "international law" was merely a cover for the use of imperialist force. International law, according to Iwakura, who echoed an argument made by Henry Wheaton, was based on positive law, in essence the agreement among states of principles of right action. But this agreement, of course, had taken place only among the Christian nations of Europe and did not attempt to take into account the experiences or needs of non-European nations. If no higher law, no natural order, existed, then international law was simply a tool for the strong to control the weak.[30]

Regarding the second issue, extraterritoriality, Iwakura's letter provided the first specific evidence of a changing attitude toward the practice. It will be recalled that the Tokugawa had not considered it an inherent evil, but rather a traditional way of holding foreigners responsible for their own affairs, and one fully sanctioned by international custom. While few sensational consular cases had yet developed, Iwakura's criticism of extraterritoriality was based on the interpretation that it existed not by "special compact" between Japan and Western nations, as approved by theorists such as Wheaton, but rather that it was imposed.[31] At the very core of Iwakura's argument lay a Western notion of sovereignty, brought to Japan by its international experience.

Iwakura's letter clearly was not a mere intellectual exercise, but had real and immediate policy implications. In arguing that extraterritoriality and the basing of foreign troops in Japan could be ended only through a substantial rewriting of the Ansei treaties, the letter broke through the years of bakufu reticence and pushed the old Tokugawa strategy beyond its tactic of negotiating moderate changes in treaties or erecting new boundaries. Iwakura's feeling had no doubt been intensified in previous months by a Western note of July 1868 informing the Meiji leaders that French and British troops would, at least temporarily, take a more prominent position in defending Yokohama, due to uncertainty over the course of the civil war.

Yet Iwakura's letter was not limited simply to analyzing Japan's international relations. It clearly reflected a Meiji concern with pacifying public opinion—meaning the mid- and upper-level samurai ranks on whose support the government depended. It is unlikely that Iwakura was serious about using military force against the West, at least in the short term, but he was phrasing his argument in terms amenable to that important sector of the public. Moreover, in urging Sanjō to discuss these issues at court, Iwakura anticipated an imminent government plan to engage just those samurai in such issues. This, of course, was a major departure from the bakufu culture of restricting any type of outside interference in policy-making. The Meiji leaders had used public opinion to help oust the Tokugawa, and did not want to fall victim to their own tactic.

Accordingly, the first point of the Meiji Five Charter Oath, issued a year earlier, on April 6, 1868, had proclaimed, "An assembly widely convoked shall be established and all matters of state shall be decided by public discussion."[32] As part of the ongoing attempt to co-opt disparate samurai elements, the Meiji leaders had created a deliberative body of approximately two hundred mid-ranking samurai from every domain, called the *Kōgisho*. Opened on April 18, 1869, it was the second such body and was superseded only four months later by yet another deliberative group. Yet in its short lifetime, it heard and debated various issues relating to both domestic and foreign policy.[33]

In its first two months, the Kōgisho directly considered the nature and future of Japan's treaty relations when the government presented it with two memorials on the international situation. The two memorials, divided into four and seventeen articles respectively, were prepared by the Foreign Office and published in the Kōgisho's in-house journal, *Kōgisho nisshi*, both being submitted May 28, 1869.[34] The first memorial was concerned solely with currency matters, ranging from the indemnities owed to the West that had been carried over from the Tokugawa era, to exchange rates and counterfeiting. The second was broader in scope, and it summed up the totality of the foreign situation in early 1869.

Its seventeen articles were modeled on the famous seventh-century "Seventeen Article Injunction" that served as the first expression of

Japanese political principles. Article 1 opened with a recapitulation of the range of views in Japan over foreign affairs:

> The question of opening or closing [the country] has from long ago until now been greatly discussed [with various opinions]: the foreigners are birds and beasts to whom we should not get close; or, as we are not yet strong and rich [*fukoku kyōhei*], we should take their riches to supply our needs and then expel them; or, we should fully change our teachings to the Western style, and open schools of Western technology, then, having diligently trained in gunnery, sweep them out; or, we should cut down all foreigners. Such arguments continue even today. If [Japan] is to open up, should we continue relations as now or should we construct a different path?

Subsequent articles concerned the antiforeign movement that was represented in the Kōgisho, the nature of international relations, and the question of pursuing a Western or an Asian path, which would be decided by whether Japan maintained the open ports as the nexus of the two cultures.[35] Finally, the Foreign Office urged the Kōgisho to choose either peace or war once and for all, having emphasized the necessity of strengthening Japan and not provoking Westerners in the near future, and warning that to relax for even one step would be to invite disaster.

While neither the *Kōgisho nisshi* nor the Foreign Office archives record a direct response to this memorandum, it was a signal document in illuminating the government's thinking during early Meiji. The Foreign Office documents presented before the Kōgisho revealed that early Meiji foreign policy was far from being a settled issue and that the leaders indeed did not yet know how they ultimately would conduct relations with the West. The Foreign Office clearly was concerned about the continuing antiforeign sentiment and acts of violence against Westerners, particularly in the wake of the Kobe and Sakai incidents.

A further significance of the memorial lay in its very existence, suggesting that the leaders now accepted, if grudgingly, that foreign affairs was a legitimate issue for this modestly defined "public realm." Abe Masahiro's polling of the daimyō regarding Perry back in 1853 had been the first acknowledgement that any response to the threat from the West required the support of the national elite. The Meiji leaders did not want to make the same mistake Ii Naosuke had, by trying to close that door once it was opened.

The document repeatedly referred to foreign troops stationed in Japan, primarily in Yokohama, but also Kobe. By May 1866, the British had pulled out the majority of their marines, and in early 1869, only several hundred European troops were in Japan, not the three thousand claimed by the Foreign Office. Nonetheless, the office rued that "it is an unheard of situation for foreign troops, according to international law, to be established anywhere other than a country's own colonies" (Article 11).[36] Domestic resentment of foreign troops was potentially as dangerous to the government as elite demand to have a voice in the issues of the day.

By far, most Kōgisho samurai were conservative and held major reservations about the wisdom of opening Japan to unfettered foreign influence.[37] As with its older Western counterparts, the Kōgisho preferred to avoid a clear-cut decision, and the government was, undoubtedly to its relief, free to craft a policy on its own. Ōkubo, Iwakura, and the others had no intention, of course, of broadening the actual sphere of decision-making, but they recognized that such issues had to be discussed in councils broader than just the ruling elite. This, of course, was a far cry from true popular representation or participation, but it nonetheless reflected the slow expansion of civil society in early Meiji.

Iwakura's concerns about the existing treaty system, and the Kōgisho's reservations about foreign relations were exacerbated by the fourth treaty the Meiji government was forced to sign with a Western nation. Just five months after the Kōgisho received the seventeen articles, the new Austro-Hungarian monarchy concluded a trade treaty with Japan. The Japanese negotiators were Sawa Nobuyoshi, foreign minister (*gaimukyō*) of the newly organized Foreign Ministry (*Gaimushō*), and Vice Minister Terajima Munenori, both of whom had prior experience in the Foreign Office. The pact, which they and the Austrian representative Baron Anthony Petz signed on October 18, 1869, altered previous treaties on the issues of residence and mobility rights, extraterritoriality, and certain tariff regulations.[38]

The agreement represented, in many respects, a major break in the treaty structure and it directly challenged the basis of trade relations set up more than a decade before. A crucial change concerned the physical boundaries of the treaty system. Article 3 breached those boundaries by adding a port on the island of Sado as a trading site.[39] In addition, the right of Japanese authorities to determine the sites of

Austrian residences was circumscribed, being reserved primarily to Austrian officials. More important and symbolic, Sawa and Terajima widened the travel boundaries for the Austrians, delineating areas in Osaka and Tokyo where mobility was permitted, a subject on which previous treaties had been silent.

Earlier treaties had been equally vague on the boundaries of Japanese authority over problems that seemed to lie in both Western and Japanese jurisdiction. For example, it was unclear who would resolve physical altercations among foreigners that occurred outside the settlements or adjudicate disputes over property bought by Westerners outside the ports (but within the twenty-five-mile travel limit). Article 5 of the Austrian treaty ended any Japanese authority over such cases: "All questions in regard to rights, whether of property or of person, arising between Austro-Hungarian citizens residing in Japan shall be subject to the jurisdiction of the imperial and Royal Authorities. In like manner, the Japanese Authorities shall not interfere in any question which may arise between Austro-Hungarian citizens and the subjects of any other Treaty Power."[40] Moreover, consular jurisdiction was now extended to cases involving both Japanese and Austrians, a change from the Ansei treaties and further confirmation of Iwakura's argument that extraterritoriality was an unfair constraint put on Japan by European powers who avoided such treatment toward each other.

The treaty also included significant changes in trade regulations. Numerous tariff alterations were made, filling in lacunae in other treaties, always to the detriment of the Japanese treasury. Article 9 settled the long-standing problem of whether foreigners could land cargo at an open port and then re-export it to another port with no duty payment. This was now allowed, as was the right of Austrians to "ship all kinds of Japanese produce bought in one of the open ports in Japan to another open port in Japan without the payment of any duty" (Article 11). This article thus opened up the lucrative field of coastal shipping to the Austrians, which had hitherto been kept solely in Japanese hands. Article 12 weakened the Japanese ability to levy internal taxes, stipulating that all imported goods, on which duties had been paid, could be transported by either Austro-Hungarians or Japanese (whoever was the owner) "into any part of the Japanese Empire without the payment of any tax or transit duty whatever."

Minor changes addressed problems long-plaguing treaty relations, primarily coinage (Article 16) and physical improvements to harbor facilities (Article 17). Foreign coin was to be exchanged freely at the mint for Japanese coin of equal value, and either foreign or Japanese coin could be used for purchases. Left unresolved was whether to value Japanese coin by weight or constituent metal, a problem dating back to Harris and the original 1858 treaties. Tokyo, further, accepted for the first time the considerable expense of erecting lighthouses, lights, buoys, and beacons in the port areas, although the government had already hired a Scottish engineer, Richard Brunton, to take charge of these and other vital construction projects.[41]

The changes in the Austro-Hungarian treaty mattered, of course, not because Austria-Hungary was a major trading partner, but because they accrued to all fourteen other treaty powers through the most-favored-nation (MFN) clause. Britain and France could now compete for domestic shipping, the tariff revisions benefited all the powers, and foreigners obtained more freedom of movement than ever before in the major cities of Osaka and Tokyo—this last point being a line in the sand once defended by the bakufu but now surrendered by the imperial government. Those concessions of October 1869 were clear examples of the grievances voiced earlier in the year by Iwakura, and they added urgency to the question of overall relations earlier raised by the Foreign Office in the seventeen articles memorial.

From an international perspective, the Austro-Hungarian treaty moved Japan firmly toward the conditions that Great Britain had imposed on China in the 1858 Tianjin Treaty. Though it did not lose a war, and thereby suffer an imposed settlement, the Meiji government was nonetheless negotiating away Japan's autonomy to a greater degree than had the bakufu. In response to Tokyo's diplomatic weakness, elements of the Meiji revision policy would slowly coalesce in the coming months.

Feeling for a New Path: Preparation for Revision, 1870–1871

During the two years following the signing of the Austro-Hungarian treaty, the Japanese increased their planning for eventual revision. At the same time, they confronted unexpected Western demands to renegotiate after July 1872, the earliest the treaties could officially be changed. Ultimately, the pace of revision was taken out of Tokyo's hands, forcing it to modify its strategy and timetable.

During 1870, planning for treaty revision took a back seat to domestic politics, and preparation for the task was concomitantly limited. In May, approximately half a year after concluding the Austro-Hungarian treaty, the Foreign Ministry conceived a plan to study Great Britain's various treaties and international agreements. This seemed to be a natural outgrowth of the circulation in Japan of works on Western international law, in which the various features of treaties were minutely discussed and exceptions to the norm analyzed.[42] The idea behind the plan was that such a study would be a guide to uncovering specific discrepancies between the principles that Western nations included in treaties among themselves and those they imposed on Japan.

This was a complex proposal, because the Foreign Ministry made no claim that Japan was an equal in power or political tradition to Western nations. Instead, the proposal harked back to the general concept of the law of nations and the logic inherent in treaty negotiations that Iwakura had spoken of in his 1869 memorandum. This was made clear by the ministry's statement that "although the governmental systems of the Western countries that have made treaties with each other are different from the [systems of the] various Asian nations, nonetheless, referring to those treaties will provide a basis for discussion" of revision.[43]

This argument acknowledged the diverse nature of states, yet claimed that careful legal analysis could benefit precisely those countries (in this case Asian) whose political and social structures varied considerably from the Western nations that had created the framework of the treaty system. The underlying premise was that inhering in the Western treaty system itself was a general logic, based on natural law, and that to identify discrepancies between this logic and reality could be the wedge for conforming the Japan treaties to the treaty ideal.

Six months later, in November, Sawa and Terajima at the Foreign Ministry established a special "office for dealing with treaty revision"[44] and charged it with undertaking a complete analysis of the revision problem. The office was given five months, until April 1871, in which to complete its investigation. Its members would then participate in a joint conference of all the major government ministries to finalize a revision policy. Negotiations with foreign consuls were to commence the following month, in May, though the Foreign Ministry understood that the actual parleys would not necessarily be easy, noting that "for every two articles we remove, they will seek to add five."[45]

The entire plan rested on the strength of the revision proposals. The Foreign Ministry fell behind schedule, but by June 1871 the special office had completed a draft treaty under the leadership of Kanda Kōhei and Tsuda Mamichi.[46] Both had served in the Tokugawa bakufu's Institute for the Study of Barbarian Books, and Tsuda also had studied abroad in Leiden with Nishi Amane in the mid-1860s and was soon to become a forceful advocate of judicial and prison reform.[47] Kanda and Tsuda also were later to be members of the influential society of Meiji intellectuals, the *Meirokusha*. Neither man, however, had extensive diplomatic experience.

Kanda and Tsuda decided on a measured path for revision, arguing for a gradual alteration of various deficiencies in the treaties. They settled on six main goals. The first was to maintain the prohibition on free travel in the interior except for diplomats. Second, they hoped to obtain Western agreement for Japanese officials to take over total administration of the open ports and foreign settlements. Third, they wanted to overturn the Austrian treaty and end Western shipping between open ports, while the fourth goal was to collect duties on Japanese goods shipped from the interior for export. Fifth, they tackled the question of Japanese legal authority by proposing mixed consular courts for criminal and civil cases. Finally, they sought to make the MFN clause reciprocal for Japan. In conclusion, the two argued that revision negotiations should be postponed for three to five years to allow Japan to begin its development, so as to present Westerners a more modern face across the negotiating table.[48]

Despite the fact that it advocated a gradualist approach to revision, the Kanda–Tsuda draft was a milestone in the development of a new Meiji strategy and reflected the emergence in certain circles of a distinct diplomatic culture. First and foremost, Tsuda and Kanda based their argument on political reality, stressing that Japan was far less "developed" than its European treaty partners, and thus could not seek revision based on a law of nations argument. This was a confirmation that the law of nations, and from it the treaty structure, was firmly anchored in Western political traditions, and therefore applicable primarily to those states sharing the attributes of advanced Western nations. Second, the draft argued by implication that the treaty regime was now more inequitable due to the changes brought about by the pact with Austria-Hungary. In particular, the provisions to limit interior travel to diplomats, to end coastal shipping, to collect transshipment duties, and to obtain reciprocal MFN status resulted from a desire to overturn changes that had accrued to each treaty power.

From this standpoint, it was natural to conclude that revision would follow some level of Japanese westernization, a specific identification of development with the European model. There was no greater contrast with the Tokugawa bakufu than this stark assertion, and indeed it was antithetical to the bakufu's whole strategy. This viewpoint was particularly evident in the call for mixed consular courts, which would require a major, if not revolutionary, change in Japanese legal codes, far beyond what the Meiji government was proposing during the drafting of new laws in 1869 and 1870.[49] Such a broad policy reorientation required breathing space in which Japan could plan and begin its "development." Despite the comprehensive nature of the draft, the Foreign Ministry did not release it, undoubtedly fearing that traditionalist elements, such as the samurai of the old Kōgisho, would rebel in dissatisfaction. Despite these concerns, the draft was a skillful melding of a new strategy with elements of the old.

The key challenges to the Kanda–Tsuda plan, however, came from inside the government. One of the most influential came in the spring of 1871 from a leading junior member of the oligarchy, Itō Hirobumi. Itō, a Finance Ministry official, had been studying banking and economic policy in the United States since late 1870. A Chōshū samurai, he had played only a minor role in the restoration, but the new leaders early on noted his promise.[50]

Itō was assigned to the Finance Ministry and was representative of the modernizing mind-set prevalent there. He was allied with Ōkuma Shigenobu, head of the ministry, who was perhaps the leading advocate of Western-style reforms. Ōkuma's own patron was Kido Kōin, Ōkubo Toshimichi's main political rival. Ōkuma and Itō planned to reform Japan's taxation system and harness it to a newly centralized local government structure. This goal put them at odds with Ōkubo, who favored an approach more sympathetic to local domainal concerns as a means to prevent any of those domains from opposing the new government. The tension between the two groups was exacerbated by the incorporation of the Ministry of Civil Affairs within the Finance Ministry in the autumn of 1869. This greatly expanded the reach of the modernizing bureaucrats and extended their influence down to the domainal level. The new power of Ōkuma forced Ōkubo first to split the two ministries and then reamalgamate them under his personal control in August 1871. Itō's memorandum on revision thus had serious implications for domestic as well as foreign policy, and it revealed the breach within the Meiji leadership.

Itō's studies in the States had convinced him of the importance of focusing on the economic inequalities of the treaties, and not on the political weaknesses, as had Iwakura two years previously. In Itō's American-influenced view, the Meiji leaders had been right all along to adopt as their slogan, "Rich Country, Strong Army," for a vigorous economy would lead to national strength and the ability to deal with the West on its own terms. In early spring 1871, the thirty-year-old Itō revealed the lessons he learned abroad, sending a long memorandum to top Meiji leaders that argued for a major revision in the tariff structure inherited from the Tokugawa.

In this letter of April 18, Itō urged that Japan "adopt a protective tariff like that of the United States, which will allow our production to flourish; then, having achieved that, we can follow the British example of supporting free trade."[51] Further, Japan should reform its monetary policy and establish a national bank to stabilize economic transactions and keep control over capital investments. Finally, Itō argued that Japan needed to send its best officials to the West to discuss revision and learn how Western nations had raised themselves to greatness.

Given Itō's later prominence in the government, it is easy to overrate the importance of his memorandum. It is incontestable, however, that it was influential in framing the goals of revision, as tariff reform became a major tenet of the Foreign Ministry's policy in mid-1871. Itō's primary contribution to the emerging debate over revision was thus to offer the first major challenge to the existing tariff system. Tariff rates had not been a major concern of the bakufu when it negotiated the 1858 treaties, being seen as secondary to the goal of maintaining various boundaries vis-à-vis the West (see chapter 5). By 1866, however, some bakufu officials had become influenced by then-current Western free trade arguments, and they put forth differing plans to lower duties as a way to expand trade and increase government revenue.

Itō, however, broke with late-Tokugawa thinking by placing tariffs, not territorial integrity, at the center of Japan's treaty system, thereby investing them with an importance hitherto lacking. He was particularly influenced by the United States, whose protective tariff had reached a general level of 47 percent by 1869. Although by 1872 the tariff on all manufactures was to fall to 10 percent, Itō was familiar with immediate post-Civil War America and argued for applying similar policies to Japan. Tariffs were important to Itō because he argued that Japan was irreversibly enmeshed in a global economic system in which the British in particular sought "free trade" for their own benefit, not Japan's. Merely limiting the presence of Westerners was an unrealistic strategy, one that would keep Japan weak. This was an intellectual nail in the coffin of the old Tokugawa style of diplomacy, and as much a harbinger of a new culture as the thoughts of Kanda and Tsuda. For Itō, the new world was in many ways an economic one, and he believed that Japan had to build up its productive base radically, for that was what made Western nations strong and thus able to defend themselves.

Based on the differences between the Kanda–Tsuda plan and the Itō proposals, Tokyo now faced a strategic choice: Would it follow to its logical conclusion the Tokugawa policy of boundary maintenance combined with gradual westernization, as reflected in the Foreign Ministry draft, or would it embrace a wholly new policy, by mandating substantial change at home in an effort to become an equal to the Western powers themselves, as urged by Itō? The Meiji leaders chose to equivocate, attempting to meld the two approaches, thereby keeping one foot tentatively in the diplomatic tradition started by the bakufu.

The fruits of this approach became apparent almost at once. In late April 1871, Terajima Munenori, who had become Tokyo's point man on revision, presented a preliminary list of demands to British minister Harry Parkes. The list included Itō's goal to revise tariff schedules as well as the Kanda–Tsuda proposals to modify the regulations for the foreign settlements. Terajima, who would serve as foreign minister from 1873 to 1878, was fast becoming the most important official in the ministry and he guided the formation of this preliminary list.

The pace of relations, however, was soon taken out of Terajima's hands. Treaty revision was an earnest goal of the Meiji leaders, but they also saw it as a long-term process. The official draft of Kanda and Tsuda had, as noted above, recommended a three- to five-year postponement of revision, thus acknowledging that Japan was in a weak position to make any extensive demands on foreign countries. For that very reason, perhaps, Western diplomats wanted treaty changes made as soon as possible. In May 1871, the U.S. and British ministers informed Tokyo of their countries' desire to seek revision.[52] The other treaty powers soon followed suit. Terajima, Sawa, and other top leaders now understood that revision was no longer a one-sided game, for Westerners would undoubtedly push their own timetable and seek to expand their trading rights in ways that could prove detrimental to Japan.

To British diplomats, revision meant far less than to the Japanese. It was a nuts-and-bolts process of garnering better trading conditions, and had no political or cultural importance. They went about the business of planning by canvassing the opinion of their nationals in the treaty ports. At the same time that Parkes had sent his letter to Sawa and Terajima, he addressed a circular to the primary British merchants in Yokohama, Osaka, and Hyogo, asking for their opinions on revision. The Osaka and Hyogo merchants replied that they favored a system similar to that operating in China, whereby they would have the right to trade anywhere in Japan, as well as the ability to travel in the interior. Unsurprisingly, they did not favor the opening of additional ports, preferring to maintain their monopoly over trade.[53]

Other Western diplomats placed more importance on revision. Parkes's initial stab at formulating a policy coincided with the presentation of a detailed plan by the German minister, Max August Scipio von Brandt. Envisioning an eventual joint Western call for negotiations, von Brandt wrote a long memorandum in May that went beyond anything yet considered by a Western representative. In many ways it looked to a transformation of Japan, a transformation designed to bolster Germany's trading position to be sure, but one that would lead to a different country. Its complexity and length led it to serve as the basis for future Western discussions of revision. In essence, it sought to efface the remaining physical and economic boundaries between Japanese and Westerners, though it did not call outright for abolition of the settlements.[54] Nonetheless, taken as a whole, the von Brandt plan would further deprive Tokyo of tariff autonomy, while dismembering the long-standing boundaries established by the Tokugawa.

Faced with these Western proposals for revision, Tokyo was edging closer to forming a concrete plan to send an embassy abroad to discuss treaty revision. This feeling was exacerbated when, after exchanging revision notification with the powers, Tokyo found itself negotiating yet another treaty, this time with the Hawaiian Kingdom, which was represented by the U.S. minister Charles De Long. The treaty, signed on August 19, allowed extraterritoriality for Hawaiians in Japan but not vice versa.[55] This treaty posed two problems for Tokyo. First, Meiji government thinking was moving away from confirming extraterritoriality as a given in bilateral relations, yet here it was granted to a minor kingdom. Second, since Japanese could now travel freely abroad, the continuing lack of extraterritorial rights for them, even in an island kingdom, raised both legal and moral questions. Given the vagaries of the MFN clause, it was conceivable that a precedent could be set not only for future pacts, but also that the Hawaiian treaty could adversely affect the renegotiation of existing ones. Combined with the changes effected by the Austro-Hungarian agreement, the balance of the treaty structure was more and more tilting against Japan.

The summer of 1871 was a delicate time for the Meiji leaders. Treaties were just part of the increasing pace of political change sweeping the land. Most important was the central domestic political reform undertaken by the government: the abolition of the domains and the establishment of the prefectural system, which was a crucial turning point in early Meiji politics.[56] Needless to say, Ōkubo, Iwakura, and other top Meiji leaders had no idea if their order would precipitate full-scale civil war, taking away as it did the power of the 250 or so domainal lords who still controlled vast numbers of armed samurai. The order was promulgated on August 29, the same day Iwakura Tomomi became foreign minister. By the autumn, the dissolution of the domains was a success and the government could relax its guard. Attention could turn back to the looming treaty revision scheduled for the following summer. By now, obtaining a postponement in revision was becoming the chief goal of top policymakers.

In mid-October, chief councillor Sanjō Sanetomi, the top-ranking Meiji official, sent a letter to Iwakura outlining the goals and dangers of treaty revision. Sanjō's letter reflected the fundamental changes that had taken place in the minds of the Meiji leaders since they had seized power three years previously. Sanjō clearly felt the existing treaties were one-sided, writing, "Although there exists a natural right of equality between nations, [our] treaties lack that equality." It was necessary, therefore, to overhaul the entire treaty structure, though "this is not something that can be finished in a day."[57] He did express hope for a favorable outcome in the upcoming revisions, but he supported the argument of lower officials such as Itō and Kanda that Japan needed to put domestic reform first, and thus required a delay in revision negotiations.[58]

The letter encapsulated the foreign policy thinking that had come to animate the Japanese government: the treaties were unfair and must change, but change at home was the key to gaining that goal. To this end, Sanjō argued that an embassy to the treaty powers should therefore be dispatched with three primary goals: to pay formal state visits, to discuss the Japanese goals for revision, and to engage in a detailed study of Western society and institutions. An ancillary goal was, of course, to gain postponement of the scheduled 1872 negotiations.

By the fall of 1871, then, the top Meiji leadership shared a common understanding of the world and Japan's place in it. They had agreed it was necessary to send a major embassy to the treaty powers as a first step to remaking Japan's position in the world. Their thinking, however, harked back to the bakufu's tactic of sending missions when attempting to secure agreements favorable to Japan. That tactic had a mixed record, succeeding in 1862 and failing two years later (see chapters 3 and 4). This latest plan seemed a safer bet, if only because it initially limited the scope of its negotiating activities to slowing down the pace of revision, and not in trying to impose a new plan on the treaty powers. The final two months before the embassy set sail in late December saw not only a flurry of diplomatic and organizational activity within Japan but also the planting of the seeds of confusion regarding the actual aims of the embassy.

Iwakura had decided to head up the mission himself, thus giving it the highest imprimatur, and he and Terajima began contacting major foreign representatives to discuss its goals. Twice during November, Iwakura met with F. O. Adams, who was in charge of the British legation while Parkes was back in England on leave. After their second meeting, Adams sent a note to Foreign Secretary Lord Granville, relaying the Japanese satisfaction that Parkes would be in London during Iwakura's visit and thus could aid the embassy in its objectives.[59] Iwakura was undoubtedly basing his expectations on his knowledge of how the Tokugawa had used Rutherford Alcock in London back in 1862.

In any case, Iwakura's messages to the British contained several problems, given Tokyo's stated goal of postponing negotiations for three to five years. The first problem was the apparent Japanese desire to fully discuss all points for revision. While this presumably was not the same as actual negotiation, there was no clear line drawn between simply informing the British of the specific Japanese grievances and discussing or resolving them. But clearly Tokyo did not intend the latter, for to enter into such discussions would be to place itself in precisely the unfavorable situation it hoped to avoid by postponing negotiations. This confusion over procedure was the result of Japanese unfamiliarity with the nuances of Western diplomacy, but Tokyo could not expect guidance from the treaty powers in this delicate issue.

A related problem was that while the British believed substantive negotiations on revision would start after the embassy had returned, perhaps in early 1873, Iwakura's messages through Adams did not make clear that Tokyo envisaged a three- to five-year delay. Parkes, it will be remembered, had made clear the British desire to seek revision as well, and there was no British talk of postponing the negotiations.

With these hidden problems growing, the court officially announced the planned embassy on November 20. Iwakura was to head it and to have the title of envoy extraordinary-ambassador plenipotentiary.[60] Four vice ambassadors were chosen: Ōkubo Toshimichi, Kido Kōin, Itō Hirobumi, and Yamaguchi Naoyoshi.[61]

Once the embassy had been announced, Terajima attempted to explain its goals to Adams more fully. Seeking to place it in a wider context, Terajima wrote that "the views and wishes of my Government are to render the friendly intercourse which exists at present with the Treaty Powers more intimate . . . we must conduct our internal reforms after the model of the systems in force in civilized countries, and consolidate this country into one whole." Then, he went on, Tokyo would undertake revision after carefully considering the information gained abroad.[62] Meanwhile, Iwakura sent a letter to the United States in which he specifically mentioned that the Japanese would discuss the situation of foreign troops in Japan and the issue of consular courts.[63]

On December 15, only two weeks before setting sail, however, Iwakura had secured from the court the "separate imperial instructions" that threatened to upset the carefully crafted government revision plan. These instructions included far-reaching provisions that, if

implemented, would fundamentally change the nature of treaty relations. The goals were to:

1. Abolish separate foreign settlements at the open ports and
   cities, and establish mixed residence within the ports.
2. Reject any further open ports or cities and not allow foreigners
   to live outside the current ones, but allow them interior travel
   based on a passport system.
3. Place foreigners under the jurisdiction of Japanese law and
   establish courts for both Japanese and foreigners based on
   Western law.
4. Establish a supreme court at Tokyo and local courts throughout Japan, and allow foreigners to sit as judges on the supreme
   court.
5. End the consular court system.
6. Incorporate both civil and criminal law in the new courts.[64]

These last-second instructions to Iwakura were a mix of plans both
reactionary and revolutionary. They also represented the boldest gamble
yet to secure equality with the treaty powers and thus ran counter to
the basic thinking that had guided the more cautious bureaucratic
plans drawn up in the Foreign Ministry. In essence, Iwakura had proceeded along a track independent of both the foreign and finance ministries. His plan could be traced to months of discussions held in private
with U.S. minister Charles De Long and an American legal consultant
to the Japanese government, Erasmus Peshine-Smith, and for which
few records were kept.

To at least some degree, the imperial instructions represented an
American plan for revision, in contradistinction to the "indigenous"
plan of Kanda and Tsuda. They focused on "modernizing" the Japanese law codes to bring them into conformity with what was seen as
civilized by the West. The introduction of an entirely new structure of
courts was in itself a centralizing tactic that would benefit the government, but it required a quick extension of Tokyo's bureaucratic apparatus throughout the country. The proposed legal changes would
also irreversibly eat away at the remaining status distinctions among
Japanese. This was a goal of the government, but to embark on it too
hastily could cause grave dissent from the samurai who were losing

their privileges. Moreover, from a negotiating standpoint, the instructions presented as provisions the very goals that Kanda and Tsuda, along with Sanjō, assumed could be achieved only after significant social, economic, legal, and political reform in Japan.

The clearest breaks with earlier plans involved extraterritoriality and foreign settlements. Until Iwakura's April 1869 letter, the former had been viewed as a necessity, perhaps even beneficial, to Japan. In the years after 1858, indeed, the primary complaints about extraterritoriality came from Western traders who believed they could not get justice under Japanese civil codes for fraudulent trades of which they were the victims.[65] Western diplomatic representatives, however, were not eager to give up the practice, convinced that the Japanese penal system was too arbitrary and cruel to subject their citizens to it.

Iwakura's 1868 ruminations on extraterritoriality had represented the first theoretical questioning of the policy by a top figure. After private discussions with De Long and Peshine-Smith, he had identified specific changes to be made in the extraterritorial system. These must be based above all on Western law, he understood, but implemented on the authority of the Japanese government. In fact, the reforms envisioned by Iwakura, De Long, and Peshine-Smith reflected the new consular system adopted in Egypt in October 1870, in which various Western laws were introduced and mixed courts were being tried out.

Equally radical were the changes the court proposed for foreign settlements, which were to be abolished. In their place, foreigners would be allowed to live side by side with Japanese, but only in the current open ports and cities. Moreover, free passage throughout Japan, subject to passport restrictions, would be granted to all foreign residents. This latter provision would have been a serious blow to the Tokugawa strategy of maintaining physical boundaries between Japanese and foreigners.

It is unclear to what extent Iwakura conferred with other Meiji leaders on the imperial instructions. His solitary discussions with De Long, however, were reported back to Washington, with the minister noting at several points that "Ewackura" agreed with him that all of Japan must be opened to trade and settlement.[66] It is hard to gauge how accurately De Long relayed Iwakura's opinions, but there had been no suggestion at all within the Meiji councils of such a far-reaching proposal, as far as the records show. The instructions symbolized, in their grandeur and isolation from the other policies of the government, a radically new diplomatic vision, one shared perhaps only by Iwakura and his American counterparts. However, if these were to be mere talking points reserved for eventual negotiation after a suitable delay, then they might not have seemed to conflict with the Foreign Ministry and Itō's plans as combined by Terajima Munenori.

As the Iwakura Mission prepared to sail from Yokohama on December 23, 1871, the Japanese leadership had come to a view of treaty relations substantially different from what had prevailed since 1858. The treaty regime had played an integral part in the early years of Meiji rule. On the foreign level, it had led the new leaders to reassess their views of Japan's international situation and to accept the reality of trade relations. At the domestic level, the continued anti-Western sentiment had forced Iwakura, Ōkubo, and their colleagues to strengthen central control, so as to prevent further attacks on foreigners like those in early 1868, and also pushed them into seeking advice on foreign questions from leading political segments of Japanese society, such as the samurai legislative body, the Kōgisho.

In these four years, a distinct Meiji diplomatic culture emerged. The existence in the new government of former bakufu diplomats and foreign officials assured that certain Tokugawa ideas, such as physical boundaries, remained a part of Meiji thinking. Yet the new leadership's own experience of treaty relations led to new concepts of how the treaties should be changed, and more important, how Japan needed to change to respond to the challenge of the West.

From mid-1871, extraterritoriality, tariffs, and MFN would constitute the core items of reform. The Tokugawa influence to maintain the limits on the number of open ports and cities accorded with Meiji thinking, for most of the leaders no more wanted to open Japan to an unregulated flood of foreigners than had their Tokugawa counterparts. In addition, Meiji leaders hoped to reverse concessions they had made, particularly in the 1869 Austro-Hungarian treaty. These included the new foreign right to undertake domestic shipping in Japan, the abolition of all transit taxes, and the trends toward unregulated travel and possibly residence in the interior. In certain ways, the Meiji goals were not so different in spirit from the proposals first made in 1857 by Iwase Tadanari, in his attempt to recenter bakufu foreign relations and regain control over those relations for both foreign and domestic reasons.

Although the Iwakura embassy was not officially invested with the power to sign any treaties, it was nonetheless about to present the major Western governments with specifics for discussion. The Japanese did not understand that for all purposes these appeared to be actual negotiating points, nor were they aware of the vagueness in their instructions separating talks from negotiations. Moreover, although Tokyo's policy was to delay formal negotiations for three to five years, the treaty powers, whose revision goals and timetables did not match those of the Japanese, only understood that Japan wished to postpone negotiating until after the embassy returned home. Perhaps most important, the embassy would be the first attempt by an Asian state to begin the process of substantive treaty renegotiation. The entire enterprise thus opened a whole new realm of political questions for the treaty powers. The possibilities were rife for miscommunication and confusion.

CHAPTER SEVEN

Negotiating the Future: The Iwakura Mission in America and Britain

Sailing away from Yokohama in December 1871, Iwakura Tomomi could not know that he was traversing not merely an ocean but also historical epochs. The policy of centralization pursued by Iwakura and his fellow leaders since 1868 had resolved certain immediate political problems, but it had not been designed to open the floodgates to radical social change. Nor did he see his embassy as a turning point in Japanese history, though it might have given him pause to realize that it was perhaps the first time since Peter the Great's peregrinations around Europe at the end of the seventeenth century that a nation's top leadership left for an extended journey to foreign lands. Yet a turning point it was, for far from being a coda to the story of treaty relations, the Iwakura Mission was irrevocably to bury the old diplomatic culture and give birth to a new era in Japan's international history.

The mission's port of embarkation itself was a symbol of the vast changes in Japan that had caused the dispatch of the top leaders. Yokohama's very existence, of course, was a direct result of the treaties. For nearly a decade, the old Tokugawa goal of maintaining boundaries between the Japanese and the Westerner had been slowly eroding, yet its framework still stood. As protecting those boundaries was a goal similarly shared by Iwakura and his compatriots, their worries grew commensurately with the size of the foreign population in Japan.

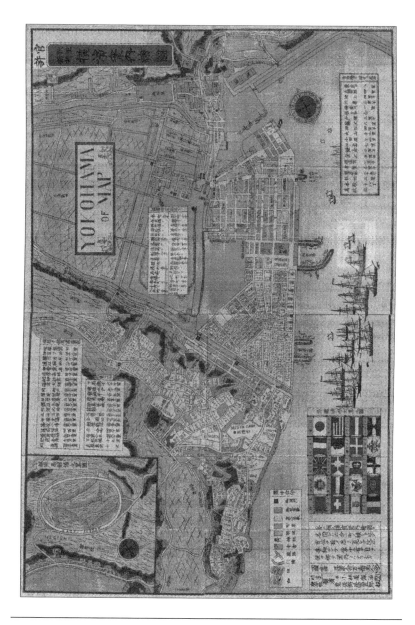

Map of Yokohama, 1870. Courtesy of the Map Collection, Sterling Memorial Library, Yale University.

A comparatively small Western contingent of more than one hundred permanent residents at Yokohama in 1861 had grown to almost 950 in 1870, including 513 British and 146 Americans.[1] Moreover, by 1870 some 10,000 seamen a year were visiting for varying lengths of time. This resulted in approximately 3,000 people residing in Yokohama at any given moment.[2] Such numbers inevitably meant the testing of treaty boundaries, unsanctioned Western travel into the interior, and ultimately complaints by both the bakufu and later the new imperial government.

In fact, as early as 1861, Rutherford Alcock had been pressured by the bakufu to enjoin British subjects from spending too much time with Japanese villagers and from lodging in towns other than Yokohama. As a result, Alcock had issued the "Rules and Regulations for the Peace, Order and Good Government of British subjects within the domains of the Tycoon of Japan" in late November 1861; it prohibited Britons from "taking up residence or sleeping during the night at any town or village away from the Foreign location at the Port where they are domiciled."[3] The rules were all but ignored over the succeeding decade. By the 1870s, the Meiji government likewise saw such unregulated contacts as a direct threat to Japan's culture and stability.

The new government's concern was not entirely misplaced. For many Japanese, the 1860s were the dawn of a new world. Both the bakufu and the Meiji governments produced maps that attempted to reify the supposedly firm physical boundaries within Yokohama. In official pictorial representations, the foreign settlement and the "Japan-town" were isolated from each other. These maps, reproduced by private printers, gave the impression of strong central control at the key location where foreigner and Japanese met.

In reality, of course, such cartographic boundaries were transgressed on a daily basis. Even before the Meiji era, some wealthy merchant families in Yokohama were experimenting with Western foods and hair fashions, and tentatively attempting to learn English.[4] Cheap woodblock prints gave rudimentary and often incorrect "grammars" of English.[5] Maids and grooms served in the households of Western merchants, while adventurous Westerners wandered freely through the streets of the native sections and traveled in areas beyond the treaty limits.[6] Woodblock artists such as Hashimoto Sadahide and Ichimōsai Yoshitora produced hundreds of prints realistically portraying resident

Westerners and the various forms of interaction between them and Japanese in the port cities. Japanese and Western photographers recorded life on both sides of Yokohama.[7] Through their efforts a new international culture was emerging, drawing Japanese and foreigners alike to the port, and disseminating itself to increasing numbers of Japanese not able to participate directly in its activities.

The question for Iwakura, then, was one that had bedeviled the bakufu: how to reconcile the government's desire to strengthen Japan and maintain control over the foreigner with the reality of a steadily increasing Western trading and cultural presence. Treaty revision provided no answers, but it had forced this question to the forefront of relations.

If Iwakura, Ōkubo Toshimichi, and the others hoped to use their Western visit to weigh realistic alternatives to this dilemma, they were soon to find themselves carried along on a rushing current of discussion over revision, the very situation they all agreed they must avoid. During the first year of the mission, the ambassadors found themselves deeply involved in a complex set of unexpected talks over when, where, and how far formally to negotiate.[8] Marlene Mayo rightly called the experience a "catechism of Western diplomacy," arguing that the mission's experience, primarily in the United States, formed the background to all subsequent Meiji applications of diplomacy and international law.[9]

In terms of diplomacy, however, the mission must be considered in the context of previous negotiations over treaty alterations and an evolving Japanese diplomatic culture. In this light, the miscalculations of the ambassadors take center stage, and the various specifics of the proposed draft treaties assume importance precisely because of their differences from earlier negotiations. Iwakura's primary mistake was not merely to enter into sudden negotiations but also to question radically the nature of the treaties themselves, something that had not been discussed even in Japan. In short, an unexpected bid for near-equality with the West destabilized the entire treaty structure, and was firmly rejected by the treaty powers.

Even here, however, the Japanese were faced not with a unanimous Western response, but with different countries expressing different goals. The mission considered the most important responses to be the American and the British, and they concentrated their efforts accordingly.

In for a Penny, In for a Pound: The Japanese in Washington, January–July 1872

Iwakura and his fellow travelers landed in San Francisco on January 16, 1872. While few public reports of the embassy's activities circulated in Japan, the American press took immediate notice of the mission. The Japanese may have considered themselves first and foremost on diplomatic business, but to the U.S. media, they were a portent of the spread of American culture across the Pacific.

Some reports, such as in *The New York Times*, delved into the intricacies of American influence on Japan's new coinage system, but others focused on the cultural exchange taking place and the profound impact it would have on Japan.[10] The *San Francisco Bulletin*, for example, devoted an entire column to the roles of Japanese and American women in their respective societies. The article noted that the five Japanese women accompanying the embassy would undoubtedly benefit from their time in the States since "in America, woman [*sic*] commanded more respect than in Japan, and was not the slave of her husband."[11] To these observers, the embassy had come to learn, not to horse-trade.

The mission journeyed overland through the United States, stopping in Salt Lake City and Chicago, among other cities, where they were hosted by local dignitaries and followed by curious onlookers. Symbolically, all the ambassadors except for Iwakura shed their Japanese dress for Western business suits, and cut their samurai topknots during their travels across the continent. Thus "reborn," they and Iwakura finally arrived in Washington, D.C., at the end of February 1872. After a week's rest they had an official audience with President Ulysses S. Grant on March 4. This meeting paralleled the Meiji emperor's reception of the top Western diplomats three years previously and marked the first official Japanese visit to the U.S. capital since the initial bakufu mission back in 1860.

The warmth of the response to their arrival surprised the ambassadors and may have influenced them to go beyond their original intention of merely outlining treaty issues.[12] Such, in any case, was the road they followed once they commenced discussions with Secretary of State Hamilton Fish on March 11. By the end of the very first day, the ambassadors had outstripped their original brief, and the problems inherent in the mission's conflicting goals had surfaced.

The confusion that had reigned in Tokyo over the mission's agenda (see chapter 6) quickly spilled over into the Washington talks. Most crucial, the mission's framers had never clarified the line between simple discussions and formal negotiations, nor had they decided how far such discussions were to bind Japan and its treaty partners. Fish immediately recognized this ambiguity, and he pressed Iwakura to define the goals of the mission clearly and to state whether it had the power to sign a protocol. As Fish knew, in Western diplomacy a protocol was a binding agreement that guided later, formal negotiations.[13] It is unclear whether Iwakura clearly realized its significance, for the Japanese had not yet encountered such subtleties of international negotiation.

Domestic American politics also pushed the ambassadors further into negotiations than they originally intended. Fish pressured Iwakura to sign a full agreement, explaining that 1872 was a presidential

The Iwakura Mission, 1872. Left to right: Kido Kōin, Yamaguchi Naoyoshi, Iwakura Tomoni, Itō Hirobumi, Ōkubo Toshimichi. Courtesy of Ōkubo Toshihiro.

election year. He warned the Japanese that, depending on the makeup of the next government, it was uncertain whether anything they agreed to, yet had not signed, that year would later be acted upon.[14] Since Washington earlier had informed Tokyo of its desire to renegotiate, Fish did not feel bound to let the Japanese determine the pace of the deliberations. Indeed, he took the questionable legal position of asserting to Iwakura that the current treaty would lapse in July 1872, and thus gave the impression that a new agreement had to be signed within the year.[15]

The crucial moment in the still-fresh negotiations came when Fish asked Iwakura to specify the points he wished to negotiate. This was the door through which the senior leadership knew it should not walk, but the moment swept Iwakura along. Rather than demurring, he enumerated all the Japanese negotiating goals, thus immediately laying open his entire position. The goals he mentioned were a mix of his, Itō Hirobumi's, and the Foreign Ministry's various proposals from the previous several years. Most important, Iwakura informed Fish that Japan sought to set tariff rates freely, to end consular jurisdiction, and to prohibit the landing of foreign troops in Japan. Other issues included a definition of neutrality, new currency regulations, and extradition of criminals.[16]

Iwakura had already informed Fish that Japan would seek similar revisions from all the powers, so this discussion seemed to foreshadow a revolutionary change in treaty relations. Perhaps more crucial, this first salvo—declaring Japan's desire fundamentally to change the treaty structure—allowed the United States and later the Europeans to demand equally sweeping changes in the treaties, most of which ran directly counter to the post-1858 Japanese strategy. Iwakura quickly would learn how drastically the negotiating environment had now changed.

Given the green light by Iwakura's naiveté, Fish hastily prepared a U.S. counterproposal, which he presented two days later, on March 13.[17] At this point, the Japanese might have tried to step back and halt the process now gathering momentum. Iwakura, Ōkubo, and Kido Kōin, however, had allowed Itō Hirobumi and Mori Arinori, who was the Japanese representative in Washington, to convince them to seek a formal treaty settlement, although this was diametrically opposed to the original plan to postpone negotiation for several years. Iwakura accordingly opened the March 13 meeting with Fish by announcing that one of the ambassadors would be sent back to Tokyo to obtain the signing authority that the secretary had requested. Within two days, then, the nature of the mission had formally and radically changed.

Fish then presented his twelve-point counterproposal, which had been drawn up with input from Charles De Long, who also had influenced the "imperial instructions" Iwakura had received back in Tokyo. De Long, who had accompanied the mission to Washington, firmly believed the imperial government was no better than the Tokugawa, and that a joint Western front was required to make any significant headway in Japan. Indeed, months before the mission set forth, De Long had sent to Washington a letter that could just as well have come from Rutherford Alcock in 1861. Decrying the lack of trade between Japanese merchants and their American counterparts, De Long directly blamed the Meiji bureaucracy, writing bitterly that "the system of treaty ports is the great method by which this government is enabled to carry on this system of extortion against foreigners." The guardhouses that control the foreign settlements, he noted, allowed Tokyo to control the trade therein and extract extra duties from Japanese merchants after they had purchased goods in the foreign quarters. Moreover, he complained, imperial officers set exorbitant prices for passports, minutely inspected all foreign freight in order to discourage traders, and required that Japanese working for Westerners pay an illegal employment tax.[18]

De Long's observations fulfilled the grim predictions made by Harry Parkes on the conclusion of the 1866 Tariff Convention that the Japanese government could continue its control over trade almost unimpeded regardless of what promises it agreed to. The sense of isolation and lack of control felt by Western diplomats was as keen four years after the restoration as it was ten years before it.

De Long's solution, too, did not differ much from that of Alcock and Parkes, as he wrote Fish in the same dispatch, "the cabinets of the great powers can open Japan to civilisation [*sic*] by concerted action." De Long had used the May 1871 proposals of German Minister Max August Scipio von Brandt as the basis for his reports back to Washington; these later influenced his input into Fish's draft presented on March 13.[19] In essence, these were the same demands that Western representatives had been making to Japan for more than a decade, and that the Japanese government, either bakufu or Meiji, had been parrying. The Meiji leaders, however, had now put themselves in the position of formally receiving them in a negotiating conference.

To the ambassadors, though, the discussions seemed to be heading their way. Fish had agreed that Japan's initial proposal of two days earlier could be the starting point for discussions, despite having submitted a draft of his own. The secretary was amenable to such a tactic, for both he and De Long aspired to increase American influence in Japan and Asia, and thus were prepared to temper their negotiating demands for that greater goal. This followed America's tradition in treaty relations with Japan, going back to Townsend Harris and Robert Pruyn.

Fish seemed sympathetic to Iwakura's main goals, remarking, for example, that the United States would be "very happy" to see the end of consular courts once the Japanese adopted a Western-style legal system and local court organization. Moreover, he assured the Japanese that Washington supported Tokyo's desire for a clear definition of neutrality that would shield Japan from any conflicts among Western traders whose respective countries happened to be engaged in hostilities. Finally, Fish expressed his sympathy toward the Japanese desire for tariff autonomy, though he did not promise his support for that particular goal.

Two long meetings, on March 16 and 18, followed this encounter, covering numerous issues, including future port openings, land-buying rights, religion, neutrality, and currency reform. Then, on March 20, Ōkubo and Itō left Washington to return to Tokyo, where they hoped to obtain the authority required to sign a formal treaty. Before boarding the train to San Francisco, they sent a memorandum to Iwakura summarizing their views on how to mesh the Japanese and American proposals.[20] The memorandum showed not only that a great deal of headway had been made in a short period of time but also that Meiji negotiating tactics still contained a fair share of Tokugawa-era ideas. Thus, even as Fish was giving tentative approval to the end of consular jurisdiction and tariff restrictions, the Meiji leaders attempted in a traditional way to maintain control over crucial aspects of the treaty relationship.

Most significant was the Japanese stance toward open ports. In their memorandum, Ōkubo and Itō noted first that the negotiators had obtained American acquiescence in their refusal to allow Western ships the freedom to visit closed ports in Japan. However, this was followed by an apparent softening of the restriction on the number of open ports. "Instead of allowing foreign ships the right to visit unopened ports," they wrote, "trade should be kept as it is currently, eventually increasing the number of open ports."[21] While this may have seemed a dramatic change from the bakufu-inspired boundary policy, the scheme would have continued to limit the Americans to a select number of sites. Further, the ports the two suggested opening, Tsuruga in Echizen, Ishinomaki in Sendai, and Otaru in Hokkaidō, were each located in isolated areas, far from the politically and economically dominant regions of Japan. Finally, they had offered these sites in response to De Long's push to open Kagoshima, Wakayama, and Kōchi, each of which were substantial cities.

The tactic exemplified how Ōkubo and Itō hoped to satisfy Western demands with the minimum concessions possible. The Meiji leaders clearly were no more ready than their Tokugawa predecessors had been to demolish all remaining boundaries between Japanese and Westerners. But the ambassadors were forced to bargain, taking two steps forward and one step back. For example, Ōkubo and Itō strongly argued in their memorandum that Japan had to preserve the right to set up local regulations in the port areas. This, if achieved, would offset the possibility of a wider diffusion of Westerners by allowing Tokyo to establish the rules under which they had to live.

Similarly, Ōkubo and Itō recorded that Japan needed to make clear to the Westerners that "once a court system has been established and come into effect for our people, foreigners will have to directly obey" the laws.[22] Thus, although the two foresaw recasting the Japanese legal system to some degree in the Western image, foreigners would have to surrender any extraterritorial rights and understand that they would be held accountable to, and judged under, the same laws in the same courts as Japanese.

Finally, the memorandum touched on the issue of taxes and duties, one of Itō's main concerns. Fish was relatively amenable to the Japanese demand to gain tariff autonomy. Ōkubo and Itō noted, "As for taxes, it is vital that we demand that [foreigners] recognize our country's right to treat tariffs and the various internal tax laws as one. Moreover, in the future, we must defend our power to deny foreign countries any connection with our internal affairs."[23] With old boundaries altering, Ōkubo and Itō were proposing new ones, still based on the legal protection of treaties.

The memorandum revealed the basis of the Japanese strategy in 1872. In response to American demands for a greater presence in Japan, Ōkubo and Itō, as well as the rest of the mission's members, were far from ready to accept Western interior travel and residence. They were equally unyielding in their desire to control the expansion of open ports, and were unwilling to surrender the old Tokugawa prerogative to establish and enforce treaty port and settlement regulations.[24] There was, however, a keen understanding that, in order to control the likely increase in foreign contact, they would have to appear to compromise while attempting to strengthen their control over the administrative system as a whole.

Much as the Tokugawa had, the Meiji ambassadors sought to institute direct and indirect delays in fulfilling those provisions they deemed nonbeneficial, the clearest case being an attempt to delay the opening of further ports while "surveys" were undertaken. This was a tactic employed by Kido during a discussion with Fish in late March. He agreed the ports would open within two years, but tied it to completion of the surveys. During this same discussion, Iwakura and Kido indicated that five, not three, ports would be opened, the additional sites being Kagoshima in Kyūshū, the former Satsuma capital that was bombarded in 1863, and Shimonoseki on the western edge of Honshu, former main port of Chōshū, bombarded by an allied fleet the following year.[25] Trade at these two ports, of course, would benefit the homelands of the top leadership, most of whom came from one of these two former domains.

On the whole, the initial negotiations proved more favorable than the mission could have expected. They were not misreading the situation, for when Fish met with the British ambassador in Washington, Edward Thornton, around March 20, he reaffirmed the substance of the negotiations. Thornton reported to London that Fish did not object to the abolishment of consular courts once a regular and complete judicial system was established, which he expected to take many years, and that Fish did not believe the Japanese should be denied the right to control their tariffs. In particular, Fish was pleased with obtaining more open ports, but he opposed Ōkubo and Itō's plan for sole Japanese control of harbors, dues collection, and taxation of the foreign population. Finally, Fish informed Thornton that he had urged freedom of conscience, religious toleration, and full protection of Christians.[26]

Although it looked as though a new treaty satisfactory to all sides was within reach, the delicate nature of the negotiations was shortly to be thrown into disarray. Even as Fish and Thornton were meeting, the Japanese made a tactical miscalculation that eventually would undo the process. This was Mori Arinori's March 18 request to Thornton to hold a conference of joint treaty powers in Europe to consider revision.

Mori and the ambassadors were playing a complex and contradictory game with this request. On the first level, Iwakura had already told Fish that the Japanese sought an agreement with Washington in the hope that the other treaty powers would accept a new pact hammered out by only two players, Japan and the United States. This was reminiscent of the bakufu's decision to sign a treaty with Townsend Harris back in 1858 before being subjected to British and French pressure. The second level of Iwakura's plan involved getting Great Britain to accept the new treaty, for, as Mori informed Thornton, a treaty approved by London would not be refused by the other European powers.[27] The ambassadors here were following the same script the bakufu had back in 1862: working with the Americans to get the acquiescence of the most powerful of the treaty signatories, and thus automatically forcing the other treaty powers into line.

Yet Iwakura's third level was more tricky, for the Japanese also wanted to use British pressure to force the United States into a European treaty conference, thereby dealing with all the powers at one time, and signing, in essence, a new joint treaty. Without American participation in Europe, the whole deal could fall apart, for Japan might not be able to use the relatively favorable treaty Fish and the ambassadors were crafting. The mission instead would be forced to negotiate with the Europeans directly, from whom they did not feel they could obtain as promising a document.

This complex Japanese plan created two new problems. The immediate result of the ambassadors' stratagem was to alienate Fish. A defender of both the American tradition of aloofness from European power politics and that of the special Japanese–American relationship, Fish immediately rejected any participation in a European conference. He stated that any U.S.–Japan agreement must be signed either in Washington or Tokyo, but not in concert with other states. More ominously, Fish made it clear that he reserved the right to make alterations in the treaty as he saw fit up to its time of signing.[28]

The second problem the ambassadors faced was with Great Britain. Foreign Secretary Lord Granville had quickly authorized Thornton to tell Mori that London approved of the idea of a European conference, which the British believed would probably take place without the Americans.[29] However, opposition to this scheme came from the British chargé d'affaires in Tokyo, F. O. Adams, due to yet another unforeseen complication. In mid-May, Foreign Minister Soejima Taneomi had requested that Adams postpone or waive the remaining installments of the 1864 Shimonoseki indemnity.

Of the total indemnity of $3 million, which was to be remitted in six installments, half had been paid by 1872. Of the remaining $1.5 million, the United States was to receive $375,000, but Washington had taken steps to release the Japanese from that obligation. Soejima hoped to persuade Adams to recommend that Britain adopt the American course.[30] Two days after Soejima met Adams, chief councillor Sanjō Sanetomi told the Englishman that Japan now wanted to revise the treaties as soon as possible at the proposed European conference.

In Adams's eyes, Tokyo had asked too much, too quickly, without possessing the status for making such demands. Moreover, the imperial government had made these sweeping proposals without offering anything in return. If this was indeed the new Japanese policy, it was far out of balance with the treaty structure established nearly fifteen years previously. Adams reported to Granville that he did not support the Japanese treaty plan and lambasted Tokyo for its strategic challenge to the treaty powers:

> The great aim of the Japanese rulers is to make it appear that their country is the equal of all other nations . . . and nothing would flatter their vanity more than to have a great Conference in Europe, assembled, as it were, at the bidding of the Japanese. . . . The Ambassadors, too, would naturally be elated with the idea of this European Congress, where the affairs of their country would be discussed by them in the eyes of the whole civilized world."[31]

But the dizzying array of various revision plans on all sides left Adams unsure as to just how far his government had committed itself. Was there to be quick revision or a delay in negotiation, as Adams believed? If the former, then bilateral revision was one thing, but an international meeting was quite another. A few days later, Adams wrote to Soejima and Vice Foreign Minister Terajima Munenori that he did not understand the Japanese goal of a European conference, since Great Britain had agreed even before Iwakura left Japan to postpone revision until the mission's return.[32]

Adams's strong stance immediately clarified for London the stakes of the Japanese proposal. After receiving Adams's dispatches, Granville quickly cooled to the idea of early revision and completely dropped the idea of a conference. To add injury to insult in Japanese eyes, London never seriously considered waiving the Shimonoseki indemnity. The audacity of the Japanese plan was now clear, for it seemed nothing less than an attempt to extend to Japan the mechanism of the Concert of Europe.

By convening a great international conference, as Adams noted, London and the other great powers would in essence be recognizing joint European adjudication of Japanese–Western treaty issues. Although Tokyo would still be a petitioner, it would have to be involved in the deliberations to some degree, as it had been on treaty issues since 1858. This entrée would allow the government more input in later discussions. However, it was unheard of for a non-European power, and certainly one considered peripheral to the concert system, to demand the convening of a conference to discuss questions related to its several bilateral treaties. This extended the purview of the system far beyond any boundary it hitherto had respected and would add to the strains it was already under.

By the 1870s the concert was beginning the final phase of its long collapse, which would culminate in the maelstrom of the Great War. The 1854–1855 Crimean War had been the first breakdown in its collective deliberation mechanism and had the side effect of influencing Japan's earliest treaty arrangements with the British and Russians (see chapter 1). Then, beginning in 1866 with the unification of Germany, Chancellor Otto von Bismarck forged an increasingly dense and complex web of alliances and security arrangements; these undercut the very core of the cooperative diplomacy of the 1815 system.

Most important in relation to Japan, the concert had never dealt with non-European questions, the Ottoman Empire aside, and was ill prepared to include Asia in its purview.[33] Moreover, Adams noted that it would be all but impossible to negotiate the myriad details of a treaty in Europe and not on the spot. Furthermore, the Japanese would likely, in his opinion, conclude new treaties with whichever nations agreed to Tokyo's call for a European conference. The result, he feared, would poison relations among the treaty powers in Japan.[34] Such an outcome could create new tensions that could ripple throughout East Asia.

The precedent of a non-European country calling for an international conference could be enormously destabilizing to the entire European conception of international relations. Indeed, seemingly innocuous changes in the treaty process could have repercussions on a grand scale, quite possibly across the globe. For the Japanese, the issue was local, concerned with their own homeland. There is no evidence that the Meiji leaders understood the complexity of what they were asking. Their vision was not yet global in the sense that it would become in later decades. They saw a procedural problem and devised a way to solve it as easily as possible. In their eyes, lacking a reciprocal most-favored-nation (MFN) clause in the Ansei treaties, a conference seemed simply to be a convenient device to secure the agreement of all the treaty powers in one fell swoop. Beyond this, of course, such a conference would clearly announce Japan's new degree of participation in the international state system, one shared by no other non-Western power.

For the Europeans, however, the issues the Japanese raised went much deeper. Great Britain and the other powers had allowed themselves to be maneuvered into this corner by their acceptance of negotiation as the primary mechanism of treaty relations with Japan since 1858. The nature of the Japanese–Western treaty regime thus raised for Europe key questions of imperialism, in particular the paradox by which legal mechanisms, embodied as treaties and negotiations, attempted to coexist with power-oriented relations. Western treaties in East Asia, Latin America, and the Levant shared this inherently unstable basis. This was an insoluble problem that would require the devastation of two world wars before being settled in the second half of the twentieth century.

Given the global repercussions of the issue, it was almost a foregone conclusion that the Japanese ultimately would snatch defeat from the jaws of victory. Moreover, the ambassadors now believed they had been mistaken to try for so lofty a goal. As early as late March, with the change in Fish's attitude, Kido had written that there were no benefits to be gained from concluding a treaty while in the West, rather that Japan was in danger of losing more of its independence.[35] Yet since negotiations had already been set in motion, neither the Americans nor the Japanese felt they simply could end the discussions, and both continued halfheartedly to search for common ground.

Negotiation, for a decade and a half the means by which Japan sought to maintain a voice in treaty relations, now seemed a trap from which the ambassadors could not escape. Even as their plans began to disintegrate in the spring of 1872, they continued their parleys with the Americans. The two sides exchanged three draft treaties between April and July, each of which moved the two sides further apart. The Japanese draft treaties in particular retreated more and more from the liberalization that Iwakura had once promised De Long, but that his fellow leaders had never contemplated. Iwakura had not reverted to any type of isolationist position, but rather felt, along with Kido, that events were moving too quickly to ensure the demolition of the long-standing boundaries between Japan and the West could occur in a controlled manner.

Iwakura's penultimate draft, delivered on April 22, was a good example of the ambassadors' attempt to have it both ways. This draft seemed to break down more barriers to the Western presence—for example, by promising to open more treaty ports and to establish a new legal system as a prelude to the establishment of mixed courts.[36] Yet each proposal, already made in the past, was now hedged by conditions designed to delay its implementation.

By the time this draft was exchanged, however, Fish already had lost faith in the Japanese. Not only was he now deeply involved in arbitration with Great Britain over Civil War claims, he still was waiting for Ōkubo and Itō to return with full signing powers. Moreover, he had already declared himself irrevocably opposed to any European conference. It is not surprising, then, that he did not offer a counterdraft until June 8, more than a month and a half later.[37] His proposals focused on ways to blunt the Japanese move toward full control over trade and port administration, such as by expanding the powers of the consuls. It also split hairs about the timing of port opening. Most promising from the Japanese point of view, though, it allowed tariff freedom (albeit buried in the appendix), but the Americans had not yet decided how many months' notice they wanted from the Japanese before Tokyo instituted a change in tariff rates. When Fish did pass the draft over to the Japanese, however, the ambassadors were already seeking to end their long deliberations in America. Iwakura and Mori held out hope the European conference could still come off, but agreed with Kido that the Fish negotiations were now dead.

On July 10, during a short one-hour meeting at Fish's summer estate near West Point, New York, Iwakura made a last attempt to change Fish's opposition to the European conference.[38] As a palliative, he handed over the final Japanese draft treaty. This copy, however, showed negotiations were more or less at a standstill, for the Japanese made no effort to accommodate provisions from the U.S. June draft, repeating instead the main points of their April proposal.[39] Iwakura was less interested in an exchange of ideas than in discovering if the European conference plan could be salvaged.

His hopes were in vain, and on July 22, just as Ōkubo and Itō returned from Japan, he decided to break off negotiations with Fish. Although his newly assumed power from Tokyo allowed him to sign treaties, Iwakura asserted to the secretary that he could complete only a joint treaty with all the powers in Europe. He thus withdrew as gracefully as possible before doing any more harm to Japanese–American relations. Within two weeks, the mission was on its way to England, having abandoned most hopes for either a treaty or a conference.[40]

The Final Act: London, November–December 1872

It is tempting to view the post-America phase of the Iwakura embassy as the start of the mission's reorientation toward cultural exchange. While that indeed happened, the ambassadors did not yet surrender entirely their diplomatic objective. On the one hand, they saw negotiations in London as the last chance perhaps to sweep away Western objections to Japan's revision goals. On the other hand, and more realistically, they realized their sojourn in England was, as well, an attempt to understand more clearly the Western prerequisites for a new treaty, and thus learn just how Japan would have to change to accomplish that goal.

Although the mission arrived in England in mid-August, it was not until late November that Iwakura sat down for any substantive talks with Granville. The months preceding the negotiations were filled with tours of the country, visits to factories, and meetings with Japanese students living in London, among other activities.[41] This alone should have indicated to the ambassadors the sea change in their status from negotiators to observers. When the two sides finally did meet, all outstanding issues were crammed into three days of discussion, on November 22 and 27, and December 6.

Iwakura entered the talks with an ambiguous brief. Partly he hoped to discover a way to resurrect the conference idea, but only if it came with no cost for Japan. More so, though, he had moved past the stage of expecting a revision miracle and now wanted to assure the British that Tokyo was sincere in its desire to conform with Western legal and social norms as they related to the treaty structure. To buy Japan breathing space, and not coincidentally to put revision back on the half-decade time frame, he conveyed the Japanese awareness that such reform would take time. Chastened by the American debacle, Iwakura clearly asserted that only after a domestic transformation would Tokyo push for full treaty revision.

Iwakura's sober new stance was apparent in his first interview with Granville, on November 22. There he spelled out clearly this cautious approach: "The policy of the Mikado and his Government is to endeavour to assimilate Japan as far as possible to the enlightened states of the West. . . . [The Embassy was] sent to England in order to study her institutions, and to observe all that constitutes English civilization, so as to adopt . . . whatever they may think suitable."[42] This seemed clearly to express the new mind-set animating Japan's diplomats.

Having surrendered the offensive, Iwakura was immediately put on the defensive by Granville's position, specifically his call for unfettered interior travel for Westerners. Without a clear Japanese revision plan, the old British demands, repeated since bakufu days, now reappeared at center stage. The Japanese may have come to a new view of their country's relations with the world, but Westerners continued to focus exclusively on their trading advantage. Equally disillusioning, Iwakura was forced to fall back on bakufu stalling tactics. Thus, he replied to the issue of interior travel by stating that he feared the "ignorance of the rural population, and other difficulties, made it impossible to allow foreigners to travel freely in the interior for the present."[43] Whether true or not, these were the same objections that Kuze Hirochika and Andō Nobumasa had raised with Alcock back in 1862. Similar vagueness, and a similar appeal to domestic unrest, was again employed to parry an old demand.

Not until the second meeting, on November 27, did Iwakura fully understand how far the embassy, with all its various demands and recantation, had overreached, and how completely the maneuvering room exploited by Japan since 1858 had disappeared. In this discussion on municipal administration, Iwakura all but surrendered to Britain a symbolic and materially vital point: the "right" to determine Japan's level of progress as a prerequisite for revision. Granville made explicit what had been implicit in all the negotiations undertaken by the Japanese and the Westerners, declaiming that "the policy of the British Government was to yield the local authorities jurisdiction over British subjects in *precise proportion to their advancement in enlightenment and civilization.*"[44] There was little riposte to this pronouncement, even though it arrogated to London the right to determine Japan's level of development, for it mirrored what Iwakura had pledged at the first meeting. The foreign secretary made clear that London would control the terms of the revision process and that "enlightened" Britain would continue to sit in judgment on Japan. In making no objection, Iwakura accepted that considerations of power solely structured the Anglo–Japanese relationship, and that negotiation was no longer the primary mechanism of treaty relations.

With this declaration, the interviews moved away entirely from any discussion of revision. The last meeting between the two, on December 6, reaffirmed that negotiation was no longer a means for Japan to defend itself against the policies of the West. It was clear that Westerners would consider granting Japan equality only after the boundaries that had protected the Japanese for so long had been torn down. It would then be a different, perhaps defenseless, Japan that would await judgment on its petition.[45] Despite this, it was clear to Iwakura, Ōkubo, and the others the path that Japan now had to follow. The final collapse of the bakufu's old physical, intellectual, and ideological boundaries had come.

How far from the headiness of six months previously, when it appeared to the ambassadors that a treaty would be concluded that, while not perfect, would have answered many of their long-standing complaints. Within ten days, the mission left England, travelling to a dozen European countries, where nary a word about revision would be said. Taking shape during those months, however, was a new policy of modernization, informed by a common understanding of the world shared by most of Japan's top leaders.

The Path to Revision, 1872–1894

Treaty revision remained the top diplomatic goal of the Meiji government, although it would not be achieved until 1894. Despite this continuity, the Iwakura Mission represented the end of the first phase of Japanese–Western treaty relations. In the next decades, Japan followed new paths, both domestic and foreign, that would set the pattern of its modern history. While a detailed analysis is beyond the scope of this book, our narrative will end with a brief account of the revision movement. The changes already evident in Japan by 1872 foreshadowed its modern future. In that year alone, a national postal system was organized and the first railway, linking Yokohama and Shinbashi in Tokyo, opened in the presence of the Meiji emperor.[46] The same year, news of the Iwakura Mission reached Kyoto not by the centuries-old post-horse relay system, which was now abolished, but by Japan's first telegraph line. The founding of the Asiatic Society of Japan by diplomats and missionaries in Yokohama propelled the country into the world of global intellectual exchange, providing a forum for Westerners studying the country's history, culture, and social system, and soon embracing Japanese members as well.

By the summer of 1873, a national bank, one of Itō Hirobumi's pet projects, was established. Reforms in the educational system, the military, agriculture, and the like were poised for takeoff. Within months of the mission's return, Ōkubo Toshimichi began to gather great power into his own hands as head of the new Home Ministry and initiated institutional and policy reforms designed to transform Japan into an industrialized society run by centralized state planners.[47] Japan was beginning to resemble the kind of "civilized" nation that British Foreign Secretary Granville demanded it become.

In these new conditions, symbolism suffused the policy of treaty revision. Revision was understood to be international recognition that Japan had taken its place with the first rank of nations. Intellectually the treaties were now stigmatized as "unequal," and thus revision became as much a moral as a political crusade. Numerous writers exhorted Japan to throw off the yoke of inequality, some championing modernization, some a return to traditional values.[48] But the Meiji government accepted the treaties as a short-term reality that could be overthrown only once Japan had dramatically changed.

The new diplomatic culture that had crystallized during the Iwakura Mission's sojourn in Europe contained within it a new approach to Japan's regional foreign relations. By increasing its influence in Asia, Tokyo would gain leverage against the treaty powers as well as demonstrate that it could act globally in the same way as the leading international states. The model for this new policy was clear: the very treaty system introduced into Japan in 1858.

Korea was Japan's main focus, as it had been in the late sixteenth century during Toyotomi Hideyoshi's invasions and in the early seventeenth century with Tokugawa attempts at stabilizing a new diplomatic system.[49] By the time the Meiji leaders took power, samurai calls for action on the peninsula had again emerged, inflamed by the Korean court's refusal to acknowledge the superiority of the Japanese sovereign. The Meiji leaders, though, understood that the way to Korea was through China. After two missions to the Qing Court in 1870 and 1871, the Japanese, represented by the former lord of Uwajima, Date Munenari, signed a treaty of equality.[50]

The Sino–Japanese Treaty of Amity, signed on September 13, 1871, was Japan's first "equal" treaty; more important, it was, as Key-Hiuk Kim pointed out, the first treaty based on Western international law concluded between East Asian nations. Although the Chinese refused to refer to the Japanese emperor as *tennō*, given the term's connotation of equality with the Chinese monarch, the rest of the treaty established equal relations between the two. The main departure from the Ansei treaties, quickly reported to Charles De Long by F. F. Low, American minister to China, was that consular jurisdiction extended only to the treaty ports in each country; outside the ports, Chinese and Japanese would be subject to the host country's laws.[51] However, there was no MFN clause, and Japanese were not allowed either to trade in China's interior or to wear swords on Chinese territory. The treaty nonetheless was indeed epochal, and marked the beginning of the collapse of the traditional Chinese tributary system.

The failure of the Iwakura Mission the following year, however, pushed Tokyo to adopt a more aggressive policy on the continent, where it appeared that it could have more freedom of action than in Japan itself. By 1873, strident anti-Korea voices were calling for an expedition to assert Japan's superiority over the peninsula. This celebrated clash (*sei-Kan* in Japanese) split the Meiji oligarchy and ultimately resulted in the triumph of the more conservative Ōkubo approach, which stressed nation-building over military expansion.[52]

Nonetheless, Ōkubo understood that post-Iwakura Mission Japan had to act like a great power in order to be considered one. He therefore supported a more-tempered plan to force Korean acceptance of Japanese superiority through the means that had failed in China, an "unequal" treaty based on Western principles. As an immediate sop to the anti-Korea forces, headed by Saigō Takamori, the Meiji leaders authorized a military expedition to Taiwan in early 1874, ostensibly to extract vengeance for the murder of fifty-five Ryūkyūan sailors on the island three years previously.

This was primarily a decision reflecting domestic tensions, namely, the growing restlessness of unemployed samurai, many of them from Satsuma. In order to quell any Chinese opposition to the expedition, Foreign Minister Soejima Taneomi, an ardent expansionist, made a crucial visit to China to gain recognition of Japan's right to act against the Formosans. This was the first example of Japan's new diplomacy in Asia, based on the 1871 Chinese acceptance of Japan's equality.[53] Soejima succeeded, and the Qing not only surrendered their nominal suzerainty over Formosa, but accorded Soejima diplomatic superiority over the Western representatives in Beijing. Soon after, Meiji troops embarked on the expedition to Taiwan. Although Tokyo eventually pulled back its forces, after receiving an Ōkubo-wrangled indemnity from China, the action set the stage for further Japanese action in Asia.[54]

Within two years, the Meiji leaders felt strong enough to aim for their major regional goal. In the summer of 1876, Tokyo sent its three warships and a ragtag fleet to Korea to carry out Ōkubo's plan to open treaty relations. This time the Japanese succeeded, and Korea accepted a trade treaty securing for Japan the one-sided privileges normally held by Westerners. The 1876 Treaty of Kanghwa symbolized the emergence of Japan as a regional power playing by Western rules, specifically through the imposition of "unequal treaties." Though it made no territorial claims, Tokyo used gunboat diplomacy to extract a Western-style treaty from one of China's most conservative tributary partners, in the process forcing Korea to accept "equality" with Japan and thus sundering its subordinate status to the Qing. Tokyo was quickly learning how to act like an imperialist power, and was doing so for a combination of long-standing domestic reasons and recent foreign ones.[55]

Moving in tandem with this new foreign policy were domestic reforms designed specifically to answer the grievances of the treaty powers and create the conditions by which Japan would be able to shed the Ansei treaties. Most important was the issue of Japan's criminal and civil codes. Legal reform gathered speed after 1872. An initial legal revision of 1871 based on Japan's ancient eighth-century codes was amended two years later by the "Revised Fundamental and Supplementary Laws," based on European models, which abolished torture and restricted use of the death penalty.[56] Ōkubo considered these reforms too limited and established a special Justice Ministry committee headed by a French legal scholar, M. Boissonade. Those concerned to meld the new laws with Japan's traditional social structure slowed the entire process, however. The code was not finished until mid-1880 and was promulgated in January 1882. Concurrent with this, work on a civil code commenced, but all the French legal revisions were soon to be supplanted by German models more suited to an increasingly powerful central government.

Public opinion now played a major role in Japan's foreign politics, and had come to do so based in part on the agonizingly slow pace of revision negotiations. Although after 1872 various revision proposals were floated about, the most important attempt to reach agreement occurred in 1878 between Japan and the United States. By this time the major actors in Tokyo since 1868 had completely turned over. Iwakura, though surviving until 1885, was increasingly marginalized by the former samurai-cum-bureaucrats. Kido Kōin died of disease in 1877, the same year Saigō Takamori committed suicide during his failed Satsuma rebellion. A year later, Ōkubo Toshimichi was assassinated by a disgruntled former samurai. The leadership now passed to younger men, primarily Itō Hirobumi, Inoue Kaoru, Yamagata Aritomo, and later Ōkuma Shigenobu.

In these new circumstances, Tokyo moved cautiously on partial treaty revision and primarily on a bilateral basis. For the time being, the new leaders shied away from grand revision schemes such as that of the Iwakura Mission. Given the difficulties of drafting an acceptable criminal and civil code, tariff issues seemed easier to resolve. Hamilton Fish had been replaced in Washington by William Evarts, who was sympathetic to Tokyo's desire to overturn the 1866 Tariff Convention. Almost twenty years to the day that Townsend Harris signed his treaty, the two sides reached agreement on a pact that would have returned to Japan tariff autonomy. The plan, however, was scuttled by Harry Parkes, still serving as British minister, who did not want to see higher tariffs on British goods, and who would at the most consider only a new tariff, not tariff autonomy.[57]

Inoue Kaoru, who had become foreign minister in 1879, believed that Britain's ability to block the bilateral Japan–U.S. agreement left Tokyo no option but to try to resolve all outstanding issues at a joint meeting of the treaty powers. Though this harked back to the Iwakura

Mission's strategy, Inoue succeeded in convening such a conference in Tokyo starting in January 1882. Support from the United States and Germany was instrumental in pushing the aging Parkes into agreeing to the plan. The first round of meetings lasted only until July of that year, however, throttled by Parkes' refusal to contemplate far-reaching changes to the extraterritoriality and tariff clauses of the treaties. A second conference did not open until four years later, in May 1886.

The issue of mixed consular courts, first proposed back in 1871 by Tsuda Mamichi and Kanda Kōhei, was reintroduced in this 1886 meeting by the British and Germans. The mixed courts would hear cases involving foreigners and would have a majority of foreign judges, as was implemented in Egypt in 1876. Japanese public opinion, however, inflamed by daily newspaper reporting on the various treaty and legal issues, turned against Foreign Minister Inoue, who had accepted in principle the idea of the foreign-controlled mixed courts.[58] Opposition in the streets was matched by tension within the government, and in July 1887, Inoue adjourned the conference sine die until such time as Japan's legal provisions were unambiguously accepted by the treaty powers. This, along with a plan to have the powers approve Japan's new legal codes before their promulgation, resulted in public demonstrations and Inoue's resignation in August 1887.

Inoue's successor was the liberal politician and opposition member Ōkuma Shigenobu, who took from Inoue's failure at joint revision the lesson that Japan should revert to bilateral negotiations. Within one year of taking office, in November 1888, Ōkuma negotiated an equal treaty with Mexico, primarily to obtain free travel for Mexicans in Japan (of which there were none), who would be subject to Japanese law. He hoped this would serve as a precedent for future revision negotiations.

During the next year, Ōkuma succeeded in negotiating new draft treaties with the United States and Germany, but again found difficulties with the British. This time, though, evidence of Japan's "liberal" reforms was evident in the promulgation of the Meiji Constitution on February 11, 1889, and the provision for the opening of the Diet the following year. Added to the cabinet system, which had been introduced in 1885, Japan now boasted a judicial, legislative, and administrative structure on a par with Western nations. Even Britain seemed ready to sign a new treaty, agreeing to Ōkuma's proposal that mixed courts be abolished twelve years from the date the new treaty came into force.

The success of these bilateral negotiations was abruptly stalled in mid-October 1889, when Ōkuma narrowly survived an assassination attempt by a member of a new nationalist organization, the *Gen'yōsha*. The resulting crisis led to the resignation of Prime Minister Kuroda Kiyotaka and a temporary halt to further negotiations. It was clear that public dissent now constituted a more serious obstacle than the treaty powers themselves. For the Meiji leaders, revision would have to be total, or they risked a public explosion. This was indeed the endpoint of the process initiated nearly four decades earlier, when the Tokugawa senior councillor Abe Masahiro had first sought daimyō opinion on how to respond to Matthew C. Perry.

From the point of view of the treaty powers, however, Japan no longer looked like the country with which the Ansei agreements had been negotiated. They feared that, much stronger now than back in the days of the Iwakura Mission, Japan might unilaterally abrogate the treaties, again with untold consequences for all Western diplomatic relations. This pushed America and France, in particular, to continue the bilateral negotiations with Tokyo. Foreign Minister Aoki Shūzō worked through 1891–1892 and was succeeded, after a short term by former bakufu official Enomoto Takeaki, by Mutsu Munemitsu in August 1892. Mutsu was part of Itō's second ministry, which held the Diet in an iron fist and suppressed any public dissent similar to that which had toppled Kuroda. Among the foreign powers, Britain held the key to changes in the treaty structure, as it had from the beginning of treaty relations, but this time found its recalcitrance opposed by almost all the other treaty powers.

Faced with the inevitable, London agreed in July 1894 to a new Treaty of Commerce and Navigation, by which extraterritoriality would end on July 17, 1899, and tariff autonomy would be restored to the Japanese in 1911.[59] The Aoki–Kimberley Treaty, as it was known, marked for all intents and purposes the end of the Ansei agreements. Within two years the remaining original treaty powers concluded new pacts with the Meiji government.

Thirty-six years after the Harris–Iwase treaty was signed, Japan finally negotiated its equality with the leading global powers. Negotiation, though frustrating and uneven, had protected Japan's independence and given the country a voice with which to respond to the West.

Conclusion

In the space of fifteen years, Japan's international relations underwent a radical change. This book has identified the particular experience of treaty relations as a starting point of the transition to modern Japan. Yet it has also attempted to understand diplomacy not simply as a set of policies or a practice, but rather as the reflection of a shared interpretation of the world—in short, a culture. It was the evolution of Japanese diplomatic culture that sparked the decisions leading to that profound historical transition.

When Western powers arrived in Japan in the mid-1850s, they encountered a distinct diplomatic culture, one influenced by the ideology and policies at the core of two and a half centuries of Tokugawa rule. By 1858, that culture rested on three interlinked boundaries that formed concentric circles emanating from Edo Castle. The innermost boundary was ideological, protecting the authority and position of the shogun, who ordered the foreign and domestic realm. Outside this lay the intellectual boundary, cutting Japan off from foreign knowledge that might lead to new conceptions of the polity. The outermost boundary was the physical, embodied in the seventeenth century maritime edicts, separating Japan from contact with foreigners except for a handful of controlled relationships.

These three boundaries served to defend the bakufu from foreign threat and domestic interference in the conduct of foreign policy. The grand strategy of the Tokugawa was to preserve these boundaries at all costs, to maintain its ordering of the world. This strategy became the response to the West.

Although faced with overwhelming Western power, or at least the perception of such, the Tokugawa chose neither to surrender nor to fight a hopeless battle. Rather, after 1858, they chose to engage the West by relying on the most promising tactic available, one provided by the Westerners themselves: negotiation. This choice was informed both by their knowledge of China's disastrous attempts to oppose British demands in the 1830s and by some understanding of the kingdom of Siam's more equitable relations with Great Britain. This strategy created a specific pattern of treaty relations in which both sides quickly accepted that negotiation was the bedrock of Japan's contact with its treaty partners.

The bakufu use of negotiation, and its acceptance by the West, allowed the voice of the Japanese to be heard in treaty relations. Though that voice was neither consistent nor unchallenged within either the bakufu or Japan, it maintained its role nonetheless. For a decade, bakufu officials engaged Western representatives in a dynamic, multilayered space in which both sides could pursue their strategies without risking conflict. Negotiation thus became a continuous dialogue about the nature and limits of the treaty regime. As the weaker party, though, the bakufu came to see any type of response to the West as a form of negotiation. Under these conditions, resistance to the presence of foreigners could equally masquerade as negotiation, as in the attempts to isolate Westerners in the new port of Yokohama in 1859.

Tokugawa attempts to defend their boundaries entailed defining them in the light of the new types of interaction between Japanese and foreigners. Negotiation, then, occurred at various levels, not only with the West, but also within the bakufu and among various groups inside Japan. This process of negotiation forced Japan's central and regional leaders, as well as its nonelite, to reconsider the boundaries surrounding their culture, society, and politics. Within the bakufu, various bureaucratic factions pitted men such as Iwase Tadanari and Mizuno Tadanori against each other. Soon, domestic actors, such as the domains of Satsuma and Chōshū, began to challenge shogunal authority over foreign affairs. Through it all, public voices kept up a running commentary through widely distributed prints and pamphlets.

For the bakufu, the physical boundary was the most crucial to protect. It was the first line of defense and the most visible symbol of

Tokugawa foreign authority. Its breach, therefore, could have untold domestic effects. Ii Naosuke in particular believed that he could circumvent, and perhaps control, the superior power of the West by adapting the boundary policy to the idea of open trading ports. The result was Yokohama. Designed by Ii as a new Dejima, the port was the physical manifestation of the bakufu's diplomatic culture. It was meant to send a clear message to Westerners and Japanese alike that the world would not fundamentally change despite the reality of the commercial treaties.

Yet the force of Ii's vision not only outlived its creator but also had a very different result from what he intended. Yokohama served more as a gate than a barrier. Its fluid nature began to seem a threat to the regime's ideological and structural stability. Ii could not have foreseen that Yokohama's great commodity would be exchange—of goods, of ideas, and of people. Though it did keep the foreigners contained in the early years, it could not harness a force that proved impervious to political control. Yokohama attracted Japanese and foreigner alike, some for trade, others for a glimpse of a new world. Artists such as Hashimoto Sadahide proselytized this culture through their vivid prints and descriptions. Sober Japanese merchants reordered their households to take part in the new international life offered by the port.

Yokohama was representative of the evolving nature of treaty relations. Over time, the bakufu found its room for negotiation increasingly circumscribed both because of the increase in the Western presence and the interference in foreign affairs by domains such as Chōshū and Satsuma. The very complexity of treaty relations meant that the ideological and intellectual boundaries of Tokugawa diplomatic culture came under increasing strain.

Indeed, the demands of treaty relations made step-by-step changes in strategy almost unavoidable. While on the one hand the bakufu tried to reassert its physical boundaries through the 1862 London Protocol, on the other it sought new types of knowledge outside its borders, sponsoring large-scale translation projects and fostering a whole generation of foreign affairs intelligentsia such as Nishi Amane and Tsuda Mamichi. Throughout the 1860s, moreover, Edo unsuccessfully sought to deal with threats it perceived from the growth of Yokohama. The combined weakening of these physical and intellectual defenses ultimately pierced the ideological boundary that had ordered Japan's shogun-centered world.

This final breach had a lasting effect on internal politics. The domestic political actors who had begun to question the ideological bases of Japanese diplomacy were increasingly emboldened in their larger challenge to Tokugawa authority. The incursion of the West pushed those actors, long isolated from foreign policy, to seek a role in treaty relations, whether by questioning bakufu competency or by engaging directly with the foreigners. Satsuma and Chōshū, in particular, took advantage of the new conditions forced on the bakufu. Both these domains paid a heavy price for their newly found activism, yet they capitalized on the weaknesses and treaty responsibilities of the bakufu, and ultimately sped its collapse.

Before their fall from power, though, top bakufu leaders such as Tokugawa Yoshinobu began to interpret the world in new ways. They realized that they could benefit from closer relations with the treaty powers and that Japan was now permanently part of a larger, complex international environment. This was the extent to which the Tokugawa could change, but it nonetheless marked a true evolution in their international understanding. Most important, perhaps, the bakufu had prepared the ground for a more radical transformation in Japan's culture.

Partly because the new Meiji leaders did not have a distinct diplomatic culture of their own, they initially borrowed the strategy of the Tokugawa. Pressed by the need to deal with the treaty powers, the imperial leaders quickly abandoned their old antiforeign platform, just as had their bakufu predecessors. Yet they, too, sought to limit the points of contact between Japanese and Westerner, not least because they feared that foreign affairs could be used by anti-imperial forces to upset their tenuous hold on power in the same way they had taken advantage of bakufu weakness. At the same time, though, they drew on their own experience of international relations during their domainal days as well as on the heritage of Western studies promoted by the bakufu during its last years. The result was a continued evolution in Japanese diplomatic thinking.

What resulted was a hybrid vision of the world in the early 1870s. On the one hand, it sought to preserve some of the same boundaries, primarily the physical, as the Tokugawa. On the other, it was committed to a redefinition of Japan's role in the world, which was based on the leaders' understanding of international law and diplomatic practice. In actual treaty relations, however, the Meiji leaders found themselves negotiating away some of those precious boundaries, especially in the 1869 Austro–Hungarian treaty.

In part from this and in part from their reading of international economics and law, the structures of meaning that guided Meiji diplomacy coalesced by 1872 into a new understanding of their international environment. The Iwakura Mission was intended to reassert those boundaries that seemed essential, but the culture of Japanese diplomacy had irrevocably changed. The leadership, gorged on experiences in America and Europe, no longer ascribed to the notion that Japan ordered the world. The mission surrendered the idea of maintaining boundaries, and instead set the stage for the transformation of Japanese culture as a whole.

Ultimately, then, though treaty relations spanned two political regimes, they were played out on a single, evolving continuum from 1858 through 1872. The negotiation that took place through these years became a discussion about the future of Japan, for foreign affairs were inseparable from domestic concerns. As such, this was the period when, as William Beasley put it, the "major decisions were taken about the shaping of the Japanese state."[1] In the broadest sense, then, the path for modern Japan emerged from these fifteen years.

Imperialism, Diplomacy, and Japan

After 1872, the pace of change accelerated, moving Japan ever further from what it had been in 1858. From the vantage point of the international system, Japan became yet another society transformed by dint of its encounter with the West. Was Japan's negotiation with imperialism, then, meaningless? Were the Japanese no better than the Melians, who chose to challenge the might of the Athenians and paid for that expression of "freedom" in the sacking of their city and the scattering of their people? Or did negotiation itself preserve Japan's freedom, offering alternatives not available had the bakufu and Meiji government simply surrendered their right of action?

The answer to this question rests on one's view of imperialism, either as an irresistible systemic force or as a set of relations unique to each locality in which it operated. Japan's encounter with the West showed that imperialism was not monolithic, even within as bounded a region as East Asia. The style of informal imperialism practiced by Great Britain differed greatly between China and Japan. Actions in

China that brought Rutherford Alcock fame got him recalled from
Edo. Japan's relative freedom of action resembled that of Siam more
than China, due in no small part to the country's geopolitical position.

Nonetheless, imperialism was real, even if informal. It enmeshed
Japan within a regional, if not international, economic structure that
was animated by a distinct Western political conception of treaty relations. Western diplomats interacted with the Japanese based both on
their understanding of international relations and their specific instructions from their home countries. Among the Western powers
themselves, different policies often brought them to odds, particularly
between the British and the Americans and French. As much as
possible, the Japanese took advantage of these cleavages to gain favorable treatment or to push their own policies. At the end of the day,
though, Japan could not escape being drawn into this system and
found itself being defined by its traditional economy, society, and
politics.

This meant that, unlike in areas such as industry or legal thought,
Japan had no time to study Western analogues. From the first appearance of Townsend Harris, the Japanese were forced to interact with
Westerners, without breathing space and without the chance to test
whether their policies were adequate to the new challenge. Yet this
abrupt plunge into the cauldron of international diplomacy triggered
an almost automatic cultural response.

It is here that the Tokugawa strategy of boundary maintenance and
the actions of individuals influenced Japanese history, changing it as
much as the encounter with imperialism did. By adopting negotiation,
the Japanese chose to act, despite the overwhelming power of the
West and the unforeseen consequences of entering the Western international system. Men such as Ii Naosuke or Iwakura Tomomi, however, saw a space in which to influence treaty relations. To apply Sidney
Hook's insight, the lesson of negotiating with imperialism was that
"these ideals, plans, and purposes are causally rooted in the complex
of conditions, but they take their meaning from some proposed *reworking* of conditions to bring them closer to human desire."[2]

Each particular reworking was a rational response to events, even
though contingency decided the outcomes. Rutherford Alcock, for
example, believed that Ii's Yokohama strategy firmly controlled Westerners in the first years of trade. Similarly, once the bakufu successfully postponed the opening of the two ports and two cities in 1862,

there was no guarantee that those sites would ever open, and that the bakufu could not simply continue negotiating away their existence in perpetuity. Indeed, contingency alone can explain the particular set of events leading up to the bombardments of Satsuma and Chōshū, which ultimately led to those two domains turning their attentions toward toppling the bakufu rather than expelling the foreigner.

Because of the unknowable outcome of such policies, diplomacy throughout these years reduced itself to the undeniable importance of the daily, lived actions of those policymakers we call elite and whose lives we cavalierly consider to be either the most free or the most circumscribed. These men, although constrained by custom, talent, and policy, acted in the space between quiescence and revolt, as James Scott puts it, fundamentally influencing the encounter with the West, even though they could not control the end result.[3] For these individuals, negotiating with imperialism was in fact a "personal experience," equal to the "thoughts, knowledge, poetry, music, love, friendship, hates, passions of which real life is compounded . . . the concrete and multi-colored reality of individual lives."[4]

Negotiating held an immediacy for the Japanese diplomats. They did not approach it from a structural perspective, theorizing patterns of regional trade or conflict. Rather, it daily ordered their actions and influenced their ideas, just as it did for the Japanese grooms, maids, and shopkeepers in Yokohama. And, in the end, it permanently changed those who shared in the experience.

Negotiation, and the culture that sustained it, was thus a process deeply woven into the texture of life. It was, in fact, the very essence of Japan's encounter with the West. The actors recounted in these pages, as well as their Western counterparts, rationally approached their responsibilities. They worked within a general historical condition, that of imperialism, but were free to attempt to rework it in light of their own understanding of the multiplicity of relations, interactions, and potentialities they saw around them.

Equally important, diplomacy and negotiation were not limited to the elite in Edo. Regional leaders, as noted earlier, engaged both bakufu and foreigner. Popular artists made known their hopes and fears in their prints and pamphlets. Foot-weary Japanese, traveling for days to visit or move to Yokohama, became part of the encounter between Japan and the West. Each of them negotiated in their own way with the new world.

In the end, a Japanese leadership that itself was profoundly altered, consciously chose the sweeping changes that occurred after 1872. These policies were not accepted easily inside the country, and were accompanied by vociferous popular dissent. Domestic modernity was brought forth from the treaty system, handing a "victory" to the government in its foreign relations, but leaving open the question of the price of that success. Yet during those years of transformation, the international system saw only Japan's challenge to the Western treaty structure, the first by an Asian nation. The enduring domestic changes were interpreted by Western nations only in the light of whether they brought Japan into alignment with narrow definitions of civilization and enlightenment.

After the Iwakura Mission it took Japan more than two decades, until 1894, to adapt to the new world and respond to the West on its own terms. But treaty relations had led to an evolution in Japanese diplomatic culture, and then to society as a whole. The negotiation that marked those relations led to a belief in possibilities, and it was this belief that changed the Japanese, drove them, and finally freed them from negotiating with imperialism.

Appendixes
Abbreviations
Notes
Acknowledgments
Index

Treaties of Friendship and Commerce Signed by the Tokugawa Bakufu and the Meiji Government, 1858–1871

Country	Signing Date	
	Japanese Calendar	Western Calendar
1 United States*	Ansei 5/6/19	7/29/1858
2 Holland*	Ansei 5/7/10	8/18/1858
3 Russia*	Ansei 5/7/11	8/19/1858
4 Great Britain*	Ansei 5/7/18	8/26/1858
5 France*	Ansei 5/9/3	10/9/1858
6 Portugal	Man'nen 1/6/17	8/3/1860
7 Prussia	Man'nen 1/12/14	1/24/1861
8 Switzerland	Bunkyū 3/12/29	2/6/1864
9 Belgium	Keiō 2/6/21	8/1/1866
10 Italy	Keiō 2/7/16	8/25/1866
11 Denmark	Keiō 2/12/7	2/1/1867
12 Sweden–Norway	Meiji 1/9/27	11/11/1868
13 Spain	Meiji 1/9/28	11/12/1868
14 North German Confederation	Meiji 2/1/10	2/20/1869
15 Austro–Hungary	Meiji 2/9/14	10/18/1869
16 Hawaii	Meiji 4/7/4	8/19/1871

*Indicates one of the original "Ansei Five Country" signatories.

Key Japanese and Western Diplomats

Name	Position		Date of Appointment or Arrival in Japan	Date of Dismissal or Departure from Japan
Bakufu				
Ii Naosuke	senior councillor		4 June 1858	24 March 1860 (assassinated)
Andō Nobumasa	sr. cncllr		6 February 1860	9 May 1862
Kuze Hirochika	sr. cncllr		21 April 1860	28 June 1862
Ogasawara Nagamichi	sr. cncllr		2 November 1862	24 July 1863
Abe Masato	sr. cncllr		27 July 1864	18 November 1865
Iwase Tadanari	foreign magistrate		16 August 1858	11 October 1858
Mizuno Tadanori	for. mag.		16 August 1858	24 September 1859
		(reappt.)	19 June 1861	8 August 1862
Nagai Naomune	for. mag.		16 August 1858	28 March 1859
		(reappt.)	1865	4 April 1867
Inoue Kiyonao	for. mag.		16 August 1858	28 March 1859
		(reappt.)	17 September 1862	20 January 1863
Takemoto Masao	for. mag.		22 November 1859	29 July 1862
		(reappt.)	27 January 1863	8 December 1864
Ikeda Nagaaki	for. mag.		24 October 1863	24 August 1864
Meiji Government (key diplomatic post held by persons listed)				
Date Munenari	foreign office head		January 1868	July 1869
Sanjō Sanetomi	foreign office head		January 1868	March 1868
Higashikuze Michitomi	foreign office head		January 1868	November 1868
Ōkubo Toshimichi	(junior) councillor		January 1868	May 1878
Kido Kōin	(junior) councillor		January 1868	March 1876

Terashima Munenori	(deputy) foreign minister	January 1868	September 1879
Itō Hirobumi	foreign ministry	January 1868	July 1871
Sawa Nobuyoshi	foreign minister	July 1869	August 1871
Mori Arinori	minister to United States	October 1870	October 1872
Iwakura Tomomi	foreign minister	August 1871	November 1871
Soejima Taneomi	foreign minister	December 1871	October 1873
United States			
Townsend Harris	consul/minister	21 August 1856	26 April 1862
Robert H. Pruyn	minister	30 April 1862	28 April 1865
Robert B. Van Valkenburgh	minister	4 May 1867	11 November 1869
Charles E. De Long	minister	11 November 1869	7 October 1873
Great Britain			
Rutherford Alcock	minister	26 June 1859	24 December 1864
Edward St. John Neale	charge d'affaires	April 1862	March 1864
Harry Parkes	minister	8 July 1865	July 1883
France			
Duchesne de Bellecourt	minister	6 September 1859	27 April 1864
León Roches	minister	27 April 1864	June 1868
Ange-Maxime Outrey	minister	June 1868	October 1871
Prussia/Germany			
Max August Scipio von Brandt	agent/minister	September 1860	November 1874
Holland			
Jan Hendrik Donker Curtius	head of factory	April 1852	October 1860
Jan K. de Wit	consul	January 1860	April 1863
Dirk de Graeff von Polsbroek	minister	April 1863	March 1870

Treaty of Amity and Commerce between the United States and Japan, July 29, 1858

The President of the United States of America and His Majesty the Ty-Coon of Japan, desiring to establish on firm and lasting foundations the relations of peace and friendship now happily existing between the two countries, and to secure the best interest of their respective citizens and subjects by encouraging, facilitating, and regulating their industry and trade, have resolved to conclude a Treaty of Amity and Commerce for this purpose, and have, therefore, named as their Plenipotentiaries, that is to say: the President of the United States, his Excellency Townsend Harris, Consul General of the United States of America for the Empire of Japan; and His Majesty the Ty-Coon of Japan, their Excellencies Ino-oo-ye [Inoue Kiyonao], Prince of Sinano [Shinano-no-kami] and Iwasay [Iwase Tadanari], Prince of Hego [Higo-no-kami]; who after having communicated to each other their respective full powers, and found them to be in good and due form, have agreed upon and concluded the following Articles:

Article I

There shall henceforth be perpetual peace and friendship between the United States of America and His Majesty the Ty-Coon of Japan and his successors.

The President of the United States may appoint a Diplomatic Agent to reside at the city of Yedo, and Consuls or Consular Agents to reside at any or all of the ports in Japan which are opened for American commerce by this Treaty. The Diplomatic Agent and Consul General of the United States shall have the right to travel freely in any port of the Empire of Japan from the time they enter on the discharge of their official duties.

The Government of Japan may appoint a Diplomatic Agent to reside at Washington, and Consuls or Consular Agents for any or all of the ports of the United States. The Diplomatic Agent and Consul General of Japan may travel freely in any port of the United States from the time they arrive in the country.

Article II

The President of the United States, at the request of the Japanese Government, will act as a friendly mediator in such matters of difference as may arise between the Government of Japan and any European Power.

The ships-of-war of the United States shall render friendly aid and assistance to such Japanese vessels as they may meet on the high seas, so far as it can be done without a breach of neutrality; and all American Consuls residing at ports visited by Japanese vessels shall also give them such friendly aid as may be permitted by the laws of the respective countries in which they reside.

Article III

In addition to the ports of Simoda [Shimoda] and Hakodade [Hakodate], the following ports and towns shall be opened on the dates respectively appended to them, that is to say: Kanagawa, on the 4th of July, 1859; Nagasaki, on the 4th of July, 1859; Nee-e-gata [Niigata], on the 1st of January, 1860; Hiogo [Hyogo], on the 1st of January, 1863.

If Nee-e-gata is found to be unsuitable as a harbor, another port on the west coast of Nipon shall be selected by the two Governments in lieu thereof. Six months after the opening of Kanagawa, the port of Simoda shall be closed as a place of residence and trade for American citizens. In all the foregoing ports and towns American citizens may permanently reside; they shall have the right to lease ground, and purchase the buildings thereon, and may erect dwellings and warehouses. But no fortification or place of military strength shall be erected under pretence of building dwellings or warehouses; and, to see that this

Article is observed, the Japanese authorities shall have the right to inspect, from time to time, any buildings which are being erected, altered, or repaired. The place which the Americans shall occupy for their buildings, and the harbor regulations, shall be arranged by the American Consul and the authorities of each place, and, if they cannot agree, the matter shall be referred to and settled by the American Diplomatic Agent and the Japanese Government.

No wall, fence, or gate shall be erected by the Japanese around the place of residence of the Americans, or anything done which may prevent a free egress and ingress to the same.

From the 1st of January, 1862, Americans shall be allowed to reside the city of Yedo; and from the 1st of January, 1863, in the city of Osaca [Osaka], for the purposes of trade only. In each of these two cities a suitable place within which they may hire houses, and the distance they may go, shall be arranged by the American Diplomatic Agent and the Government of Japan. Americans may freely buy from the Japanese and sell to them any articles that either may have for sale, without the intervention of any Japanese officers in such purchase or sale, or in making or receiving payment of the same; and all classes of Japanese may purchase, sell, keep, or use any articles sold to them by the Americans.

The Japanese Government will cause this clause to be made public in every part of the Empire as soon as the ratifications of this Treaty shall be exchanged.

Munitions of war shall only be sold to the Japanese Government and foreigners.

No rice or wheat shall be exported from Japan as cargo, but all Americans resident in Japan, and ships, for their crews and passengers, shall be furnished with sufficient supplies of the same. The Japanese Government will sell, from time to time at public auction, any surplus quantity of copper that may be produced. Americans residing in Japan shall have the right to employ Japanese as servants or in any other capacity.

Article IV

Duties shall be paid to the Government of Japan on all goods landed in the country, and on all articles of Japanese production that are exported as cargo, according to the tariff hereunto appended.

If the Japanese Custom House officers are dissatisfied with the value placed on any goods by the owner, they may place a value thereon, and offer to take the goods at that valuation. If the owner refuses to accept the offer, he shall pay duty on such valuation. If the offer be accepted by the owner, the purchase-money shall be paid to him without delay, and without any abatement or discount.

Supplies for the use of the United States navy may be landed at Kanagawa, Hakodade, and Nagasaki, and stored in warehouses, in the custody of an officer of the American Government, without the payment of any duty. But, if any such supplies are sold in Japan, the purchaser shall pay the proper duty to the Japanese authorities.

The importation of opium is prohibited; and, any American vessel coming to Japan for the purposes of trade having more than three catties (four pounds avoirdupois) weight of opium on board, such surplus quantities shall be seized and destroyed by the Japanese authorities. All goods imported into Japan, and which have paid the duty fixed by this Treaty, may be transported by the Japanese into any part of the empire without the payment of any tax, excise, or transit duty whatever.

No higher duties shall be paid by Americans on goods imported into Japan than are fixed by this Treaty, nor shall any higher duties be paid by Americans than are levied on the same description of goods if imported in Japanese vessels, or the vessels of any other nation.

Article V

All foreign coin shall be current in Japan and pass for its corresponding weight of Japanese coin of the same description. Americans and Japanese may freely use foreign or Japanese coin in making payments to each other.

As some time will elapse before the Japanese will be acquainted with the value of foreign coin, the Japanese Government will, for the period of one year after the opening of each harbor, furnish the Americans with Japanese coin in exchange for theirs, equal weights being given and no discount taken for re-coinage. Coins of all description (with the exception of Japanese copper coin) may be exported from Japan, and foreign gold and silver uncoined.

Article VI

Americans committing offences against Japanese shall be tried in American Consular courts, and, when guilty, shall be punished according to American law. Japanese committing offences against Americans shall be tried by the Japanese authorities and punished according to Japanese law. The Consular courts shall be open to Japanese creditors, to enable them to recover their just claims against American citizens; and the Japanese courts shall in like manner be open to American citizens for the recovery of their just claims against Japanese.

All claims for forfeitures or penalties for violations of this Treaty, or of the Articles regulating trade which are appended hereunto, shall be sued for in the Consular courts, and all recoveries shall be delivered to the Japanese authorities.

Neither the American or Japanese Governments are to be held responsible for the payment of any debts contracted by their respective citizens or subjects.

Article VII

In the opened harbors of Japan, Americans shall be free to go where they please, within the following limits:

At Kanagawa, the River Logo [Rokugo] (which empties into the Bay of Yedo between Kawasaki and Sinagawa), and 10 ri in any other direction.

At Hakodade, 10 ri in any direction.

At Hiogo, 10 ri in any direction, that of Kioto [Kyoto] excepted, which city shall not be approached nearer than 10 ri. The crews of vessels resorting to Hiogo shall not cross the River Engawa, which empties into the Bay between Hiogo and Osaca. The distance shall be measured inland from Goyoso, or town hall of each of the foregoing harbors, the ri being equal to 4,275 yards American measure.

At Nagasaki, Americans may go into any part of the imperial domain in its vicinity. The boundaries of Nee-e-gata, or the place that may be substituted for it, shall be settled by the American Diplomatic Agent and the Government of Japan. Americans who have been convicted of felony, or twice convicted of misdemeanors, shall not go more than one Japanese ri inland from the places of their respective residences, and all persons so convicted shall lose their right of permanent residence in Japan, and the Japanese authorities may require them to leave the country.

A reasonable time shall be allowed to all such persons to settle their affairs, and the American Consular authority shall, after an examination into the circumstances of each case, determine the time to be allowed, but such time shall not in any case exceed one year, to be calculated from the time the person shall be free to attend to his affairs.

Article VIII

Americans in Japan shall be allowed the free exercise of their religion, and for this purpose shall have the right to erect suitable places of worship. No injury shall be done to such buildings, nor any insult be offered to the religious worship of the Americans. American citizens shall not inure any Japanese temple or *mia [miya]*, or offer any insult or injury to Japanese religious ceremonies, or to the objects of their worship.

The Americans and Japanese shall not do anything that may be calculated to excite religious animosity. The Government of Japan has already abolished the practice of trampling on religious emblems.

Article IX

When requested by the American Consul, the Japanese authorities will cause the arrest of all deserters and fugitives from justice, receive in jail all persons held as prisoners by the Consul, and give to the Consul such assistance as may be required to enable him to enforce the observance of the laws by the Americans who are on land, and to maintain order among the shipping. For all such service, and for the support of prisoners kept in confinement, the Consul shall in all cases pay a just compensation.

Article X

The Japanese Government may purchase or construct in the United States ships-of-war, steamers, merchant ships, whale ships, cannon, munitions of war, and arms of all kinds, and any other things it may require. It shall have the right to engage in the United States scientific, naval and military men, artisans of all kinds, and mariners to enter into its service. All purchases made for the Government of Japan may be exported from the United States, and all persons engaged for its service may freely depart from the United States; provided that no articles that are contraband of war shall be exported, nor any persons engaged to act in a naval or military capacity, while Japan shall be at war with any Power in amity with the United States.

Article XI

The Articles for the regulation of trade, which are appended to this Treaty, shall be considered as forming a part of the same, and shall be equally binding on both the Contracting Parties to this Treaty, and on their citizens and subjects.

Article XII

Such of the provisions of the Treaty made by Commodore Perry, and signed at Kanagawa, on the 31st of March, 1854, as conflict with the provisions of this Treaty are hereby revoked; and as all the provisions of a Convention executed by the Consul General of the United States and the Governors of Simoda, on the 17th of June, 1857, are incorporated in this Treaty, that Convention is also revoked.

The person charged with the diplomatic relations of the United States in Japan, in conjunction with such person or persons as may be appointed for that purpose by the Japanese Government, shall have power to make such rules and regulations as may be required to carry into full and complete effect the provisions of this Treaty, and the provisions of the Articles regulating trade appended thereunto.

Article XIII

After the 4th of July, 1872, upon the desire of either the American or Japanese Governments, and one year's notice given by either party, this Treaty, and such portions of the Treaty of Kanagawa as remain unrevoked by this Treaty, together with the regulations of trade hereunto annexed, or those that may be hereafter introduced, shall be subject to revision by Commissioners appointed on both sides for this purpose, who will be empowered to decide on, and insert therein, such amendments as experience shall prove to be desirable.

Article XIV

This Treaty shall go into effect on the 4th of July, 1859, on or before which day the ratifications of the same shall be exchanged at the City of Washington; but if, from any unforeseen cause, the ratifications cannot be exchanged by that time, the Treaty shall still go into effect at the date above mentioned.

The act of ratification on the part of the United States shall be verified by the signature of the President of the United States, countersigned by the Secretary of State, and sealed with the seal of the United States.

The act of ratification on the part of Japan shall be verified by the name and seal of His Majesty the Ty-Coon, and by the seals and signatures of such high officers as he may direct.

This Treaty is executed in quadruplicate, each copy being written in the English, Japanese, and Dutch languages, all the versions having the same meaning and intention, but the Dutch version shall be considered as being the original.

In witness whereof, the above-named Plenipotentiaries have hereunto set their hands and seals, at the City of Yedo, this 29th day of July, in the year of Our Lord 1858, and of the Independence of the United States of America the eighty-third, corresponding to the Japanese era, the 19th day of the sixth month of the 5th year of An-sei, *Mma.*

Text taken from William G. Beasley, *Select Documents on Japanese Foreign Policy, 1853–1868* (London: Oxford University Press, 1955), 183–189.

Abbreviations

BDFA	*British Documents on Foreign Affairs, Japan, 1860–1878: Reports and Papers from the Foreign Office Confidential Print*
BGKM	*[Dai Nihon Komonjo] Bakumatsu gaikō kankei monjo* (Tokyo University, 1911–)
CHOC	*Cambridge History of China* (Cambridge: Cambridge University Press)
DNISK	Dai Nihon ishin shiryō kōhon (Historiographical Institute, University of Tokyo)
FRUS	*Foreign Relations of the United States*
F. O.	Foreign Office records
NARG	National Archives (U.S.) Record Group
NGB	*[Dai] Nihon gaikō bunsho* (Tokyo, 1936)
P. P.	*Parliamentary Papers* (Great Britain), including *Correspondence with Her Majesty's Envoy Extraordinary and Minister Plenipotentiary in Japan* (1860)
P. P.:CRAJ	*Parliamentary Papers* (Great Britain), *Correspondence Respecting Affairs in Japan*
YSS	*Yokohama-shi shi* (Tokyo: Tōshoinsatsu kabushiki gaisha, 1959)

Notes

Introduction

1. Commissioners for maritime defense, *kaibō-gakari,* were advisers to the bakufu on foreign affairs and conducted the first negotiations with foreign diplomats. They were replaced by *gaikoku bugyō* (foreign magistrate) in August 1858.
2. The phrase "structures of meaning" is from Akira Iriye, *Cultural Internationalism and World Order* (Baltimore: Johns Hopkins University Press, 1997), 3. Equally helpful in understanding the idea of particular cultures within a meta-culture is T. S. Eliot's recognition that even a subculture "should also have a way of life somewhat peculiar to its initiates, with its own forms of festivity and observances." T. S. Eliot, "Notes Towards the Definition of Culture," in *Christianity and Culture* (New York: Harcourt Brace Jovanovich, 1968), p. 88, note.
3. Chapter 1 explores the specific nature of Japan's diplomatic culture.
4. Rosalind O'Hanlon and David Washbrook, "After Orientalism: Culture, Criticism and Politics in the Third World," in *Mapping Subaltern Studies and the Postcolonial*, ed. Vinayak Chaturvedi (London: Verso, 2000), 198.
5. See Mary C. Wright, "The Adaptability of Ch'ing Diplomacy: The Case of Korea," *Journal of Asian Studies* 17:3 (May 1958): 363–381. A current formulation of the paradigm as it relates to domestic society is given by C. A. Bayly in *Rulers, Townsmen, and Bazaars: North Indian Society in the Age of British Expansion* (Cambridge: Cambridge University Press, 1983).
6. See William G. Beasley, *The Meiji Restoration* (Stanford: Stanford University Press, 1972), especially chapters 7–8.

7. C. A. Bayly, "Rallying around the Subaltern," in Chaturvedi, *Mapping Subaltern Studies*, 120.

8. James C. Scott, *Domination and the Arts of Resistance: Hidden Transcripts* (New Haven: Yale University Press, 1990), 190–193.

9. James C. Scott, *Weapons of the Weak: Everyday Forms of Peasant Resistance* (New Haven: Yale University Press, 1985), xvi–xvii.

10. Scott, *Domination*, 199.

11. This was the rallying cry of the early subaltern studies school, before a theoretical shift toward exposing the historicism of the Enlightenment worldview. See Vinayak Chaturvedi, "Introduction," in Chaturvedi, *Mapping Subalten Studies*, ix.

12. See Richard Langhorne, *The Collapse of the Concert of Europe: International Politics, 1890–1914* (New York: Macmillan, 1981).

13. I am influenced by the argument in Hannah Arendt, *On Revolution* (New York: Viking, 1963), 9–11. I am indebted to Steven Smith for pointing me toward this book.

14. Ronald Syme, *The Roman Revolution* (Oxford: Oxford University Press, 1939), p. 4.

15. Beasley, *Meiji Restoration*, 116.

1. The Style and Substance of Treaty-Making

1. Laurence Oliphant, *Narrative of the Earl of Elgin's Mission to China and Japan in the Years 1857, 58, 59*, vol. 2 (Edinburgh, 1859), 235–236.

2. *The Times*, April 9, 1860.

3. The picture was rediscovered in 1998 (see page 48). *Asahi Shinbun*, August 25, 1998.

4. Oliphant, *Narrative*, vol. 2, 246.

5. Alcock to Lord John Russell, March 17, 1862. William G. Beasley, ed., *Select Documents on Japanese Foreign Policy, 1853–1868* (London: Oxford University Press, 1955), 212.

6. Townsend Harris, *The Complete Journal of Townsend Harris*, 2nd ed. (Rutland, Vt.: Charles E. Tuttle, 1959), 130–131, 156.

7. Ibid., 150.

8. James Hevia, *Cherishing Men from Afar: Qing Guest Ritual and the Macartney Embassy of 1793* (Durham, N.C.: Duke University Press, 1995), especially page 123. See also Mark Mancall, *China at the Center: 300 Years of Foreign Policy* (New York: Free Press, 1984), chapter 2.

9. Ronald Toby, *State and Diplomacy in Early Modern Japan: Asia in the Development of the Tokugawa Bakufu*, 2nd ed. (Stanford: Stanford University Press, 1991), especially 232–235; Nakamura Hidetaka, "Taikun gaikō no kokusai ninshiki," *Kokusai seiji* 51 (1974): 1–24.

10. Toby, *State and Diplomacy*, 142–161.

11. The term comes from Alastair Iain Johnson, *Cultural Realism: Strategic*

Culture and Grand Strategy in Chinese History (Princeton: Princeton University Press, 1995), ix.

12. Rutherford Alcock, *The Capital of the Tycoon: A Narrative of Three Years Residence in Japan,* vol. 2 (London, 1863), 330.

13. The best treatment remains George B. Sansom, *The Western World and Japan* (New York: Knopf, 1949), especially chapters 5–7.

14. See George A. Lensen, *The Russian Push toward Japan: Russo-Japanese Relations, 1697–1875* (Princeton: Princeton University Press, 1959), especially chapter 4.

15. For a copy of the Perry convention, see Beasley, *Select Documents,* 119–122.

16. See John King Fairbank, "The Creation of the Treaty System," in CHOC, vol. 10: *Late Ch'ing, 1800–1911,* part 1, 216–217.

17. Ibid., 218.

18. The following is based on Joseph Fletcher, "The Heyday of the Ch'ing Order in Mongolia, Sinkiang, and Tibet," in CHOC 10, 377–383.

19. Ibid., 378–379, 383.

20. Ibid., 383.

21. Fairbank, "Creation," 217.

22. Ibid., 224–225.

23. Inoue Kiyoshi, *Jōyaku kaisei* (Tokyo: Iwanami Shoten, 1955), 4.

24. Ishii Takashi, *Nihon kaikoku shi* (Tokyo: Yoshikawa Kōbunkan, 1972), 3.

25. Katō Yūzō, *Kurofune zengo no sekai,* 2nd ed. (Tokyo: Chikuma Gakugei Bunko, 1994), 167.

26. Fairbank, "Creation," 214; see also John K. Fairbank, *Trade and Diplomacy on the China Coast: The Opening of the Treaty Ports, 1842–1854* (Cambridge, Mass.: Harvard University Press, 1954).

27. For a brief review, see Jonathan D. Spence, *The Search for Modern China,* 2nd ed. (New York: Norton, 1999), 180–183.

28. Katō, *Kurofune,* 483–485.

29. See C. A. Bayly, *The New Cambridge History of India,* 2.1: *Indian Society and the Making of the British Empire* (Cambridge: Cambridge University Press, 1988), 5.

30. Anthony Webster, *Gentlemen Capitalists: British Imperialism in Southeast Asia, 1770–1890* (London: Tauris Academic Studies, 1998), 149.

31. A. J. Stockwell, "British Expansion and Rule in Southeast Asia," in *The Oxford History of the British Empire,* vol. 3, *The Nineteenth Century,* ed. Andrew Porter (Oxford: Oxford University Press, 1999), 375; Webster, *Gentlemen Capitalists,* 156.

32. Webster, *Gentlemen Capitalists,* 162.

33. Articles 4 and 5 of the Anglo-Siamese treaty, at BGKM, vol. 14, document no. 291.

34. Webster, *Gentlemen Capitalists,* 156; Stockwell, "British Expansion," 380–381.

35. C. Rajchagool, *The Rise and Fall of the Thai Absolute Monarchy* (Bangkok: White Lotus, 1995); Stockwell, "British Expansion," 388.

36. Ian Brown, *The Elite and the Economy in Siam, 1890–1920* (Singapore: Oxford University Press, 1988) esp. chapters 1, 3, conclusion.

37. Mitani Hiroshi, "Kaikoku-kaikō o meguru shodaimyō no taigai iken," in Yokohama Kaikō Shiryōkan-Yokohama Kinsei shi Kenkyūkai hen, *19-seiki no sekai to Yokohama* (Yokohama: Yamakawa Shuppansha, 1993), pp. 25.

38. See Tokugawa Nariaki's December 1857 letter to this effect in Beasley, *Select Documents*, pp. 168-169.

39. See, for example, the 1857 Dutch Supplementary Treaty in Beasley, *Select Documents*, 149–155.

40. See the 1855 Russo–Japanese treaty, where all three terms are included. BGKM 8:193, 410–426; also the Japanese translation of the Anglo–Siamese treaty, BGKM 14:291, 829–906.

41. Richard T. Chang, *The Justice of the Western Consular Courts in Nineteenth-Century Japan* (Westport, Conn.: Greenwood, 1984). Moreover, the most famous extraterritoriality problem, the *Normanton* case, did not occur until 1886.

42. F. C. Jones, *Extraterritoriality in Japan* (New Haven: Yale University Press, 1931), 6.

43. Derek Massarella, *A World Elsewhere: Europe's Encounter with Japan in the Sixteenth and Seventeenth Centuries* (New Haven: Yale University Press, 1990), 115–116.

44. BGKM 8:193, 410–426.

45. BGKM 14:291, Article 2.

46. Harris, *Complete Journal*, 316–317.

47. BGKM 18:204, 709.

48. Garrett Mattingly, *Renaissance Diplomacy* (Boston: Houghton Mifflin, 1954), 67–68.

49. *Times*, November 10, 1858.

50. YSS, vol. 1, 192–193.

51. Bob Tadashi Wakabayashi, "Rival States on a Loose Rein: The Neglected Tradition of Appeasement in Late Tokugawa Japan," in James W. White et al., *The Ambivalence of Nationalism: Modern Japan between East and West* (Lanham, Md.: University Press of America, 1990), 12–15.

52. Marius Jansen, *China in the Tokugawa World* (Cambridge, Mass.: Harvard University Press, 1992), 74–76; Fairbank, "Creation," 218–219.

53. Beasley, *Select Documents*, 179–180, emphasis added.

54. P. J. Cain and A. G. Hopkins, *British Imperialism*, vol. 1: *Innovation and Expansion, 1688–1914* (New York: Longman, 1993), 45.

55. Quoted in Jones, *Extraterritoriality in Japan*, 13.

56. See Article 7 of the treaty, BGKM 14:291.

57. For the classic informal empire argument, see John Gallagher and Ronald

Robinson, "The Imperialism of Free Trade" in *Economic History Review* 6:1 (1953), pp. 1–15.

58. For a general discussion of the cartographic imagination during the Edo period, see Marcia Yonemoto, *Mapping Early Modern Japan: Space, Place, and Culture in the Tokugawa Period (1603–1868)* (Berkeley: University of California Press, 2003), especially chapter 1.

59. See Brett L. Walker, *The Conquest of Ainu Lands: Ecology and Culture in Japanese Expansion, 1590–1800* (Berkeley: University of California Press, 2001), 227–232.

60. Known as the *bakuhan* system, an amalgamation of "bakufu" and "han" (domain).

61. See Donald Keene, *The Japanese Discovery of Europe, 1720–1830*, rev. ed. (Stanford: Stanford University Press, 1969), 39–43.

62. See Article 2 of the treaty, BGKM 8:193, 411–412.

63. A print of Harris in Edo is at *Edo no taihen: kawaraban* (Tokyo: Heibonsha, 1995), 68; some Perry prints are in *Nichibei kōryū no akebono* (Tokyo: Edo-Tokyo Hakubutsukan, 1999), 133–136.

64. See memorandum from Hotta Masayoshi in Beasley, *Select Documents*, 131–134.

2. Negotiating Space

1. See Townsend Harris, *The Complete Journal of Townsend Harris*, 2nd ed. (Rutland, Vt.: Charles E. Tuttle, 1959), 468–480.

2. DNISK, magnetic tape roll no. AN085–0189.

3. On Abe's poll and its effects on the civic realm, see Mitani Hiroshi, "Kaikoku-kaikō o meguru shodaimyō no taigai iken," in *19-seiki no sekai to Yokohama* (Tokyo: Yamakawa Shuppansha, 1993), 3–25. See also Mitani Hiroshi, *Meiji ishin to nashonarizumu* (Tokyo: Yamakawa Shuppansha, 1997), chapter 5.

4. On bakufu organization, see Conrad Totman, *Politics in the Tokugawa Bakufu, 1600–1843* (Berkeley: University of California Press, 1988), chapter 2.

5. See Matsuoka Hideo, *Iwase Tadanari: Nihon no kaikoku saseta gaikōka* (Tokyo: Chūō Kōronsha, 1981); on early relations with other diplomats, see Doi Ryōzō, *Bakumatsu gonin no gaikoku bugyō* (Tokyo: Chūō Kōronsha, 1997), 40–41.

6. BGKM 18:89, 327–331; see also BGKM 18:90, 332–336.

7. Ibid., p. 328.

8. See Robert Leroy Innes, *The Door Ajar: Japan's Foreign Trade in the Seventeenth Century* (Ann Arbor: University Microfilms, 1980), 2 vols. See also Herman Ooms, *Tokugawa Ideology: Early Constructs, 1570–1680* (Princeton: Princeton University Press, 1985).

9. BGKM 18:89, p. 329.

10. BGKM 18:90, 329.

11. Doi, *Bakumatsu gonin*, 27.

12. Translation of Mizuno's letter in William G. Beasley, ed., *Select Documents on Japanese Foreign Policy, 1853–1868* (London: Oxford University Press, 1955), 170–174.

13. See Ishii's analysis of the two in Ishii Takashi, *Nihon kaikoku shi* (Tokyo: Yoshikawa Kōbunkan, 1972), 259.

14. BGKM 18:173.

15. Harris to Cass, August 7, 1858. NARG no. 133, roll 2, no. 27.

16. Harris, *Complete Journal*, 515–516. Sebastopol (Sevastopol) was the site of a major stalemate in the recently concluded Crimean War.

17. Ibid., 548.

18. Ibid., 508. Harris's account of the entire day's proceedings can be found in his *Complete Journal*, 505–513.

19. Inoue and Iwase first suggested that the consul live between Kanagawa and Kawasaki, one station closer to Edo. See BGKM 18:178, 558.

20. BGKM 18:196, 655.

21. Harris, *Complete Journal*, 551–552.

22. Ibid., 427.

23. See F. L. Hawks, *Narrative of an Expedition of an American Squadron to the China Seas and Japan, Performed in the Years 1852, 1853, and 1854, Under the Command of Commodore M. C. Perry*, vol. 1 (Washington, 1856), 338–344.

24. Photostats of original treaties in the Historiographical Institute, University of Tokyo. Japanese written in formal Chinese style (*kanbun*) was used as an official government version.

25. Hawks, *Narrative*, 338–339.

26. Harris, *Complete Journal*, 428. Englebert Kaempfer was a German physician attached to the Dutch factory at Dejima from 1690 to 1692. He wrote perhaps the most widely circulated Western history of Japan soon after his return to Europe.

27. See Appendix 3 for a copy of the treaty.

28. For Hotta's Kyoto mission, see Ishii, *Nihon kaikoku*, 285–322; see also William G. Beasley, *The Meiji Restoration* (Stanford: Stanford University Press, 1972), 129–139.

29. The daimyō estate was divided into three groups: *shinpan* daimyō were related by blood to the Tokugawa, *fudai* daimyō had allied with Tokugawa Ieyasu before he became shogun in 1603, and *tōzama* daimyō were lords from outer regions maintaining an independent, sometimes hostile, stance toward Edo. See Totman, *Politics*, chapters 6–8.

30. See Ii's order at DNISK AN111–1109.

31. See Hara Takeshi, *Bakumatsu kaibōshi no kenkyū: zenkokuteki ni mita Nihon no kaibō taisei* (Tokyo: Meicho Shuppan, 1988).

32. See Doi, *Bakumatsu gonin*, especially chapters 7, 14.

33. BGKM 21:345.
34. Not to be confused with the castle town of the same name in the domain of Kaga.
35. BGKM 21:137.
36. See also YSS, 195.
37. Ibid., 196.
38. BGKM 22:101, 271.
39. Ibid., 272; for an 1865 map of the area, see *F. Beato bakumatsu Nihon shashinshū* (Yokohama: Yokohama Kaikō Shiryōkan, 1987), 29–30.
40. BGKM 22:101, 273.
41. Ibid., 280.
42. Ibid., 281.
43. BGKM 22:118; see also YSS, 198.
44. BGKM 22:126, 379.
45. The historian Ishii Takashi believes that the bakufu simply did not want to use the cumbersome designation of "Kanagawa-Yokohama" when referring to the site, and therefore was not distorting the truth when it claimed that Yokohama was indeed Kanagawa. Yet Ishii's own analysis of the Yokohama issue relies heavily on the importance of Iwase Tadanari's December 1857 letter urging the opening of the isolated Yokohama village, and of his being opposed by Mizuno's rejection of both Kanagawa and Yokohama. Ishii, *Nihon kaikoku,* 269–270.
46. BGKM 22:150, 476.
47. *The Education of Henry Adams* (New York: Viking, 1983), 840.
48. Harris to Cass, March 24, 1859. NARG 59/133/2, no. 14.
49. YSS, 199.
50. DNISK AN145–0894.
51. Harris to Cass, July 4, 1859. NARG 59/133/2, no. 3.
52. Alcock to Malmesbury, July 9, 1859, F. O., 46/3, no. 8.
53. Alcock to foreign magistrates, July 12, 1859, F. O. 46/3, no. 9 and enclosures.
54. Alcock to foreign magistrates, July 19, 1859, BGKM 24:8.
55. Alcock to Russell, Sept. 7, 1859. P. P.: *Correspondence with Her Majesty's Envoy Extraordinary and Minister Plenipotentiary in Japan* (1860), no. 21.
56. Russell to Alcock, October 7, 1859, F. O. 46/2, 76–77.
57. Even after the establishment of the legation in Tokyo, the British kept a consul in Yokohama, but continued the fiction that the consulate was located in Kanagawa. See Iwao Seiichi, *List of the Foreign Office Records Preserved in the Public Record Office in London Relating to China and Japan* (Tokyo: Tōhō Gakkai, 1959).
58. Check, for example, letters from Minister Robert Pruyn in FRUS 1864:3, 450.

59. Ishii, *Nihon kaikoku*, 401. Ishii sees this as a complete distortion of reality by Manabe, but it jibes with Alcock's view.
60. Rutherford Alcock, *The Capital of the Tycoon: A Narrative of Three Years Residence in Japan*, vol. 2 (London, 1863), 386.
61. Ibid., 389.
62. Ishii, *Nihon kaikoku*, 406.
63. Beasley, *Select Documents*, 202.

3. Negotiating Time

1. For the purge, see George M. Wilson, "The Bakumatsu Intellectual in Action: Hashimoto Sanai in the Political Crisis of 1858," in *Personality in Japanese History*, ed. Albert M. Craig and Donald H. Shively (Berkeley: University of California Press, 1970), 234–263.
2. Niigata did not open for trade until 1869 and never became an important port.
3. BGKM 18:89.
4. For studies of nativist thought, see Harry Harootunian, *Toward Restoration: The Growth of Political Consciousness in Japan* (Berkeley: University of California Press, 1970); J. Victor Koschmann, *The Mito Ideology: Discourse, Reform, and Insurrection in Late Tokugawa Japan, 1790–1864* (Berkeley: University of California Press, 1987).
5. Ono Masao, "Daimyō no Ahen sensō ninshiki," in *Iwanami kōza: Nihon tsūshi* 15: *Kinsei* 5 (Tokyo: Iwanami shoten, 1995), 299–311; see also Bob Tadashi Wakabayashi, "Opium, Expulsion, Sovereignty: China's Lessons for Bakumatsu Japan," *Monumenta Nipponica* 47:1 (Spring 1992): 1–25.
6. See the debate with Harris of February 2, 1858, BGKM 18:200, especially 674–76; see also BGKM 18:204.
7. Townsend Harris, *The Complete Journal of Townsend Harris*, 2nd ed. (Rutland, Vt.: Charles E. Tuttle, 1959), 527.
8. See Edwin B. Lee, "The Kazunomiya Marriage: Alliance Between the Court and the Bakufu," *Monumenta Nipponica* 22:3–4 (Winter 1967): 290–304. William Beasley, for one, sees this as the origin of the postponement issue as well as the beginning of the bakufu's ill-fated dual policy of trying to appease both the court and the Westerners; see William Beasley, *Select Documents on Japanese Foreign Policy, 1853–1868* (Oxford: Clarendon Press, 1955), 196–198.
9. This is a point stressed by Ōkubo Toshiaki, "Bakumatsu seiji no tenkai," in Bannō Junji et al., *Nihon rekishi taikei fukyūban* 12: *Kaikoku to bakumatsu seiji* (Tokyo: Yamakawa Shuppansha, 1996), 155.
10. Article V of the 1858 Treaty read: "As some time will elapse before the Japanese will be acquainted with the value of foreign coin, the Japanese Government will, for the period of one year after the opening of each harbor, furnish the Americans with Japanese coin in exchange for theirs, equal weights

being given. . . . Coins of all description (with the exception of Japanese copper coin) may be exported from Japan, and foreign gold and silver uncoined."

11. The only study in English is Peter Frost, *The Bakumatsu Currency Crisis* (Cambridge, Mass.: Harvard East Asian Monographs 36, 1970); see especially chapters 2–4. In Japanese, Ishii Takashi, *Bakumatsu bōekishi no kenkyū* (Tokyo: Nihon Hyōronsha, 1944).

12. Ishii, *Bakumatsu bōekishi*, 84–87.

13. Frost, *Bakumatsu Currency*, chapter 4.

14. Harris to secretary of state, May 8, 1861. FRUS, 1862, no. 20 (Japan), 794.

15. See Patricia Sippel, "Popular Protest in Early Modern Japan: The Bushū Outburst," *Harvard Journal of Asiatic Studies* 37:2 (December 1977): 273–322.

16. See, for example, Alcock, vol. 2, 383, or the *Times*, March 1, 1862.

17. The order was known in Japanese as *gohin Edo kaisō rei* (loosely: "the order forwarding the five goods to Edo"). See Irimajiri Yoshinaga, *Bakumatsu no tokken shōnin to zaigō shōnin* (Tokyo: Sōbunsha, 1977), 205–228.

18. Bakumatsu-Meiji kawaraban archive (Ishin zengo fūshi kaku), print number 0380–17–2–2, Historiographical Institute, Tokyo University.

19. Harris to Cass, August 1, 1860. FRUS 1862, no. 26 (Japan), 793–794.

20. Trade figures are given in Kajima Morinosuke, *Nihon gaikō shi* (Tokyo: Kajima Kenkyūjo Shuppankai, 1970), 1:207. Britain accounted for $1,240,088 in 1863, which was 80.73 percent of total Japanese trade.

21. DNISK MA011–0557.

22. Thus, Ōkubo Toshiaki was wrong to claim that Alcock was resolutely against any type of postponement. See Ōkubo, "Bakumatsu seiji," 156–157.

23. Richard Sims, *French Policy Towards the Bakufu and Meiji Japan, 1854–95* (Surrey: Japan Library, 1998), 27–28. See also Meron Medzini, *French Policy in Japan During the Closing Years of the Tokugawa Regime* (Cambridge, Mass.: Harvard East Asian Monographs, 1971), 25–32.

24. DNISK MA015–0477.

25. DNISK MA018–0540.

26. The bakufu did not formally grant the land for the foreigners' cemetery until June 1861. See the order at DNISK BU013–1127.

27. Henry Heusken, *Japan Journal 1855–1861*, trans. and ed. Jeannette C. van der Corput and Robert A. Wilson (New Brunswick: Rutgers University Press, 1964).

28. DNISK BU004–0118.

29. Ishii Takashi, *Meiji ishin no kokusaiteki kankyō* (Tokyo: Yoshikawa Kōbunkan, 1957), 57.

30. Japanese ministers for foreign affairs to Alcock, May 30, 1861, in BDFA, part I, series E, vol. 1, 45–47.

31. Alcock to Russell, July 6, 1861. P. P.:CRAJ 1861, no. 1.

32. Alcock to Russell, July 25, 1861. P. P.:CRAJ 1861, no. 4.

33. DNISK BU015–0116.

34. DNISK BU016–0725; BDFA I:E:1, 73–78.

35. Alcock to Russell, August 16, 1861. BDFA I:E:1, 35–44.

36. See Ishii, *Meiji ishin*, 73.

37. Ronald P. Toby, *State and Diplomacy in Early Modern Japan: Asia in the Development of the Tokugawa Bakufu*, 2nd ed. (Stanford: Stanford University Press, 1991), especially chapters 1, 3–4; see also Robert Hellyer, "A Tale of Two Domains: Satsuma, Tsushima and the System of Foreign Relations in Late Edo Period Japan" (Ph.D. diss., Stanford University, 2001).

38. The best study is George Alexander Lensen, *The Russian Push toward Japan: Russo–Japanese Relations, 1697–1875* (Princeton: Princeton University Press, 1959); see also Glynn Barratt, *Russia in Pacific Waters, 1715–1825* (Vancouver: University of British Columbia Press, 1981).

39. See C. Pemberton Hodgson, *A Residence at Nagasaki and Hakodate in 1859–1860. With an Account of Japan Generally. With a Series of Letters on Japan by His Wife* (London: R. Bentley, 1861).

40. DNISK BU003–0336.

41. DNISK BU004–0827.

42. DNISK BU005–0681, BU006–0051.

43. For information on the bakufu ships, see Nomura Minoru, *Nihon kaigun* (Tokyo: Kawade shobō shinsha, 1997), 16–19.

44. DNISK BU007–0613. George Lensen's account of the clash states that several Japanese were killed by Russian rifle fire and several more captured, but this is not included in the domain report. See Lensen, *Russian Push*, 449.

45. DNISK BU010 0277.

46. DNISK BU014–1017. Lensen argues that Goshkevitch may not have known what the Russian captains were up to in Tsushima; Lensen, *Russian Push*, 450.

47. Lensen, *Russian Push*, 448.

48. See William G. Beasley, "The Language Problem in the Anglo–Japanese Negotiations of 1854," in *Collected Writings of W. G. Beasley* (Richmond: Curzon, 2001), 13–22.

49. DNISK BU016–0725.

50. DNISK BU019–0238.

51. DNISK BU019–0396, DNISK BU019–0466.

52. On the mission, see Masao Miyoshi, *As We Saw Them: The First Japanese Embassy to the United States* (New York: Kodansha, 1994), especially 20–24 and chapter 4.

53. For a complete list of the embassy, see Haga Tōru, *Taikun no shisetsu: bakumatsu Nihonjin no Sei-ō taiken* (Tokyo: Chūō Kōronsha, 1991), 15–18.

54. See Ishii, *Meiji Ishin*, 103-105.

55. Alcock to Russell, March 17, 1862. P. P. 1863:74, no. 15.

56. See Haga, *Taikun*, 50–73.

57. Ibid., 47, 70.

58. Ibid., 74–77.

59. Sims, *French Policy,* 232–233.

60. See, for example, articles of May 12, 14, 20, 21, and June 9, 1862.

61. Fukuzawa Yukichi, *The Autobiography of Yukichi Fukuzawa* (New York: Columbia University Press, 1966), chapter 7, especially 131–135.

62. See Beasley, *Select Documents*, 216–217.

63. DNISK BU039–0086. Spirits were taxed at 35 percent, while glassware was levied a 20 percent tariff.

64. Ishii, *Meiji ishin*, 119–120.

65. See, for example, D. C. M. Platt, *Finance, Trade, and Politics in British Foreign Policy, 1815–1914* (Oxford: Clarendon Press, 1968), 266–267; Kenneth Bourne, *The Foreign Policy of Victorian England, 1830–1902* (Oxford: Clarendon Press, 1970), 81–83.

4. The Limits of Negotiation

1. See William G. Beasley, *The Meiji Restoration* (Stanford: Stanford University Press, 1972), 179–181.

2. Harris's last journal entry was on June 9, 1858. On the American mission in Japan, see Jack L. Hammersmith, *Spoilsmen in a "Flowery Fairyland": The Development of the U.S. Legation in Japan, 1859–1906* (Kent, Ohio: Kent State University Press, 1998).

3. YSS, 790.

4. See Neale to Russell, December 3, 1862. P. P. 1864:66 (3242), included in no. 7.

5. Russell to Neale, December 24, 1862. P. P. 1864:66 (3242), no. 1.

6. Russell to Neale, December 24, 27, 1862. P. P. 1864:66 (3242), nos. 1, 2.

7. Rutherford Alcock, *The Capital of the Tycoon: A Narrative of Three Years Residence in Japan,* vol. 2 (London, 1863), 388–389.

8. See *Sankin kōtai: kyōdai toshi Edo no naritachi* (Tokyo: Edo-Tokyo Hakubutsukan, 1997); in English, Constantine Vaporis, *Breaking Barriers: Travel and the State in Early Modern Japan* (Cambridge, Mass.: Council on East Asian Studies, Harvard University, 1994).

9. Neale to Russell, January 10, 1863. P. P. 1864:66 (3242), no. 10 and enclosures.

10. Neale to Russell, February 10, 1863. P. P. 1864:66 (3242), no. 16, emphasis added.

11. Neale to Russell, March 29, 1863. P. P. 1864:66 (3242), no. 25.

12. Neale to Japanese ministers for foreign affairs, April 6, 1863. P. P. 1864:66 (3242), no. 26.

13. See meetings recorded at DNISK BU081–0750; DNISK BU085–0287; DNISK BU087–0254.
14. DNISK BU083–0775.
15. Pruyn to Secretary of State (William) Seward, May 3, 1863. FRUS 1863:2, no. 21.
16. The amount was paid in dollars, totaling $440,000. See Ernest Satow, *A Diplomat in Japan* (Tokyo: Tuttle, 1983), 79–80, illustration at 80; DNISK BU097–0440.
17. See Satow's firsthand account in *Diplomat*, 84–94. Satow blamed Neale for the botched nature of the attack, accusing him of interfering in military affairs. "We had bombarded and destroyed the greater part of the forts and town, probably killed a good many persons who were innocent of Richardson's murder, and had thereby elevated what was in the beginning a crime against public order into a *casus belli*" (93).
18. *The Times*, October 21, 1863. The casualty figures represented the information available at the time. Gosling and Wilmot were the officers killed on the *Euryalus*.
19. The events following are succinctly laid out in Beasley, *Meiji Restoration*, 191–202.
20. See Conrad Totman, "Tokugawa Yoshinobu and *Kōbugattai*: A Study in Political Inadequacy," *Monumenta Nipponica* 30:4 (Winter 1975): 393–403.
21. Neale to Japanese ministers for foreign affairs, June 24, 1863. P. P. 1864:66 (3242), no. 45.
22. DNISK BU098–0326.
23. Beasley sees a "sharp deterioration" in relations; *Meiji Restoration*, 197.
24. Pruyn to Seward, June 25, 1863. FRUS 1863:2, no. 43.
25. See Gracc Fox, *Britain and Japan, 1858–1883* (Oxford: Clarendon Press, 1969), 113–114.
26. Neale to Russell, July 29, 1863. P. P. 1864:66 (3242), no. 66.
27. Neale to Russell, September 11, 1863. P. P.:CRAJ (1864), no. 65.
28. Consular Report of February 15, 1864. P. P.:CRAJ (1865), no. 24.
29. Ishii Takashi, *Meiji ishin no kokusaiteki kankyō* (Tokyo: Yoshikawa Kōbunkan, 1957), 181–182. Later calculations have led to similarly mixed results. On the one hand, Ishii Takashi calculated that, by picul (about 133 pounds), the silk trade declined nearly 30 percent between 1863 and 1864, less than indicated in consular records. Yet more recently, Sugiyama Shin'ya has calculated that between 1862 and 1863, exports, primarily silk and tea, increased from ¥10.6 million (current prices) to ¥13.3 million, while imports increased a modest ¥500,000. On the other hand, from 1863 through 1864 only a slight decrease in exports, from ¥13.3 million to ¥12.5 million, occurred, while imports jumped nearly 30 percent, from ¥7.2 million to more than ¥10 million yen. Sugiyama Shin'ya, *Japan's Industrialization in*

the World Economy, 1859–1899: Export Trade and Overseas Competition (Atlantic Highlands, N.J.: Athlone, 1988), 46–47.

30. Alcock to Russell, June 27, 1864. P. P.:CRAJ (1865), encl. no. 1 in no. 51.
31. The best analysis is in YSS, 790–820; also see Hara Tomio, *Meiji sekken no kakuritsu katei* (Tokyo: Ochanzomizu Shobō Kan, 1957), 184–268.
32. Neale to Russell, January 30, 1864. P. P. 1865:57, no 4.
33. Ishizuka Hiromichi, "Yokohama kyoryūchizō no keisei," in *Yokohama kyoryūchi to i-bunka kōryū* (Yokohama: Yokohama Kaikō Shiryōkan, 1996), 4–5. On urban critical density and the role of the city in breaking down traditional social bonds, see Georg Simmel, "The Metropolis and Mental Life" (1903), in *Social Sciences 3 Selections and Selected Readings*, 14th ed., vol. 2 (Chicago: University of Chicago Press, 1948).
34. See Satō Takashi, "Chi'iki shakai to shinbun: bakumatsuki kaikōba no shinbun o chūshin toshite," in *Nihon kingendai shi 1: Ishin henkaku to gendai Nihon*, ed. Miyachi Masato (Tokyo: Iwanami Shoten, 1993), 175.
35. Ibid., 178.
36. Hashimoto was also known as Gyokuransai and Gountei. Hashimoto Kenichirō, *Edo-Tokyo modan: ukiyo-e ni miru bakumatsu-Meijiki no sesō* (Tokyo: Zaidan-hōjin Higashi-Nihon Tetsudō Bunka Zaidan, 1998), 120. On the importance of prints as media, see Ono Hideo, *Kawaraban monogatari: Edo jidai masu-komi no rekishi* (Tokyo: Yūzankaku Kabushiki Gaisha, 1960). William Steele has shown that the face of Commodore Perry launched a thousand kawaraban; see "Goemon's New World View: Popular Representations of the Opening of Japan," *Asian Cultural Studies* 17 (1989): 69–83.
37. See chart in Ishizuka, "Yokohama kyoryūchizō," 14.
38. Hashimoto Sadahide, *Yokohama kaikō kenbun shi* (1862), vol. 1, intro.
39. DNISK BU127–0058.
40. DNISK BU127–0268.
41. Naruiwa Sōzō, *Bakumatsu Nihon to Furansu gaiko* (Osaka: Sōgensha, 1997). See also Richard Sims, *French Policy Towards the Bakufu and Meiji Japan, 1854–95* (Surrey: Japan Library, 1998), 41 (Sims calls it a "grave disappointment"); Beasley, *Meiji Restoration*, 202; Fox, *Great Britain and Japan*, 125–126.
42. DNSIK BU131–0349; DNISK BU132–0137.
43. DNISK BU137–0006.
44. DNISK BU137–0527.
45. The negotiations there have been documented by Meron Medzini in *French Policy in Japan During the Closing Years of the Tokugawa Regime* (Cambridge, Mass.: Harvard University Press, 1971), 58–70; see also Sims, *French Policy*, 40–43.
46. Medzini, *French Policy*, 68; in French, William G. Beasley, *Select Documents on Japanese Foreign Policy, 1853–1868* (Oxford: Clarendon Press, 1955), 273–274.

47. Neale to Russell, September 11, 1863. P. P. 1864:66 (3242), no. 65.

48. Russell to Neale, January 11, 1864. P. P. 1864:66 (3242), no. 76.

49. Neale to Russell, March 1, 1864. P. P. 1865:57 (3428), no. 15.

50. Alcock to Russell, March 31, 1864. P. P. 1865:57 (3428), no. 20.

51. Alcock to Russell, April 14, 1864. P. P. 1865:57 (3428), no. 23.

52. Alcock to Russell, May 6, 1864. P. P. 1865:57 (3428), no. 34.

53. Ibid.

54. Foreign magistrate Takemoto Masao had explained to Pruyn back in July 1863 that many bakufu officials privately welcomed the initial U.S. attack on Chōshū batteries. FRUS 1864:3, no. 48. See also Conrad Totman, *Collapse of the Tokugawa Bakufu* (Honolulu: University of Hawaii Press, 1980), 128.

55. See Mark D. Erickson, "The Tokugawa Bakufu and Léon Roches" (Ph.D. diss., University of Hawaii, 1978).

56. See Fox, *Great Britain and Japan*, 130.

57. See copy in P. P. 1865:57 (3428), no. 55, encl. 4.

58. See, for example, an account of recent trade in the *Japan Herald*, July 16, 1864.

59. Russell to Alcock, July 26, 1864. P. P. 1865:57 (3428), nos. 40, 41; emphasis added.

60. Russell to Alcock, August 8, 1864. P. P. 1865:57 (3428), no. 45.

61. Russell to Alcock, August 18, 1864. P. P. 1865:57 (3428), no. 49.

62. Mizuno served as senior councillor from April 1862 to July 1866, Itakura from April 1862 to July 1864, and Inoue from October 1862 to August 1864.

63. DNISK GE020–0257.

64. FRUS 1864:3, Pruyn to Seward, August 10, 1864, no. 51.

65. See extracts from the meeting in Ishii, *Meiji ishin*, 229.

66. DNISK GE036–0629.

67. DNISK GE044–0234.

68. See especially Alcock to Russell, November 19, 1864. P. P. 1865:57 (3428), no. 88.

5. *New Horizons*

1. See Marius B. Jansen, *China in the Tokugawa World* (Cambridge, Mass.: Harvard University Press, 1992), especially chapter 1.

2. The 1894 Anglo–Japanese Treaty of Trade and Navigation ended most of the 1866 tariff restrictions, but did not come into effect until 1899, concurrent with the end of extraterritoriality. Until 1911, however, fixed tariff rates of 5–15 percent remained for numerous items.

3. See William G. Beasley, *Select Documents on Japanese Foreign Policy, 1853–1868* (Oxford: Clarendon Press, 1955), 80–83; Conrad Totman, *The Collapse of the Tokugawa Bakufu, 1862–1868* (Honolulu: University of

Hawaii Press, 1980), 161, 163; Grace Fox, *Great Britain and Japan, 1858–1883* (Oxford: Clarendon Press, 1969), 182–185; Sugiyama Shin'ya, *Japan's Industrialization in the World Economy, 1859–1899: Export Trade and Overseas Competition* (Atlantic Highlands, N.J.: Athlone, 1988), 35–36. For Japanese authors, see Mori Kenzō, "Igirusu shihonshugi to Nihon kaikō," in *Sekai shijo to Bakumatsu kaikō*, ed. Ishii Kanji (Tokyo: Tokyo Daigaku Shuppanka, 1982), 25–61; Inoue Kiyoshi, *Jōyaku kaisei: Meiji no minzoku mondai* (Tokyo: Iwanami Shoten, 1955), chapter 2.

4. See, for example, Kristin Hoganson, "Cosmopolitan Domesticity: Importing the American Dream, 1865–1920," *American Historical Review* 107 (February 2002): 55–83.

5. R. J. Evans, *The Victorian Age, 1815–1914* (London: Edward Arnold, 1968), 128.

6. D. C. M. Platt, *Finance, Trade, and Politics in British Foreign Policy, 1815–1914* (Oxford: Clarendon Press, 1968), xxxvii–xxxix, 143.

7. E. L. Woodward, ed., *Oxford History of England*, vol. 13: *The Age of Reform, 1815–1870* (Oxford: Clarendon Press, 1962), 179.

8. Evans, *Victorian Age*, 128.

9. Thomas H. Johnson, *The Oxford Companion to American History* (New York: Oxford University Press, 1966), 773.

10. Harris to Cass, August 7, 1858. NARG 59/133/2, no. 27.

11. Class I items were to be duty free; they included gold and silver, and clothing, books, furniture, etc., to be used by foreign residents. Class II imports were assessed at 5 percent; these included gear for ships and whalers, house timber, various foodstuffs, animals, raw silk, tin, lead, and coal. All intoxicating liquors (Class III) were levied a duty of 35 percent. Class IV included all other goods, such as cotton and woolens, finished textiles, glass and mirrors, wines and spirits, and mechanical goods such as watches and clocks, all of which were assessed a 20 percent tariff rate. See Townsend Harris, *The Complete Journal of Townsend Harris*, 2nd ed. (Rutland, Vt.: Charles E. Tuttle, 1959), 554–555; Beasley, *Select Documents*, 185.

12. See John K. Fairbank, *Trade and Diplomacy on the China Coast: The Opening of the Treaty Ports, 1842–1854* (Cambridge, Mass.: Harvard University Press, 1954), especially chapters 16, 19–20.

13. DNISK BU033–0257.

14. DNISK BU039–0086.

15. The text can be found in Beasley, *Select Documents*, 216–217.

16. Ibid., 218–221.

17. Yokohama was the major tea-exporting center during this period. See Ishii Takashi, *Bakumatsu bōekishi no kenkyū* (Tokyo: Nihon Hyōronsha, 1944), 95–96, tables on 84–97; Sugiyama, *Japan's Industrialization*, 140–145.

18. See Ishii Takashi, *Meiji ishin no kokusaiteki kankyō* (Tokyo: Yoshikawa Kōbunkan, 1957), 142–144.

19. Meeting of June 23, 1862; repeated in a September 22 meeting. DNISK BU050–0967.
20. All nonenumerated items were currently levied a 20 percent duty. See Ishii, *Meiji ishin*, 144.
21. DNISK BU059–0663.
22. The newly reduced tariffs were on machine parts, medicine, beer, iron, tin plate, white sugar, and clocks. DNISK BU077–0071.
23. DNISK BU083–0775.
24. DNISK BU114–0716.
25. Inclusion of Pruyn letter of October 19, 1863, DNISK BU137–0454.
26. DNISK BU137–0454.
27. See copy of convention in FRUS 1864:3, 479–480. The items in Article I were sheet lead, rattan, gypsum, solder, oil for painting, firing pans, matting, indigo, and baskets; those in Article II were machines and machinery, drugs and medicines (not including opium), pig iron, sheet iron, iron ware, tin plates, white sugar, glass and glassware, clocks, watches, wines, and spirits.
28. DNISK BU137–0791.
29. DNISK BU139–0006.
30. Totman, *Collapse*, 156–163, and Fox, *Great Britain and Japan*, 182–184.
31. The best study of Parkes is Gordon Daniels, *Sir Harry Parkes: British Representative in Japan, 1865–83* (Richmond: Japan Library, 1996).
32. The best short English treatment of the Osaka events is Totman, *Collapse*, 156–161.
33. See Western demands at DNISK KE030–1093 (November 21), KE032–0383 (November 27), and KE033–0985 (December 14).
34. Pruyn left Japan in April 1865. DNISK KE032–0600.
35. Richard Sims, *French Policy Towards the Bakufu and Meiji Japan, 1854–95* (Surrey: Japan Library, 1998), 48–53.
36. Tanabe Taiichi, *Bakumatsu gaikōdan*, vol. 2 (1898; Heibonsha, 1989), 241–243. Tanabe was a mid-level assistant to bakufu foreign affairs magistrates.
37. See entreaties at DNISK KE042–0647; DNISK KE047–0993.
38. Texts can be found at DNISK KE064–0718 and P. P. 1867:74 (3758), Parkes to Clarendon, June 27, 1866, no. 1 and enclosures.
39. Specific duties on eighty-nine imports and fifty-three exports were established, leaving twenty-four import goods at the 5 percent rate. Eighteen duty-free imports were declared, while only three exports (gold, silver, and copper) were so delineated. The silk rate was 75 bu on 100 catties. 1 bu equals 134 grains troy weight of silver; 1 catty equals 1.33 lb. English avoirdupois weight.
40. Parkes to Clarendon, July 16, 1866. P. P. 1867:74 (3758), no. 3.
41. Western knowledge of Japan was equally growing, of course, but such knowledge did not bring about any fundamental transformation in those societies, unlike in Japan.

42. See Grant K. Goodman, *Japan: The Dutch Experience* (London: Athlone, 1986); Ronald P. Toby, *State and Diplomacy in Early Modern Japan: Asia in the Development of the Tokugawa Bakufu,* 2nd ed. (Stanford: Stanford University Press, 1991), chapter 4. See also Donald Keene, *The Japanese Discovery of Europe, 1720–1830,* rev. ed. (Stanford: Stanford University Press, 1969).

43. Marius B. Jansen, *China in the Tokugawa World* (Cambridge, Mass.: Harvard University Press, 1992), 74–76.

44. The only English study of the institute is Marius B. Jansen, "New Materials for the Intellectual History of Nineteenth-Century Japan," *Harvard Journal of Asiatic Studies* 20 (1957): 567–597. For convenience, I will refer to the various incarnations simply as the institute.

45. The best treatment is Hara Heizō, "Bansho shirabesho no sōsetsu," in Hara Heizō, *Bakumatsu yōgakushi no kenkyū* (Tokyo: Shin Kinbutsu Ōraisha, 1992), chapter 3; see also Numata Jirō, *Bakumatsu yōgaku shi* (Tokyo: Tōkō Shoin, 1952).

46. Eiichi Kiyooka, trans., *The Autobiography of Yukichi Fukuzawa* (New York: Columbia University Press, 1966), 98.

47. See Fukui Tamotsu, *Edo bakufu kankōbutsu* (Tokyo: Yūshodō, 1985), 203–211.

48. See Immanuel C. Y. Hsü, *China's Entrance into the Family of Nations: The Diplomatic Phase, 1858–1880* (Cambridge, Mass.: Harvard University Press, 1960), 123–128.

49. On Wheaton's reception in Japan, see Tanaka Akira, *Kaikoku to tōbaku* (Tokyo: Shūeisha, 1992), chapter 8.

50. Henry Wheaton, *Elements of International Law,* 3d ed. (Philadelphia: Lea and Blanchard, 1846), 167–169.

51. On the complexities of translation and the shifting meaning of Western political and legal concepts, see Douglas R. Howland, *Translating the West: Language and Political Reason in Nineteenth Century Japan* (Honolulu: University of Hawaii Press, 2002); see also Alexis Dudden, "Japan's Engagement with International Terms," in *Tokens of Exchange: The Problem of Translation in Global Circulations,* ed. Lydia H. Liu (Durham, N.C.: Duke University Press, 1999), 165–191. On the problems of translating Wheaton in China, see Lydia H. Liu, "Legislating the Universal: The Circulation of International Law in the Nineteenth Century," in *Tokens of Exchange,* 127–164.

52. See Thomas R. H. Havens, *Nishi Amane and Modern Japanese Thought* (Princeton: Princeton University Press, 1970), especially chapter 3.

53. See Ogata Tomio, ed., *Edo bakufu kyūzō yōsho mokuroku* (Tokyo: Rangaku Shiryō Kenkyūkai, 1957), unpaginated.

54. Beasley, *Select Documents,* 308–309.

55. On the Summer War, see Totman, *Collapse,* chapter 8.

56. Ibid, chapter 11.

57. See Fox, *Great Britain and Japan*, 191–210; Ishii, *Meiji ishin*, 556–620.
58. See letter in *Iwakura kō jikki* (Tokyo, 1927), vol. 2, 42–43.
59. Meron Medzini, *French Policy in Japan During the Closing Years of the Tokugawa Regime* (Cambridge, Mass.: Harvard University Press, 1971), 138–140.
60. See Fox, *Great Britain and Japan*, chapter 8; Sims, *French Policy*, chapter 3; Ishii Takashi, *Meiji ishin no butaiura* (Tokyo: Iwanami shoten, 1960), chapter 7.
61. Medzini, *French Policy*, 140.
62. On the volatile postresignation days, see Michio Umegaki, *After the Restoration: The Beginning of Japan's Modern State* (New York: New York University Press, 1988), 18–49.
63. Yoshinobu's letter was written in the second and third person. Shibusawa Eiichi, ed., *Tokugawa Yoshinobu kō seiken hōkan no igi* (Tokyo, n.d.), 20–23.
64. *The Times*, February 28, 1868.

6. Rethinking Negotiation

1. The best English monographic treatment of these years is Michio Umegaki, *After the Restoration: The Beginning of Japan's Modern State* (New York: New York University Press, 1987); see also William G. Beasley, *The Meiji Restoration* (Stanford: Stanford University Press, 1972), chapters 12–15.
2. See M. William Steele, "The United States and Japan's Civil War," *Asian Cultural Studies* 25 (March 1999): 45–65.
3. Van Valkenburg to Seward, February 17, 1868, in FRUS 1868:1, 656–658.
4. Appended by van Valkenburg, FRUS 1868:1, 658.
5. See order of February 22, 1868, DNISK ME015–0535.
6. See Beasley's analysis in *Meiji Restoration*, chapter 10.
7. A. B. Mitford, *Mitford's Japan: The Memoirs and Recollections, 1866–1906 of Algernon Bertram Mitford, the First Lord Redesdale*, ed. Hugh Cortazzi (London: Athlone, 1985), 79.
8. NGB, vol. 1, document 102 (hereafter 1:102).
9. Copy of order at DNISK ME019–0494, which contains most of the material relating to the Kobe incident.
10. See Michael R. Auslin, "Terrorism and Treaty Port Relations: Western Images of the Samurai during Bakumatsu and Early Meiji," in *Image and Identity: Rethinking Japanese Cultural History*, ed. Jeffrey Hanes and Hidetoshi Yamaji (Kobe, Japan: Kobe University Press, 2004).
11. See Tosa reports, DNISK ME021–0948.
12. Japanese translation of Roches's demands dated March 12, 1868, DNISK ME023–0057.
13. Report of Higashikuze's negotiations, DNISK ME024–0552.
14. DNISK ME024–0967.

15. *Meiji tennō ki* (Tokyo: Yoshikawa Kōbunkan, 1968), 1, 635.

16. Parkes's account of the attacks and audience are at Parkes to Stanley, March 25 and 26, 1868, BDFA, part 1, series E, vol. 1, documents 126–128.

17. The era name Keiō was changed to Meiji on October 23; henceforth, era names would span the entire reign of an emperor, and not be arbitrarily changed, as before. The era name Meiji (Enlightened Rule) was the name posthumously given to Emperor Mutsuhito (r. 1867–1912).

18. The best discussion of the evolution of the Vienna system is Paul W. Schroeder, *The Transformation of European Politics, 1763–1848* (Oxford: Clarendon Press, 1994).

19. See Appendix 1 for a list of treaties entered into by Japan before 1871.

20. Copies of the treaties are at NGB 1:569, 571.

21. Inō Tentarō, *Jōyaku kaiseiron no rekishiteki tenkai* (Tokyo: Komine Shoten, 1976), 121–122.

22. The Meiji government moved to Edo, which had been renamed Tokyo (alternately pronounced, in the early years, as "Tokei" or spelled as "Tokio" by foreigners) on September 3, 1868. For treaty port affairs in general, see J. E. Hoare, *Japan's Treaty Ports and Foreign Settlements* (Folkestone: Japan Library, 1994).

23. Richard Sims, *Japanese Political History Since the Meiji Renovation* (New York: Palgrave, 2001), 78.

24. NGB 1:736, order of January 31, 1869.

25. NGB 1:745, letter of February 4, 1869.

26. NGB 1:743, letter of February 4, 1869.

27. Attachment to NGB 1:743.

28. Letter to Sanjō, in *Iwakura kō jikki*, vol. 2 (Tokyo: Iwakura kō Kyūseki Hozonkai, 1927), 696–704.

29. Ibid., pp. 698–699.

30. See Henry Wheaton, *Elements of International Law*, 3d ed. (Philadelphia: Lea and Blanchard, 1846), 40. For a stimulating discussion of the translation and reception of such concepts, see Douglas R. Howland, *Translating the West: Language and Political Reason in Nineteenth Century Japan* (Honolulu: University of Hawaii Press, 2002), 64–66.

31. Wheaton, *Elements*, 167–168.

32. Given in Beasley, *Meiji Restoration*, 323.

33. The Kōgisho deliberated over measures such as the abolition of ritual suicide and the proscription of sword bearing.

34. *Kōgisho nisshi*, no. 9, reprinted. in Inō, *Jōyaku kaiseiron*, 135–140.

35. Ibid. "Article Seven: Looking at the present situation, those who like the open ports support the path of the West, while those who wish to close the ports advocate the Japanese and Chinese [way]. If one is to be chosen, which path shall we take and definitely decide upon?"

36. Hora Tomio calculates that in 1868 only five hundred European troops were in Yokohama (three hundred British and two hundred French). Hora

Tomio, "Bakumatsu ishin ni okeru Eifutsu guntai no Yokohama chūton," in *Meiji seiken no kakuritsu katei*, ed. Hayashi Akira et al. (Tokyo: Ocha-nomizu Shobōkan, 1957), 260.

37. For discussion and examples of the debates, see Inō, *Jōyaku kaiseiron*, 141–152.
38. Copy of the treaty at NGB 4:462.
39. The port was Ebisuminato; Sado was located on the Japan Sea.
40. "Imperial and Royal Authorities" refers to Austrian officials, not to Japanese and Austrian officials acting in concert, as the Japanese version of the treaty makes clear.
41. See his memoirs, Richard Henry Brunton, *Building Japan, 1868–1876* (Folkestone: Japan Library, 1991).
42. See, for example, Wheaton, *Elements*, 3.2 and 4.4.
43. Resolution from Foreign Ministry conference, dated May 1870, NGB 3:57.
44. The office was called, in Japanese, *Jōyaku kaisei torishirabe gakari*.
45. NGB 3:58. It is unclear why Sawa or Terajima believed negotiations could begin in mid-1871, since the 1858 treaties clearly stated revision could occur only after July 1, 1872, and required a one-year prior notice by any of the contracting parties. It may have been that in setting its May 1871 target date the Foreign Ministry had in mind the earliest date when Tokyo could announce its intention to seek revision.
46. The draft was entitled the *Gishintei jōyaku sōhon*.
47. For Tsuda's reformist program, see Daniel V. Botsman, "Crime, Punishment, and the Making of Modern Japan, 1790–1895" (Ph.D. diss., Princeton University, 1999), 302–304.
48. See Ōkubo Toshiaki, *Iwakura shisetsu no kenkyū* (Tokyo: Shūkō Shobō, 1976), 17–23; Ishii Takashi, *Meiji shoki no kokusai kankei* (Tokyo: Yoshikawa Kōbunkan, 1977), 16–17.
49. For early Meiji legal reform, see Botsman, "Crime, Punishment," 266–267.
50. Itō later would become the first prime minister, in 1885, under the new cabinet system. He was the leading architect of the 1889 Meiji Constitution; would form four more cabinets and his own political party, the Seiyūkai; and served as resident-general of the Korean protectorate from 1905 until his assassination there in 1909.
51. Letter in *Itō Hirobumi den* (Tokyo: Tōseisha, 1940), 1, 592–597. On the Itō memorandum see Ishii, *Meiji shoki*, 17–20; Marlene Mayo, "Rationality in the Meiji Restoration: The Iwakura Embassy," in *Modern Japanese Leadership*, ed. Bernard S. Silberman and Harry D. Harootunian (Tucson: University of Arizona Press, 1966), 343–346.
52. NGB 4:55, note dated May 22, 1871; Parkes indicated that London wanted to revise not just the 1858 treaty, but the 1866 Tariff Convention as well. De Long sent a follow-up note on July 2, the official date for announcing the intention to revise; NGB 4:61.

53. Dated December 8, 1871, at F. O. 46/152, encl. no. 3 in Adams's no. 33.

54. Von Brandt's plan included: (1) lowering general duties below 5 percent to offset rising duties of tea and silk; (2) abolishing harbor duties in exchange for a fixed, low tonnage rate; (3) basing lighthouse and harbor taxes on tonnage, along with the possibility of having Westerners hired by the Japanese run port affairs; (4) allowing interior travel by foreigners for business and the establishment of business partnerships between Japanese and Westerners; (5) allowing Western entry into nonopen ports; (6) currency reform; (7) expanding the pleasure travel limits of all foreigners; (8) expanding the limits within which foreigners could buy land outside foreign settlements; (9) establishing Western control of treaty port settlement municipal affairs, particularly property tax collection; (10) allowing merchants interior river travel; (11) expanding freedom to practice Christianity outside treaty ports; (12) lowering various nontariff taxes; and (13) establishing mixed consular courts. F. O. 46/152, enclosure in Adams's no. 40. The second article of the 1866 Tariff Convention allowed the "readjustment of the duties on tea and silk on the basis of five per cent on the average value of these articles, during the three years last preceding"; P. P.: *Correspondence Respecting the Revision of the Japanese Commercial Tariff* (1867), no. 1. Since the price of tea and silk had risen, the tariff would also rise.

55. NARG 59/133/18, no. 231.

56. The reorganization was called *haihan chiken*. Umegaki, *After the Restoration*, chapters 3–5.

57. *Itō Hirobumi den*, 1, 999–1005.

58. See Marlene Mayo's discussion of the letter; "Rationality," 352–355.

59. Adams to Granville, December 2, 1871, BDFA 1.E.1.: 243.

60. *Tokumei zenken taishi.*

61. Yamaguchi was an assistant minister of foreign affairs. On the background of the formation of the embassy, see Inō, *Jōyaku kaiseiron,* 53–70.

62. Terajima to Adams, November 26, 1871, BDFA 1.E.1.: 244.

63. *Iwakura Tomomi kankei monjo*, vol. 7 (Tokyo: Nihon Shiseki Kyōkai, 1934), 290–291.

64. *Itō Hirobumi den* 1, 613–615.

65. See, for example, the Takasuya affair of 1860–1865 in Sugiyama Shin'ya, *Japan's Industrialization in the World Economy, 1859–1899: Export Trade and Overseas Competition* (Atlantic Highlands, N.J.: Athlone, 1988), 55–64.

66. De Long to Fish, May 16, 1871. NARG 59/133/18, no. 191.

7. Negotiating the Future

1. Ishizuka Hiromichi, "Yokohama kyoryūchizo no keisei," in *Yokohama kyoryūchi to i-bunka kōryū* (Yokohama: Yokohama Kaikō Shiryōkan, 1996), 21. J. E. Hoare, *Japan's Treaty Ports and Foreign Settlements: The Uninvited Guests, 1858–1899* (Folkestone: Japan Library, 1994), 21, gives a figure of 1,200 in 1870.
2. Hoare, *Japan's Treaty Ports,* 21.
3. Order printed in *Japan Herald,* no. 1, November 23, 1861.
4. The Yokohama merchant Yoshimura Yukibei left an extensive record of his family's "westernization," which is kept in the Yokohama Archives of History. Satō Takashi uses the archive in exploring the life of 1860s merchants. See Satō Takashi, "Chi'iki shakai to shinbun: bakumatsuki kaikōba no shinbun o chūshin toshite," in *Nihon kingendai shi 1: ishin henkaku to gendai Nihon,* ed. Miyachi Masato (Tokyo: Iwanami Shoten, 1993), 178.
5. See Ono Hidetaka, *Kawaraban monogatari* (Tokyo: Yūzankaku Kabushiki Gaisha, 1960), 252.
6. Torii Tami, *Yokohama yamate: Nihon ni atta gaikoku* (Tokyo: Sōshisha, 1977), 76–79; see also J. R. Black, *Young Japan: Yokohama and Yedo: A Narrative of the Settlement and the City from the Signing of the Treaties in 1858, to the Close of the Year 1859, with a Glance at the Progress of Japan during a Period of Twenty-one Years,* vol. 1 (London, 1880), 239–243.
7. For Sadahide and Yoshitora, see the collection in *Edo-Tokyo modanu: ukiyoe ni miru bakumatsu-Meijiki no sesō* (Tokyo: Zaidan Hōjin Higashi Nihon Tetsudō Bunka Zaidan, 1998). On photography, see Ono Takeshi, *Bakumatsu-Meiji no shashin* (Tokyo: Chikuma Gakugei Bunko, 1997); Ono Takeshi, *Bakumatsu shashin no jidai* (Tokyo: Chikuma Gakugei Bunko, 1996); *F. Beato bakumatsu Nihon shashinshū* (Yokohama: Yokohama Kaikō Shiryōkan, 1987).
8. On the cultural aspects, see Ian Nish, ed., *The Iwakura Mission in American and Europe: A New Assessment* (Surrey: Japan Library, 1998).
9. The best analysis of the mission available in English is Marlene J. Mayo, "A Catechism of Western Diplomacy: The Japanese and Hamilton Fish, 1872," *Journal of Asian Studies* 26:3 (May 1967): 389–410. In Japanese, the best treatment is Ishii Takashi, *Meiji shoki no kokusai kankei* (Tokyo: Yoshikawa Kōbunkan, 1977), 28–95.
10. *The New York Times,* February 10, 1872.
11. *San Francisco Bulletin,* January 22, 1872.
12. Hypothesized in Mayo, "Catechism," 395.
13. Ibid., 398–402.
14. Record of March 11 discussion at NGB 5: 67, 141.
15. Fish agreed on this day to extend the current treaty one year. NGB 5: 67, 140.

16. NGB 5: 67, 140–141.
17. NGB 5: 68.
18. De Long to Fish, January 19, 1871. NARG 59/133/17, no. 136.
19. The draft's key points included provisions that: foreign ships obtain the right to visit all closed ports in Japan; the boundaries of the foreign settlements, in particular Nagasaki, be more clearly determined; interior travel be allowed under a passport system; the radius of the area outside the foreign settlements in which Westerners could buy land be expanded; foreigners be more freely allowed to hire Japanese and vice versa; transshipment and port duties be lowered; freedom of religion be expanded; and most-favored-nation status be reaffirmed. De Long to Fish, May 16, 1871. NARG 59/133/18, no. 191, encl. 1.
20. Memorandum at NGB 5: 71, 164–166.
21. Ibid., 164.
22. Ibid., 165.
23. Ibid., 166.
24. Since 1867 the Japanese had been in charge of Yokohama's municipal affairs. The best account of treaty port administration is Ōyama Azusa, *Kyūjōyaku ni okeru kaishi kaikō no kenkyū: Nihon ni okeru gaikokujin kyoryūchi* (Tokyo: Ōtori Shobō, 1967). For a discussion in English, see Hoare, *Japan's Treaty Ports*, 108–118. Hoare argues that the Japanese did not want to take over control of the foreign settlement; at the least, though, they did wish to make the rules.
25. NGB 5: 74.
26. Thornton to Granville, March 22, 1872. BDFA I.E.1.: 250.
27. Thornton to Granville, March 18, 1872. BDFA 1.E.1.: 249.
28. Mayo, "Catechism," 404.
29. Thornton to Granville, March 25, 1872. BDFA 1.E.1.: 251.
30. The U.S. House of Representatives voted to waive the remaining payments on May 29, 1872, but the measure died in the Senate. Soejima met Adams on May 14, 1872.
31. Adams to Granville, May 20, 1872. BDFA 1.E.1.: 265.
32. Adams to Japanese ministers for foreign affairs, May 25, 1872. BDFA 1.E.1.: 259.
33. See Richard Langhorne, *The Collapse of the Concert of Europe* (New York: St. Martin's, 1981), chapter 1.
34. BDFA 1.E.1., no. 265.
35. Mayo, "Catechism," 405.
36. NGB 5: 76.
37. Draft at NGB 5: 86.
38. Mayo, "Catechism," 407.
39. NGB 5: 90.
40. BDFA 1.E.1., no. 253.
41. See Andrew Cobbing, "Early Meiji Travel Encounters," *The Iwakura Mis-*

sion in America and Europe: A New Assessment, ed. Ian Nish (Surrey: Japan Library, 1998). 36–53.

42. Interview between Iwakura and Granville, November 22, 1872, F. O. 46/160.

43. Ibid.

44. Interview between Iwakura and Granville, November 27, 1872, F. O. 46/160, emphasis added.

45. Interview between Iwakura and Granville, December 6, 1872. BDFA 1.E.1.: 262.

46. Planning for the railway actually had begun in the waning days of the bakufu. One of the last official communications between a senior bakufu official and the Western representatives was Ogasawara Nagamichi's approval of a plan to construct a railroad between Yokohama and Tokyo and his attachment of regulations regarding it to A. L. C. Portman on January 17, 1868. DNISK KE169–0893.

47. See Sidney D. Brown, "Ōkubo Toshimichi and the First Home Ministry Bureaucracy, 1873–1878," in *Modern Japanese Leadership,* ed. Bernard S. Silberman and Harry D. Harootunian (Tucson: University of Arizona Press, 1966), 195–232.

48. See the numerous tracts on revision, for example, *Shintei jōyaku narabi ni furoku sōan* (Tokyo, 1872); Ono Azusa, *Jōyaku kaisei ron* (1887), reprinted in *Meiji bunka zenshū,* vol. 11 (Tokyo: Nihon Hyōronsha, 1928), 409–445. The best collection of contemporary documents is in Inō Tentarō, *Jōyaku kaiseiron shiryō shūsei,* 6 vols. (Tokyo: Hara Shobo, 1994).

49. Ronald P. Toby, *State and Diplomacy in Early Modern Japan: Asia in the Development of the Tokugawa Bakufu,* 2nd ed. (Stanford: Stanford University Press, 1991), especially chapters 2, 3.

50. Key-Hiuk Kim, *The Last Phase of the East-Asian World Order: Korea, Japan, and the Chinese Empire, 1860–1882* (Berkeley: University of California Press, 1980), 140–150. See also Nagai Jun'ichi, "Nisshin shūkō jōki teiketsu kōshō to Yanagiwara Sakimitsu," *Nihon rekishi* 475:12 (1987): 61–79.

51. Low to De Long, October 31, 1871. NARG 59/133/19, no. 249, encl. 1.

52. An excellent analysis is Marlene J. Mayo, "The Korean Crisis of 1873 and Early Meiji Foreign Policy," *Journal of Asian Studies* 31:4 (August 1972): 793–819.

53. See Inuzuka Takaaki, "Meiji shoki gaikō shidōsha no taigai ninshiki," *Kokusai seiji* 102 (1993): 22–38; also Wayne C. McWilliams, "East Meets East: The Soejima Mission to China, 1873," *Monumenta Nipponica* 30:3 (Autumn 1975): 237–275.

54. Robert Eskildsen, "Of Civilization and Savages: The Mimetic Imperialism of Japan's 1874 Expedition to Taiwan," *American Historical Review* 107:2 (April 2002): 388–418.

55. For Japan's Korea policy during the period of the unequal treaties, see Peter Duus, *The Abacus and the Sword: The Japanese Penetration of Korea, 1895–1910* (Berkeley: University of California Press, 1995), chapter 1.
56. See F. C. Jones, *Extraterritoriality in Japan* (New Haven: Yale University Press, 1931), 80–91.
57. Ibid., 86–89.
58. On the influence of the media, see James L. Huffman, *Creating a Public: People and Press in Meiji Japan* (Honolulu: University of Hawaii Press, 1997), especially chapter 6.
59. On Mutsu, see Louis G. Perez, *Japan Comes of Age: Mutsu Munemitsu and the Revision of the Unequal Treaties* (Madison, N.J.: Fairleigh Dickinson University Press, 1999), especially chapters 4–8. See also Jones, *Extraterritoriality,* chapter 8; Hoare, *Japan's Treaty Ports,* chapter 4.

Conclusion

1. William G. Beasley, "Japan and the West in the Nineteenth Century," in *Collected Writings of W. G. Beasley* (Surrey: Japan Library, 2001), 131.
2. Sidney Hook, *The Hero in History: A Study in Limitation and Possibility* (Boston: Beacon Press, 1943), xiii.
3. James C. Scott, *Domination and the Arts of Resistance: Hidden Transcripts* (New Haven: Yale University Press, 1990), 199.
4. Isaiah Berlin, *The Hedgehog and the Fox: An Essay on Tolstoy's View of History* (New York: Mentor, 1957), 48.

Acknowledgments

I owe a great debt to the many people who helped in various ways as I worked on this book. I must begin with Ron Toby, friend and mentor, whose knowledge and support were crucial. Paul Schroeder and William Widenor helped me to broaden my view with respect to international relations. I am particularly grateful to Akira Iriye, who has seen this book through its various incarnations, and has continued to be a source of support.

As I struggled with the manuscript, Conrad Totman painstakingly read every line and endured hours of questions often only tangentially related to my topic. The book owes a great deal to his insightful suggestions and sympathetic ear. At Yale, my colleagues Ted Bromund, John Lewis Gaddis, Valerie Hansen, Paul Kennedy, Steven Stoll, and Jonathan Spence gave freely of their often-crucial advice.

In Japan during 1997–1998, I benefited from the kind support of Miyachi Masato and Mitani Hiroshi at the University of Tokyo and Bill Steele at International Christian University. Without the tutoring, help, and friendship of Lee Won Won, I could never have finished my research.

I am grateful to all those who helped with sources, readings, or general support over the years, sometimes just by asking the pertinent question that forced me to rethink a point or an assumption. They include Taylor Atkins, Andy Barshay, Dani Botsman, Philip Brown, Jean Cherniavsky, James Cornelius, Roger Dingman, Martin Fackler,

Michael Foster, Jeffrey Hanes, Daniel Headrick, Laura Hein, Robert Hellyer, William Hoover, James Huffman, the late Kanai Madoka, Katō Yūzō, Minh Luong, Louis Perez, Greg Pflugfelder, Brian Platt, Patricia Sippel, Patricia Steinhoff, and Brett Walker. The students in my seminar on Japan's international history read a draft of the book and took it upon themselves to help me with my writing style; to them, I offer my thanks: Matthew Louchheim, Kathryn Malizia, Mattias Ottervik, Alexandra Riguero, Zachary Safir, and Jack Snyder.

At Yale's Sterling Memorial Library, Sue Roberts and Ellen Hammond were unfailingly helpful, while Keiko Suzuki stepped in to track down some sources at the last minute. Fred Musto of the Map Collection at Sterling kindly provided a scan of the Yokohama map. Galen Amstutz of Harvard's Reischauer Institute put me in touch with Kuniko Yamada McVey of the Harvard-Yenching Library, who located and made sure I received a copy of the title page of the *Bankoku kōhō*. Both Kuniko McVey and Yasuko Makino, of Princeton University's East Asia Library, cheerfully faxed documents not available at Yale. Martin Durrant at the Victoria and Albert Museum expertly tracked down the photograph of the Japanese foreign magistrates. And Mr. Toshihiro Ōkubo very kindly provided me with a print of the Iwakura Mission originally held by his ancestor.

I would also like to thank the groups that allowed me to talk about this book at various points in its development, including the Association for Asian Studies, the Midwest Conference on Asian Affairs, the Asiatic Society of Japan, the Asian Forum at ICU, the Midwest Conference on Asian History and Culture, the Japan Forum at Harvard's Reischauer Institute, the Center for Japanese Studies at Berkeley, and Yale's International Security Studies. The suggestions and advice I received from those attending these talks were invaluable.

Without very generous funding, I could not have undertaken this project. I would like to express my gratitude to the Fulbright program's Japan–U.S. Educational Commission; the Japan Foundation; the University of Illinois; the Japan–America Society of Chicago; Yale's Council on East Asian Studies; and the Frederick W. Hilles Publication Fund of Yale University.

My editor at Harvard, Kathleen McDermott, expertly shepherded me through the publication process, all the while allowing me to consider how this work fit into future book projects. Kathleen Drummy at

Harvard University Press also patiently answered my often-repetitious questions.

I owe the most to those closest to me. My family, Donald and Myra Auslin, Tetsuo and Yoshiko Ueyama, Cele Shulman, and Daniel Auslin, has been a constant source of love and encouragement. Above all, Ginko Ueyama has given of her inexhaustible love, patience, and wisdom. She and Benjamin have fostered and supported me, and I dedicate this book with love to them.

Index

Harvard University Press is a member of Green Press Initiative (greenpressinitiative.org), a nonprofit organization working to help publishers and printers increase their use of recycled paper and decrease their use of fiber derived from endangered forests.

60683294R00166

Made in the USA
Lexington, KY
15 February 2017